Sense, Reference, and Philosophy

Sense, Reference, and Philosophy

Jerrold J. Katz

OXFORD
UNIVERSITY PRESS
2004

OXFORD
UNIVERSITY PRESS

Oxford   New York
Auckland   Bangkok   Buenos Aires   Cape Town   Chennai
Dar es Salaam   Delhi   Hong Kong   Istanbul   Karachi   Kolkata
Kuala Lumpur   Madrid   Melbourne   Mexico City   Mumbai   Nairobi
São Paulo   Shanghai   Taipei   Tokyo   Toronto

Copyright © 2004 by Oxford University Press, Inc.

Published by Oxford University Press, Inc.
198 Madison Avenue, New York, New York, 10016

www.oup.com

Oxford is a registered trademark of Oxford University Press

Library of Congress Cataloging-in-Publication Data
Katz, Jerrold J.
Sense, reference, and philosophy / Jerrold J. Katz.
p. cm.
Includes bibliographical references and index.
ISBN 0-19-515813-X
1. Language and languages—Philosophy.   2. Reference (Philosophy)
3. Semantics (Philosophy)   I. Title.
P107 .K38 2003
401—dc21   2002009479

2 4 6 8 9 7 5 3 1

Printed in the United States of America
on acid-free paper

Personally, to Virginia V. Valian

Professionally, to the memory of W. V. Quine

When you are criticizing the philosophy of an epoch, do not chiefly direct your attention to those intellectual positions which its exponents feel it necessary explicitly to defend. There will be some fundamental assumptions which adherents of all the variant systems within the epoch unconsciously presuppose.

Alfred North Whitehead

Facts of such a kind are far more numerous than many people think, disdaining as they do to direct their attention upon such simple matters.

René Descartes

Our argument is not flatly circular, but something like it. It has the form, figuratively speaking, of a closed curve in space.

Willard Van Orman Quine

PREFACE

The professional dedication for this book will be a surprise to many philosophers. "What? Has the author undergone a conversion to empiricism in his old age?" No, not at all. Regardless of ideology, philosophers owe their deepest debt to those of their predecessors who have done the most to open the way for their own work. This is the debt Kant felt he owed Hume when he described Hume as waking him from his "dogmatic slumbers." There is no twentieth-century philosopher, including Wittgenstein, to whom I am more deeply indebted than W. V. Quine. An account of this debt will provide the reader with both an explanation of this dedication and an overview of the general line of argument in the book.

My debt to Quine began in graduate school, where a reading of his essay "The Problem of Meaning in Linguistics" first made me aware of an alternative to ordinary-language-style and artificial-language-style philosophy of language. The problem of meaning could be studied within natural language, but from a scientific standpoint that allowed theory to be brought to bear in an attempt to understand language as it is.

Two other influences combined with this one to determine the nature of my thinking about the philosophy of language. One was a strong attraction to the intensionalism of Gottlob Frege and Rudolf Carnap. At Princeton, we had to do an examination on the thought of one great philosopher—"the Great Man Exam," as it was then called. I chose Carnap. The other influence was contact with Noam Chomsky, who spent a year at the Institute of Advanced Study during this period, bringing the message of generative linguistics to the philosophy graduate students.

My philosophical program, to the extent that I framed it to myself as such at the time, was to try to understand meaning in natural language using some form of Fregean intensionalism to provide a semantic theory for Chomsky's theory of generative grammar, which, remarkably for a theory of language, at the time had no semantic theory.

At MIT I set out to implement this program. Around MIT in the '60s and early '70s, Quine was the opposition. Chomsky provided this focus and was laying out what we, the younger members of the MIT linguistics and philosophy community, saw as a devastating attack on the forces of reaction located on the other side of town. We naturally joined in on this attack against both the Skinnerian learning theory that seemed to underlie Quinean semantics and Quine's empiricism itself. The arguments went back and forth in a lively manner for a decade or so.

In the early '70s, another issue came sharply into focus for me, one that indirectly reshaped my thinking about the controversy over Quinean empiricism. I had been wondering about how well Frege's realism about senses, to which I was committed, squared with Chomsky's psychologism about language, to which I also was committed. I reached the conclusion that my program could not be carried out as initially framed because a theory of abstract senses could not be fitted into a theory of concrete syntactic structures in the human mind. My solution was to adopt a realist view of grammar as a whole, a move that seemed the right choice in light of the fact that the words and sentences that grammars are theories of are plausibly regarded as types and hence as abstract objects.

The impact of this new ontological view on my conception of the controversy about empiricism was significant. The issue with which Chomsky was concerned was nativism—a psychological issue about how human beings acquire a language, whereas Quine was concerned also with the separate issue of rationalism—a philosophical issue about the epistemic character of the linguist's scientific theory of language. Chomsky could be right about the psychological issue of an innate basis for acquisition while Quine could be right about the philosophical issue of whether linguistics contains a priori knowledge. This forced a re-examination of Quine's arguments against a priori semantic knowledge.

What I found in re-examining Quine's arguments was that they seemed entirely cogent against the intensionalist semantics that he had explicitly targeted, Frege/Carnap semantics, but not effective against the intensionalist semantics I had developed. I had come to suspect that, in fashioning an intensional semantics to fit a theory of grammar in linguistics, I had developed an intensional semantics that strayed far from its Fregean origins. One indication was that my definition of sense (e.g., in *Semantic Theory* [1972]) did not relate sense to reference or make reference any part of the explanation of sense. Another was that my definition of analyticity did not involve logic. Quine's arguments more than confirmed my suspicions. They provided a "proof" that my intensional semantics was essentially different from Frege/Carnap intensional semantics. For me, the most significant statement in all of Quine's writings is the one he makes just after what appears to be a demonstration that an interchangeability argument to explain synonymy is circular. Instead of saying, "Q.E.D.!" Quine says, "Our argument is not flatly circular, but something like it. It has the form, figuratively speaking, of a closed curve in space." As I explain at length in this book, Quine is saying that the sin is not circularity, even though the curve of definability is closed. We cannot define synonymy, or any other notion in the theory of meaning, without using yet other notions in the theory, but this characteristic of certain axiomatic systems (e.g., autonomous theories of number or implication) is not one that produces circularity. Rather, the sin is irreducibility. The system of interdefined semantic notions floats there, not reducible to other systems, such as, say, the theory of reference. As a criticism of Fregean intensionalism, the criticism works, because Fregean intensionalism enshrines reducibility, first, in the definition of sense, and second, in the account of analytic truths as species of logical truths. The Fregean definition of sense is that sense is the determiner of reference, and Frege's definition of analytic truths is that they are consequences of logical truths together with definitions.

As a criticism of my intensionalism, where the theory of sense is autonomous and analytic truths are not species of logical truths, Quine's argument does not work. Quine would require an independent argument for the necessity of reducibility, but he offers none.

The story is the same with indeterminacy. Given reducibility of the theory of sense to the theory of reference, all that is available in radical translation as evidence to choose between translations are facts about referential relations, and hence in Quine's cases there is evidential symmetry and indeterminacy of translation. But with an autonomous theory of sense, there can be evidence in the form of facts about sense relations (e.g., the sense of 'rabbit' is not, but the sense of 'undetached rabbit part' is, similar to the sense of 'finger'). The possibility of these new facts blocks evidential symmetry and hence indeterminacy.

As long as an autonomous theory of sense remains an option, intensionalism remains an option, too. Hence, the issue of a priori semantic knowledge had been decided without considering all the options for a theory of meaning: it had been assumed that Frege/Carnap semantics is the only option for intensionalists. Given how widely held this assumption is, it is reasonable to think that other philosophical issues might also have been discussed without considering an alternative to Frege/Carnap semantics. I think that this is definitely the case. Virtually all of the issues that extensionalists and intensionalists debated over the last century were framed on the assumption that intensionalism is Fregean intensionalism. If there is a different form of intensionalism, many arguments now considered decisive fail.

For example, arguments like Saul Kripke's modal argument for an extensionalist view of names and Hilary Putnam's Twin Earth argument for semantic externalism become non sequiturs when the assumption is withdrawn. Examples such as Kripke's Jonah case show that names cannot have a Fregean sense, something that determines a bearer, but not that they cannot have a sense; Putnam's Twin Earth example shows that it is not the case both that intension determines extension and that knowledge of meaning is in the head, but not that it is the latter rather than the former that is false.

As might be expected in a century in which philosophy prided itself on its linguistic turn, and in which "adherents of all the various systems . . . unconsciously presuppose" that intensionalism is Fregean intensionalism, many such issues have been decided on the basis of too restrictive a consideration of the alternatives. The arguments involved in these issues are symptomatic of a mistake on which the philosophy of our epoch—analytic philosophy, as it is called—rests, a mistake that has led philosophers to accept less intuitively satisfying resolutions to issues in the philosophy of language than they could have. This mistake is the failure, as Descartes put it, "to direct [our semantic] attention to simple matters." Descartes's distinction between simple and complex matters is the distinction between mereological structure and logical structure—between, to use Frege's revealing metaphors, analyticity based on containment in the sense of "beams in a house" and analyticity based on containment in the sense of "a plant in the seed." Non-Fregean intensionalism yields the former sense of analyticity; Fregean intensionalism yields the latter.

Quine's criticism of the attempt to determine analytic sentences in terms of meaning postulates plays the same role as his criticism of the attempt to determine synonymy pairs in terms of interchangeability. In virtue of what is a sentence (e.g., 'Bachelors are single') analytic? Not, Quine showed, because, as Carnap had argued, it belongs to a set specified by arbitrarily chosen postulates. But if reducing analyticity to logical truth via meaning postulates does not work, what is left?

From the perspective of Descartes's "simple matters," there is, as before, another option. "Simple" here is naturally taken to refer to syntactic and logical simplicity. 'Bachelor' and 'single' are syntactic and logical simples and the sentence 'Bachelors are single' is logically non-complex or elementary. But none of this implies that there is no complexity of sense structure. If sense structure is mereological, then the term 'bachelor' can have a complex sense, one of whose components is the sense of 'single', and the sentence 'Bachelors are single' can be understood as analytic in virtue of a "beams in the house" containment like the traditional Kantian notion.

I think that I have explained my debt to Quine for showing that the theory of meaning cannot be explicated in logical terms à la Frege/Carnap intensionalism. I have also sketched an alternative explication. This book argues that the theory of meaning can be explained in mereological terms within a non-Fregean intensionalism. I believe that it presents the history and status of significant portions of contemporary philosophy in a new and more intuitively satisfying light.

ACKNOWLEDGMENTS

I wish to thank a number of people for helpful comments at various stages of the writing of this book: Brad Amour-Garb, David Barnett, Edward Becker, Alan Berger, Paul Boghossian, Ned Block, Arthur Collins, John Collins, Edward Ernst, Massimo Grama, Carsten Hansen, Eric D. Hetherington, Paul Horwich, Arnold Koslow, Daniel Leafe, Russell Marcus, Fritz McDonald, Elliott Mendelson, David Pitt, Paul Postal, François Recanati, Mark Sainsbury, Virginia Valian, Palle Yourgrau, and Zsofia Zvolenszky.

I owe special thanks to David Pitt for help with the preparation of the final manuscript when, for health reasons, I was unable to do it all on my own. He is responsible for very many improvements in both style and content. I also owe special thanks to Brad Armour-Garb for regular discussions of material in the book. He, too, is responsible for many improvements. I am grateful to both of them for many hours of highly enjoyable philosophy.

CONTENTS

Sense, Reference, and Philosophy

Introduction

This book sets out a new conception of the philosophy of language, and, due to the central role that language has played in twentieth-century philosophy, a new conception of many other aspects of philosophy as well. The new conception of the philosophy of language is needed because contemporary philosophy of language rests on a mistake. The mistake is the widespread assumption that the semantics of natural language is logic/reference-based. There is, of course, a sense in which the assumption is just a truism. Given the "theory of sense"/"theory of reference" ambiguity of the term 'semantics', reference is *ipso facto* a basic part of semantics. But the assumption in question makes the significant claim that the theory of sense is logic-based, too.

Gottlob Frege originated this claim. He held that expressions of a language have sense over and above reference (intensionalism), but he also held that sense and analyticity are fundamentally referential notions (Fregean intensionalism). As much as Frege's celebrated distinction between sense and reference, this conception of sense and analyticity set the agenda for much of twentieth-century semantics and philosophy of language. It polarized those fields around the issue between the intensionalist semantics of philosophers like Frege and Rudolf Carnap and the extensionalist semantics of philosophers like Bertrand Russell and W. V. Quine. One side championed a logic-based semantics with senses mediating between word and object, and the other championed a logic-based semantics without them.

Ludwig Wittgenstein in his late work was an exception, insofar as he rejected a logic-based semantics, but an exception that proves the rule. The *Philosophical Inves-*

3

tigations (1953) is to a large extent a sustained argument against Frege's, Russell's, and Wittgenstein's own earlier logic-based semantics. Wittgenstein was the first philosopher to see the basic problems with a logic-based semantics for natural language, to challenge the supposition that such a semantics is the only possible one for natural language, and to come up with an alternative semantics. But in equating formal semantics with logic-based semantics, he also posed the issue too narrowly. From the perspective of the present work, Wittgenstein led the way, but, as I shall argue, the alternative he came up with threw out the formal baby with the logical bath water.

Since a logic is a *theory* of implication, the mistake on which contemporary philosophy of language rests leads to its drawing the language/theory distinction at a point beyond the true boundaries of language. The initial Fregean form of the conception, on which just the theory of implication is encompassed within a theory of language, was the thin edge of the wedge. In the course of the last century, the rationale for expanding the boundaries of language led to more extreme forms of expansion. One instance is expressed in Wittgenstein's conception of the incompleteness of language (1953: section 18); languages, like cities, are forever extending their "suburbs" with the advancement of science. Another instance is Quine's familiar holistic view, on which the boundaries of language encompass "[t]he totality of our so-called knowledge or beliefs" (1953: 42). Frege's rationale for his own expansion was his logicist program. The early Wittgenstein and the logical positivists had their own axe to grind, namely, their program to eliminate metaphysics. Another, less ideologically based rationale for such expansion was the program of refuting the skeptic on linguistic grounds. This was to be accomplished by providing a linguistic basis for philosophical views about knowledge and, hence, a linguistic sanction for them that everyone, including the skeptic, must accept.

To be sure, none of these programs ever accomplished its goal; but, despite this poor track record, the idea that meaning is to be understood in logical terms became more and more entrenched over the years, particularly as logical apparatus came to be relied on more and more for representing the meaning/logical form of sentences. Thus, quite properly within this tradition of logical semantics, Russell's theory of descriptions (1905) came to be known as, in Frank Ramsey's phrase, a "paradigm of philosophy." As a consequence of this entrenchment, the idea that meaning is to be understood in logical terms has warped the way philosophers approach many questions, and in ways that have become more and more difficult to detect.

I am not claiming that the warping has gone completely unnoticed. As just mentioned, Wittgenstein, early on, saw signs of trouble, such as the difficulties he encountered (1961: section 6.3751) in trying to explain how elementary propositions can have logical properties. But, as I see it, he misread the signs. He took them to show that an account of meaning in terms of a *formal* theory is wrong, when what they show is only that accounts of meaning in terms of a *logical* theory are wrong. Quine also saw signs of trouble, particularly in connection with the analytic/synthetic distinction. But he, too, misread them. He took his incisive criticisms of Frege's and Carnap's accounts of analyticity to show that analyticity is bogus, rather than that Frege's and Carnap's accounts are bogus.

As it all goes back to Frege, the presentation of my new conception of the philosophy of language must begin with Frege. As we shall discover, there are really two Freges. One is the Frege of the prevalent conception of the philosophy of language, who, but for the details (later supplied, principally, by Carnap), had the last word on intensionalism. This Frege is a figure of myth. The other is the Frege who, in the pursuit of a logicist will-o'-the-wisp, got his creation, intensionalism, off on the wrong track by wedding sense to reference in his classic characterization of sense as the determiner of reference (1952: 57). This Frege, as will emerge in the course of this study, replaced the incondite intensionalism of traditional philosophers such as Descartes, Locke, and Kant with a more precise and philosophically ambitious but, as we shall see, far less philosophically and linguistically adequate intensionalism. This is the real Frege. What I think we should say about the real Frege is something like what the real Frege said (1953: 101–102) about Kant. We should say that Frege was "a genius to whom we must all look up with grateful awe" who performed a "great service" in creating robust arguments to make a distinction between sense and reference. But he was wrong about semantics. Neither sense, nor the distinction between sense and reference, nor analyticity, is what he said it is.

Frege's contributions to the philosophy of mathematics, logic, and the philosophy of language have now attained a level of renown that strikingly contrasts with their near-total neglect during his lifetime. Despite the fact that his account of the foundations of mathematics did not survive Russell's paradox and Gödel's theorem, Frege is widely considered to be the greatest philosopher of mathematics of all time. Despite the fact that his logical notation was never adopted and his logic says nothing about important contemporary branches of the subject, Frege is widely considered to be the greatest logician since Aristotle. And the same is true with respect to his contributions to the philosophy of language. Despite the trenchant criticisms of Wittgenstein, Quine, and Kripke, Frege is thought by many to be the greatest modern philosopher of language. Many, and I count myself among them, would even go so far as to say that Frege's contributions to the philosophy of language rendered virtually everything in the subject prior to them obsolete and everything after them into commentary, elaboration, and response.

However, Frege's contribution to the philosophy of language contrasts sharply with his contributions to the philosophy of mathematics and logic in two respects. On the one hand, whereas the defects of his logicist philosophy of mathematics and the limitations of his predicate logic are now fully recognized and properly understood, the defects and limitations of his intensionalism are either not recognized at all or not properly understood. Intensionalists have not recognized these problems because, in light of Frege's solutions to his puzzles (1952: 56–71) and his "fruitfulness criticism" of Kantian analyticity (1953: 99–101), they have come to see the identification of sense with Fregean sense and the identification of analyticity with Fregean analyticity as the *sine qua non* of semantics. This is the message of David Lewis's pronouncement that "Semantics with no treatment of truth conditions is not semantics" (1972: 169). Extensionalists—those who reject senses—have, of course, recognized the defects and limitations of Frege's intensionalism, but they have not properly identified their source. They have taken intensionalists at their word that senses are Fregean senses, and, as a consequence, they have mistakenly attributed problems with the Fregean notion of sense to the notion of sense per se. One of the main theses in this book is that the fundamental feature of Fregean intensionalism, its conception of sense as the determiner of reference, is the principal source of the defects and limitations that are generally attributed to intensionalism.

The term 'Fregean intensionalism', as it is often used, and as I shall use it in this book, refers not only to Frege's own views about sense, reference, and analyticity, but also to positions based on his views that have significantly developed and extended them over the years. The term covers the positions of Frege's principal disciples, Carnap, Alonzo Church, and C. I. Lewis, who, though departing from Frege's overall position in some ways, nonetheless preserve the central aspects of his thinking on sense, reference, and analyticity. The term also covers the positions of the "neo-Fregeans," a diverse group of contemporary philosophers including Michael Dummett, Hilary Putnam, Gareth Evans, and Christopher Peacocke, whose views differ more from Frege's than do those of his principal disciples. Dummett construes a theory of meaning as a theory of understanding, Putnam takes an externalist view of sense, and Peacocke characterizes concepts in terms of the conditions under which people possess them. Nonetheless, these philosophers endorse the essential tenets of Fregeanism—that senses or meanings or concepts are determinants of reference, and that semantics is logic-based.

This is clear in the cases of Dummett and Putnam, though, of course, they want semantics to include considerably more than just logic. It is also clear in Peacocke (1992). Peacocke's possession conditions for concepts build logic into them, and are governed by what he calls a "determination theory," which requires that a possession condition for a concept determine its semantic value. It is not clear why Peacocke diverges from Frege in putting the individuation conditions for concepts in these terms. Peacocke takes concepts to be abstract objects, and he distinguishes between a philosophical theory of them and a psychological theory of their possession. So it is hard to see why the former theory is required to provide psychological explanations of the circumstances under which people meet the conditions for possessing concepts, since this is just what the latter theory is required to provide. Nothing would be lost by presenting a more Fregean statement of the individuating conditions for concepts, on which they are formulated directly with respect to the features of concepts themselves. Thus, instead of talking about the need for thinkers to find the introduction and elimination rules for conjunction compelling, the philosophical theory can characterize the concept of conjunction in terms of these rules, and the psychological theory can concern itself with the circumstances under which people possess the concept of conjunction (in virtue of finding those rules compelling).

Intensionalists are not the only ones to rely on the equation of intensionalism and Fregean intensionalism. Extensionalists rely on it, too. As I have argued elsewhere (1990b), Wittgenstein, Quine, and Donald Davidson assume the equation in formulating their positions as denying the existence of Fregean senses and in constructing the criticisms of intensionalism that justify their notion of an unmediated relation between word and object.

Another of the main theses of this book is that there is a non-Fregean form of intensionalism—a position that is intensionalist in claiming that expressions have senses over and above their reference, but that claims that senses are not reference-determiners and sense structure is not logical structure. Showing that there is an alternative conception of sense shows that the automatic identification of intensionalism with Fregean intensionalism is mistaken. Recognition of this mistake raises the questions of whether intensionalists ought to be Fregean intensionalists and whether extensionalists' criticisms have been too narrowly tailored for them to apply beyond Fregean intensionalism. I will argue that there are strong reasons for thinking that intensionalists ought to abandon Fregean intensionalism and for thinking that extensionalists' criticisms do not apply to intensionalism per se, but only to its Fregean form.

Frege's extensionalist critics were right, but they drew the wrong conclusion about the source of the problems with Fregean intensionalism that they uncovered. Ironically, they made the same mistake as the Fregean intensionalists themselves, namely, identifying sense with Fregean sense. Accepting this identification, Frege's extensionalist critics attributed the problems they discovered with his intensionalism to intensionalism per se and concluded that intensionalism is unsound. This conclusion does not follow if the notion of Fregean sense lies at the heart of those problems and if there is an alternative form of intensionalism in which senses are appropriately non-Fregean.

If I am right about there being such an alternative, the central issue of twentieth-century philosophy of language—the intensionalist/extensionalist controversy—has been misformulated. Properly formulated, the issue is not whether sentences of natural languages have *Fregean* senses, but whether they have senses. As a consequence of this mistaken formulation, two misconceptions have become widespread. One is that the problems with Fregean intensionalism establish that extensionalism is the right philosophy of language, as Wittgenstein and Quine argue; the other is that those problems establish extensionalism for names and certain other terms, as Kripke and Putnam argue. And these, as we shall see (especially in the third part of the book) are by no means the only misconceptions to which acceptance of this mistaken formulation has led.

The other respect in which Frege's contribution to the philosophy of language differs from his contributions to the philosophy of mathematics and logic is that, although the defects and limitations of the latter, being recognized, had no detrimental consequences, the defects and limitations of the former, not being recognized, have had detrimental consequences for much of twentieth-century philosophy. This is only to be expected, since Frege's work in the philosophy of language brought about the so-called linguistic turn, which put questions of language and meaning at the center of philosophy and led to the founding of the most vigorous school of philosophy in the twentieth century, analytic philosophy. As a consequence, the influence of Fregean intensionalism is felt in virtually every major area of the subject.

Hume once claimed that attention to the "imperceptible" change in the course of argument from 'is' to 'ought' "wou'd subvert all the vulgar systems of morality" (1978: 469–470). I will claim that attention to the "imperceptible" change in the course of arguments from conclusions about Fregean sense to conclusions about sense would "subvert" very many philosophies of language. I will also claim that attention to the non-Fregean notion of sense—overlooked when philosophers unhesitatingly pass from conclusions about Fregean sense to conclusions about sense—would change the way that very many philosophical questions are understood and, as a result, enable us to make substantial progress in answering them.

The book is divided into three parts. The first is about sense. It criticizes the Fregean definition of sense and presents an alternative that avoids the criticisms. I argue that the basic defect of the Fregean definition is that in making the understanding of sense a matter of understanding reference, it is reductive, and that, in virtue of its reductive nature, the definition raises three insoluble problems for Fregean intensionalism. The first is that Frege's notion of sense is too restrictive in fixing extensional structure, thus ruling out what are genuine extensional possibilities. The second is that, at the same time, the notion is not restrictive enough in fixing intensional structure, thus precluding constraints on the determination of sense strong enough to prevent indeterminacy. The third problem is that the reductive nature of Frege's characterization of sense renders it incapable of explicating sense in natural language, since it erases all boundaries between senses.

All three problems are discussed in the literature in some form or other; but in each case they are wrongly attributed to intensionalism per se. The first problem was originally raised by Wittgenstein at various places in the *Philosophical Investigations* and subsequently pressed by Putnam and Kripke. The second was raised by Quine, in arguing for evidential symmetry in radical translation and the indeterminacy of translation. The third problem was also raised by Wittgenstein. It was one of the difficulties with the Frege/Russell-style semantics of the *Tractatus* that eventually led him to develop his late philosophy. All of these problems were initially presented as problems with intensionalism rather than as problems with Fregean intensionalism. In contrast, I will be concerned to show that their real source is the reductive nature of Fregean definitions of sense and analyticity. The problems arise *only* because Fregean definitions explicate sense and analyticity in terms of concepts from the theory of reference rather than the theory of sense.

To show that these problems arise only for Fregean intensionalism, I present a non-reductive definition of sense—one that explains sense and analyticity without reference to reference. Rather than determiners of referential properties and relations, senses, on this definition, are determiners of sense properties and relations. The main burden of the first part of the book is to show that these non-reductive definitions of sense and analyticity face none of those problems. The definitions are not too restrictive extensionally, they are not too permissive intensionally, and they preserve the boundaries between senses in natural language.

The second part of the book is about reference. It examines the relation between sense and reference from the perspective of my non-Fregean conception of sense. I argue that, as well as providing a better account of sense than Frege's, this conception of sense provides a better account of the relation between sense and reference. I explore in some detail the relation between theories of sense and theories of reference in natural language, showing, first, that a richer conception of the theory of reference emerges as a result of having an autonomous theory of sense together with an account of how the sense structure described in that theory contributes to referential structure, and, second, that that conception of the theory of reference sacrifices nothing of value in standard treatments of reference.

The third part of the book is about philosophy. It is concerned with the implications of the arguments in the first and second parts for twenty or so significant questions in contemporary philosophy. In including this material, I have an ulterior motive in addition to the philosopher's customary one of trying to better understand philosophical questions and make progress in answering them. I want to use the understanding and progress that are achieved to challenge the belief that the proper approach to meaning in natural language is a logic-based semantics, and to dispel the consequent bias against non-referential conceptions of semantics. It is a measure of how deeply entrenched this bias has become that Lewis can make so contentious a claim as "Semantics with no treatment of truth conditions is not semantics" without feeling the slightest obligation to give an argument and without other philosophers feeling the slightest need for one.

Such pronouncements pass unchallenged because virtually everyone thinks that non-referential semantics cannot do significant philosophical work. This thought, which I hope by the end of this book will no longer seem a truism, originates with Frege's famous "fruitfulness criticism" of Kant's semantics (1953: 99–101), which dismisses it as too conceptually impoverished to do philosophically significant work. Now, Frege never actually argued for this claim about Kantian semantics. What he argued for was rather that it did not do the philosophical work that *he* wanted to be done: the Kantian concepts of sense and analyticity are not logically rich enough to account for definition in mathematics. And what was the project for which such concepts were required? Logicism. Hence, the bias against non-referential semantics began its career as a dissatisfaction with Kantian semantics for failing to meet the needs of Frege's ill-fated logicist program.

Frege's new definition of analyticity and its role in his logicist program provided a model for subsequent philosophers with their own ideas about what philosophical work needed to be done. The early Wittgenstein and the logical positivists saw the usefulness of the definition for their campaign against metaphysics. The Fregean concept of analyticity seemed just what empiricists needed to reply to Kant's criticism of Hume. They could now reply that Kant's criticism rests on an inadequate concept of analyticity. Kant's cases of synthetic a priori knowledge are just an artifact of an unfruitful concept of analyticity. Thus, they argued that Frege's concept of analyticity discredits the metaphysician's claim that knowledge of synthetic a priori truth requires positing a special philosophical faculty for intuiting essences. Moritz Schlick claimed that it makes it possible to explain away "the showpieces of the phenomenological philosophy" as analytic (in the sense of Frege's fruitful concept) a priori truth (1949: 285).

The idea that senses have to be thick to be philosophically useful does not have an impressive track record. Neither Frege's attempt to reduce mathematics to logic nor the logical positivists' attempts to explain away synthetic a priori knowledge or to prove that metaphysical sentences are nonsense were successful. Despite such failures, no disgrace attached to the idea. Its survival in the face of its failures in explaining away "the showpieces of the phenomenological philosophy," in particular, Wittgenstein's failure to show that alleged synthetic *a priori* sentences such as (I.1)

(I.1)   Nothing is simultaneously red and green.

are analytic, is perhaps the most striking example of its survival value. Here the failure led not, as might have been expected, to rejection of the idea that senses have to be thick to do significant philosophical work, but rather to a further thickening of them. The change from Wittgenstein's early philosophy to his late philosophy was, as E. B. Allaire (1966) and others have argued, motivated in large part by Wittgenstein's failure to handle color sentences such as (I.1) within something like the logic-based semantics of the *Tractatus*. Wittgenstein thus abandoned logic-based semantics together with formal semantics in favor of a notion of sense that is based on the idea of interlocking language games making up an entire "form of life." Wittgenstein's response to the recalcitrance of sentences such as (I.1) was thus to introduce even thicker senses than those in the logic-based semantics. The idea that senses have to be thick to be philosophically useful is the best example I know of of a "teflon idea" in philosophy.

We will see later that senses have to be maximally thin to avoid philosophical trouble and to do the sort of philosophical work it is appropriate for them to do. In the third part, I will present a large number of examples to illustrate this point (one of which is that this thin notion of sense, when properly formalized, finally succeeds in showing that color sentences such as (I.1) are not synthetic, but analytic). In presenting so many examples, I am not indulging in philosophical overkill. The bias against a thin theory of meaning is now so deeply entrenched that drastic action is called for. As I see it, excess is the only thing that stands much chance of demonstrating the health benefits of thinness.

This book extends the line of argument in previous publications (1986a; 1988; 1990a; 1992; 1994; 1997) in which I undertook to develop an alternative to Fregean intensionalism. In one of those essays, I proposed a "new intensionalism" based on the non-Fregean definition of sense (1992), and, in that essay and others, I argued that the problems that have beset intensionalism over the past forty or so years stem almost entirely from the assumption that senses are reference-determiners. This book presents an extensive philosophical rationale for a theory of sense that is entirely independent of the theory of reference. It aims to be a far more systematic criticism of Frege's notion of sense, a far fuller clarification of the new intensionalism's conception of the relation between sense and reference, and a far more elaborate consideration of the philosophical consequences of an autonomous theory of sense.

This book is also directly related to the line of argument in *The Metaphysics of Meaning* and *Realistic Rationalism* (1990b; 1998b). In those books, I argued that the idea that senses must be thick, which was responsible for the rejection of intensionalism, limited our broader philosophical choices to one or another form of naturalism—in particular, some version of Wittgenstein's therapeutic naturalism or some version of Quine's scientistic naturalism. I argued that the possibility of a new intensionalism in the philosophy of language, in turn, creates the option of a viable non-naturalist philosophy. *The Metaphysics of Meaning* and *Realistic Rationalism* set out this further option. The former book shows that the arguments of Wittgenstein and Quine depend on the assumption that intensionalism is Fregean intensionalism. The latter book sets out the non-naturalist philosophy, which is realist where Wittgenstein's naturalism is anti-realist and rationalist where Quine's is empiricist. This book thus provides systematic semantic support for the philosophical position set out in those books, though it has been written to stand on its own as a treatise on twentieth-century philosophy of language.

Sense

1.1. Two definitions of sense

Two things have made Frege's characterization of sense (1952: 57) irresistible to intensionalists.[1] One is the thought that Frege's puzzle about how '$a = a$' and true '$a = b$' statements can differ semantically, which he uses to motivate the introduction of his notion of sense, cannot be solved without Fregean senses. The problem with this thought is that Fregean senses are not necessary for a solution to the puzzle. It can be handled with any notion of sense, since any notion of sense permits us to assign different senses to the symbols 'a' and 'b'. In particular, the puzzle can be solved with my non-Fregean notion of sense.

The other is the thought that a Fregean definition is able to accomplish two things that are each desirable and not otherwise jointly accomplishable. One is the reduction of the theory of sense to the theory of reference in virtue of explaining sense in terms of reference. The other is the preservation of the sense/reference distinction. Reduction is desirable because it replaces what is seen as a barren and vague notion of sense with what is seen as a fruitful and precise one. Preservation of the sense/reference distinction is desirable because it keeps philosophers from facing the situation of having to cope with Frege's puzzle without the possibility of appealing to senses in a solution to it. Intensionalists thus see a Fregean definition as letting them have their cake and eat it.

But if sense is reducible to reference within the theory of reference, it is not immediately clear why the distinction between sense and reference should survive.

If the theoretical vocabulary of the system that provides the definition base consists exclusively of referential concepts, as surely the theory of reference does, how can there be a place for a concept of sense over and above the concepts of reference? Does not acceptance of the Fregean reduction of the theory of sense to the theory of reference turn intensionalism into extensionalism? The reason it does not is that a Fregean reduction of the theory of sense to the theory of reference is not an *elimina-tive* reduction in the manner of an account of meaning like Davidson's, which de-nies that there is "anything essential to the idea of meaning that remained to be captured [once we have] a characterization of the predicate 'is true' that led to the invariable pairing of truths with truths and falsehoods with falsehoods" (1967a: 312). Rather, the Fregean characterization of sense effects a *conservative* reduction: a notion of sense and a sense/reference distinction are available in the reducing theory.

This is because the Fregean definition explains sense in terms of the role senses play in an instrument/purpose structure. Sense and reference are distinguished by their different but correlative roles in the structure. The Fregean definition is like a definition of an employer as one who hires someone. Here employing and being employed are converses with respect to the hiring relation. On the Fregean defini-tion, having a sense and having a referent are converses with respect to the referring relation. Sense is the aspect of expressions in virtue of which they refer to certain objects in the domain of the language; referents are the things in the domain to which expressions refer in virtue of their senses. Sense and reference are therefore deter-miner and determinee with respect to the referring relation.

Accordingly, our understanding of the notions of sense and reference must come from an account of reference, just as our understanding of the notions of employer and employee must come from an account of hiring. The sense/reference distinction is then a distinction within the theory of reference, between the instruments of refer-ence determination (senses) and the objects which those instruments determine (refer-ents). It is not lost on a Fregean reduction, but rather recast as a distinction within the reducing theory. So Fregean intensionalists do not pay the price extensionalists have to pay for eschewing senses. Since senses are not sacrificed, Fregean intensionalists do not face the puzzles about identity and opacity with no chance of appealing to the only objects that offer a clear route to a solution.

Notwithstanding the attractiveness of the Fregean conservative reduction in this respect, it does sacrifice something. What it sacrifices is the option of a non-reductive definition of sense, one that makes no use of notions from any theory other than the theory of sense itself. This sacrifice entails the loss of the possibility of an autonomous theory of sense, and, as a consequence, the loss of the possibil-ity of conceiving of the relation between sense and reference as weaker than deter-mination. Given an autonomous theory of sense, the question of what the relation is between the sense of an expression and its reference is the question of how a linguistic system of independent senses is related to a domain of objects. And the only constraint on an answer is the general one of capturing the role sense plays in the assignment of objects to expressions. On this conception, nothing commits us in advance to accepting an answer based on the maximally strong relation of refer-ence determination.

Intensionalists who adopt a Fregean notion of sense are like the characters in W. W. Jacobs's story "The Monkey's Paw." Their wish for "fruitful" notions of sense and analyticity is granted in a way that results in calamity. Signs of the intensionalists' calamity are everywhere. They include *inter alia* Wittgenstein's wide-ranging criticisms of their views of meaning and language, Quine's criticism of their analytic/synthetic distinction, Putnam's criticisms of their conception of natural kind terms, and Kripke's criticism of their descriptivism concerning proper names. In this book, I shall argue that intensionalists have unnecessarily opened themselves up to those criticisms. I shall also argue that pursuing the possibility of a semantics based on a non-reductive definition of sense avoids the criticisms and the calamity for contemporary intensionalism that they brought on.

Opponents of non-referential semantics assure us that such an option is not worth preserving. Neither extensionalists nor intensionalists are likely to show much interest in such an option, the former because they think intensionalism is fundamentally wrong and the latter because, being almost exclusively Fregeans, they think Fregean intensionalism is fundamentally right. But we have progressed far enough at this point not to take such assurances at face value. At this stage of my argument, of course, this option is a mere possibility. But possibilities are too important in philosophy to be dismissed without argument. Moreover, as I will show shortly, there can be no such argument in the present case, since a consistent notion of an autonomous theory of sense can be formulated.

If the possibility of non-Fregean forms of intensionalism has to be recognized, then those who think intensionalism ought to be Fregean have to argue that Fregean intensionalism is preferable to other forms of the position. In order to make clear what is required of such an argument, it is useful to distinguish between establishing (1) that a Fregean reductive definition of sense is better than any other reductive definition of sense and (2) that a Fregean reductive definition of sense is better than any non-reductive definition of sense. Both (1) and (2) have to be established to justify Frege's characterization of sense and his reduction of the theory of sense to the theory of reference.

Intensionalists have argued, successfully in my opinion, that the Fregean definition is preferable to other reductive definitions such as those that identify sense with use, illocutionary force potential, dispositions to verbal response, patterns of retinal stimulation, extension in the actual world, extensions in possible worlds, and so on. All such identifications fail "Moore's test." If, for an identification of sense with X, we ask, "Are all cases of sameness of sense cases of sameness of X and all cases of sameness of X cases of sameness of sense?" the answer is negative. For instance, the identification of sense with extension in all possible worlds fails Moore's test because there are nonsynonymous expressions—like 'the number two' and 'the even prime'—with the same extension in all possible worlds.

For present purposes, I shall assume that (1) is established. What about (2)? Here the picture is quite different. Fregean intensionalists have done next to nothing to establish (2). They either have been content to take the apparent absence of a non-referential semantics to mean that there is none or, like Lewis, have dismissed non-referential semantics out of hand as not semantics. The rationale for thinking that

Fregean intensionalism is the only tenable form of intensionalism thus comes down to Frege's fruitfulness criticism. Let us return to that criticism—something we shall do again and again throughout the book.

Frege criticized the semantics underlying Kant's notion of analyticity as having all the conceptual subtlety and constructive potential of a set of baby's blocks. Simple ideas stack up to form complex ideas, which, in turn, combine with other complex ideas to form further complex ideas. Analysis is a matter of breaking down complexes into their parts, with nothing new contributed in the process. The explicative relation in the predicate of an analytic sentence in Kant's sense merely unstacks a baby-block construction. Frege invidiously compared such semantics to his own logic-based semantics: "the more fruitful type of definition is a matter of drawing boundary lines that were not previously given at all. What we shall be able to infer from it cannot be inspected in advance; here, we are not simply taking out of the box what we have just put into it" (1953: 100–101). Frege notes that analytic truths and definitions in his sense "extend our knowledge and ought, therefore, on Kant's view, to be regarded as synthetic," and then goes on to remark, "yet [such truths] can be proved by purely logical means, and are *thus* analytic" (italics mine). Frege's suggestion is that Kant's notion of analyticity contains a conceptual confusion because propositions that ought to be taken as synthetic because they extend our knowledge, turn out to be analytic.

This criticism rests on a sleight of hand in which Frege's "proved by purely logical means" concept of analyticity and Kant's explicative concept are switched across the conjunction. The switch is accomplished with an egregiously pre-emptive use of 'thus' (German 'also'). Frege thereby presumes that his own notion of analyticity—namely, provability from logic and definition—is the only clear criterion by which to decide whether something turns out analytic. Thus, we can register (along with Benacerraf [1981: 34, n. 6]) the quite justified protest on Kant's behalf that his explicative concept of analyticity does not contain a conceptual confusion. Sentences, such as ones of the form $P \rightarrow (P \lor Q)$, which are provable logically but are not analytic, are simply not analytic in *his* sense.

For Frege's fruitfulness criticism to refute Kantian analyticity, it has to be shown that fruitfulness *is* a virtue and fruitlessness a vice. It is, of course, clear why Frege *thought* fruitfulness a virtue. His logicist program of showing that mathematical truth is analytic truth requires a fruitful concept of analyticity. With Kantian analyticity in place of Fregean analyticity, Russell would not have had to discover a contradiction in the set-theoretic foundations of Frege's logicism. It would never have gotten off the ground. But the fact that Kantian analyticity is useless for Frege's logicism shows no more than that Kantian analyticity is useless for one purpose—hardly a refutation, since concepts not useful for one purpose may be useful for others.

Frege writes as if fruitfulness were an absolute, a criterion that allows us to evaluate concepts once and for all on a single the-more-fruitful-the-better basis. But concepts are cognitive tools, and, as such, must be judged in relation to the demands of the tasks for which we intend to use them. A Swiss Army knife may be more "fruitful" than a scalpel, but the latter is better for performing surgery. Since the evaluation of concepts is task-relative, Frege has no business taking fruitfulness as a standard for making absolute judgments about the adequacy of semantic concepts.

The adequacy of a concept of analyticity, like that of a semantics as a whole, ought not to be determined on the basis of its appropriateness for the study of the foundations of mathematics, but on the basis of its appropriateness for the study of natural languages. Frege does not concern himself with whether his concepts of sense and analyticity are appropriate for that study, no doubt because he thinks study of such "imperfect" languages is only worthwhile as a point of departure for the construction of a "logically perfect" one (1952: 70). Be this as it may, the right question from the present standpoint is whether Frege's concepts are the proper ones to use in the study of natural language. Certainly many in both philosophy and linguistics think they are. But here Frege's fruitfulness criticism of Kantian analyticity contributes nothing, amounting as it does to no more than the trivial claim that his fruitful concept of analyticity is preferable to Kant's because it is more fruitful.

Linguistic definitions show their worth in explicating *linguistic* structure. The proper standard for linguistic theories is how well they account for the structure of natural languages. This means that what has to be reckoned with is the possibility that a revealing account of such structure might well require a description of the contents of the sense "boxes" associated with expressions of a natural language. If so, we are better off with a concept of analyticity that merely inventories the contents of such boxes than with a fruitful one that finds things in them that are not there. Frege's fruitfulness criticism fails even against as flawed a notion of analyticity as Kant's because it provides no reason to think that unfruitfulness is unsatisfactory.

Some contemporary philosophers employ versions of the fruitfulness criticism, but none manages to avoid the question-begging character of Frege's own version. Dummett uses a version of the criticism to object to autonomous sense theories, theories that are, as he puts it, concerned with "the nature of significance (meaningfulness) or of synonymy (sameness of meaning)" (1973: 92). He claims that those theories fail as theories of meaning for natural language because such theories are theories of *understanding*. Here Dummett expands the notion of fruitfulness beyond Frege's logical notion. A theory of meaning has to be a theory of everything involved in the speaker/hearer's understanding of utterances, including, in addition to their semantics, knowledge of their sound pattern and syntax, information necessary for on-line processing, and pragmatic features.

Like Frege, Dummett has a philosophical agenda that requires a theory of sense to be more fruitful than a mere explication of sense structure. Again, the agenda derives from concerns in the philosophy of mathematics. In Dummett's case, nothing less than a full theory of understanding will do because nothing less can provide an adequate linguistic basis for his intuitionist philosophy of mathematics. Hence, the question for Dummett, as for Frege, is this: What argument is there to show that a theory of understanding is better than an autonomous theory of sense for the purposes of explicating meaning in natural language? Dummett's argument, that "there would be no route from [an autonomous theory of sense] to an account of understanding" (1975: 100–101), assumes that a theory of meaning should be a theory of understanding, and hence Dummett begs the question. (See the discussion of Dummett's argument in Katz 1990b [84–86].)

It is surprising that Dummett says nothing about Chomsky's competence/performance distinction (1965: 3ff.), since that distinction by itself undercuts his claim that a theory of meaning for natural language is a theory of understanding. That distinction separates theories about the structure of a language from theories about how speakers produce and understand its sentences. On Chomsky's distinction, the linguist idealizes away from aspects of the use of sentences in formulating grammatical laws, in a manner similar to the way the physicist idealizes away from friction in formulating the laws of motion. On the linguist's idealization, a theory of syntax concerns not understanding, but what is understood, the grammatical structures underlying properties and relations such as well-formedness (grammaticality) and equivalence of constituent-type (sameness of syntax). Similarly, a theory of meaning concerns not understanding, but what is understood, the grammatical structures responsible for properties and relations such as significance (meaningfulness) and synonymy (sameness of meaning). On this distinction, Dummett's theory rests on a competence/performance conflation.

If there were no non-reductive definition of sense, Fregean intensionalists would not need an argument to convince other intensionalists to accept their reductive definition of sense.[2] But, as there *is* such a definition, the failure to establish (2) calls the reduction of the theory of sense to the theory of reference and the Fregean sense/reference distinction into question, thereby opening up a dialectic within intensionalism about which definition of sense is better.

The non-reductive definition of sense that I will oppose to the Fregean reductive definition is (D).[3]

(D)   Sense is that aspect of the grammatical structure of sentences that is responsible for their sense properties and relations (e.g., meaningfulness, meaninglessness, ambiguity, synonymy, redundancy, and antonymy).

On (D), senses are still determiners, but what they determine are sense properties and relations, not referential properties and relations. Sense properties and relations, like syntactic properties such as well-formedness and phonological properties like rhyme, reflect the grammatical structure within the sentences of a language, in contrast to referential properties and relations, which reflect the connection between language and the world. In taking it to be internal to sentences, (D) makes sense independent of reference, and makes the theory of sense autonomous.

The condition for the autonomy of a theory of sense with respect to the theory of reference is that its theoretical vocabulary contain no concept from the theory of reference (or from any other theory dealing with the connection between language and its domain). The condition will be met just in case, first, the terms 'meaningfulness', 'meaninglessness', 'ambiguity', 'synonymy', etc. that appear in (D) are themselves understood in terms of the notion of sense—e.g., having a sense, lacking a sense, having more than one sense, having the same sense, etc.; and, second, the account of when expressions have a sense, lack a sense, have more than one sense, have the same sense as another expression, etc. is given exclusively in terms of senses and their mereological structure.

It is hard to exaggerate the importance of this second requirement. The choice of mereological structure over logical structure as sense structure is as important as (D) itself for our theory of sense and its philosophical consequences. The choice ensures that a theory of sense is just about intralinguistic properties and relations of sentences. In delogicizing sense semantics, it reverses Frege's step of replacing Kant's "beams in the house" notion of analyticity with his own "plant in the seed" notion. In the course of this book, the reader will come to see in detail what the significance of this delogicizing is for sense, reference, and philosophy.

Lacking referential concepts, the theory of sense can state no principle concerning the relation between language and the world. Therefore, an account of that relation has to be given in the theory of reference, and, since that relation is not fixed antecedently in the theory of sense, as it is in Fregean semantics, the account of the relation can take the form of a principle weaker than the principle that sense determines reference. I shall also argue that the freedom to choose a weaker principle has important philosophical consequences.

Initially, (D) might seem circular. How much insight, it might be asked, is to be gotten from a definition that explains sense in terms of sense properties and relations? But it would be too quick to conclude that the autonomy of the theory of senses comes at the price of circularity. In the formal sciences, there are domains in which the objects are understood in terms of their properties and relations and their properties and relations are, correspondingly, understood in terms of the structure of the objects. One example is arithmetic, in which numbers and numerical properties and relations play such a complementary role. Logic is another. Quine himself defines logical truth in terms of logical properties and relations. He writes: "I defined a logical truth as a sentence whose truth is assured by its logical structure. . . . It is better to put the matter more explicitly thus: a sentence is logically true if all sentences are true that share its logical structure" (1970: 49).

Quine also remarks that terms like 'logical truth', 'logical falsity', 'logical implication', 'logical incompatibility', and 'logical equivalence' are members of "a family of closely related notions" (48). Still another example is found in linguistics, where the definitions of sound pattern and syntax make use, respectively, of the notions of phonological properties and relations and syntactic properties and relations. The sound pattern of a language is that aspect of the grammatical structure of its sentences responsible for their phonological properties and relations (e.g., rhyme and alliteration), and its syntax that aspect of the grammatical structure of its sentences responsible for their syntactic properties and relations (e.g., well-formedness and equivalence of constituent structure).

I would argue (though I shall not here) that this "family circle" is characteristic of theories in the formal sciences generally. Short of such an argument, it is worth making two related points. One is that it would be quite perilous to make an argument against autonomy in the case of the family of sense concepts. Such an argument would readily translate into an argument against autonomy in the cases of mathematical, logical, and linguistic concepts. Conversely, if autonomy is acceptable in these subjects, there is a prima facie case for the autonomy of the theory of sense. Autonomy rests on the same thing in the theory of sense as in theories in mathematics, logic, and linguistics: axiomatization that explains concepts non-reductively in terms of a systematization of the structure of objects in the domain. This rationale carries over to the theory of meaning as long as it is reasonable to suppose that an explanation of sense concepts can take the form of an axiomatic systematization of the sense structure of sentences.

(D) is not viciously circular because insight into sense is no more intended to come from (D) itself than insight into logic is intended to come from a definition like Quine's. The properties and relations that are invoked in such definitions are to be explained in terms of formal representations of the appropriate structures of sentences. Thus, insight into the nature of sense comes from the interrelations between representations of sense structure and the definitions of sense properties and relations stated in terms of them. (D) sets the stage for the construction of such representations and definitions.

Mention of Quine and circularity brings to mind the argument in "Two Dogmas of Empiricism" that many philosophers have taken to show that the attempt to individuate senses in terms of synonymy is circular. But when we look closely at what Quine actually says about the attempt, we see that he does not say that it is circular. In fact, he *denies* that it is! In summarizing his criticism of interchangeability in intensional contexts as an explanation of synonymy, Quine says the following: "Our argument is not flatly circular, but something like it. It has the form, figuratively speaking, of a closed curve in space" (1953: 30). I regard this remark as so significant a revelation that I chose it as one of the three epigraphs for this book.

The remark may be puzzling at first. How can Quine deny that the argument is "flatly circular"? Hasn't he just tried to demonstrate that it is? Isn't the argument in question one that tries to explain synonymy in terms of interchangeability, in contexts like 'Necessarily all and only bachelors are bachelors', in which necessity can be supposed to be "so narrowly construed as to be applicable only to analytic statements" (1953: 29)? *And* hasn't Quine already shown us that necessity so construed does not serve for languages with "extra-logical synonym pairs, such as 'bachelor' and 'unmarried man'" (23–24) unless we have an understanding of synonymy already? What can he mean by describing the argument as "hav[ing] the form, figuratively speaking, of a closed curve in space"? How are the metaphors "closed curve" and "space" to be unpacked? My initial inclination, which I suspect many readers of "Two Dogmas" shared, was to take the remark as more stylistic than substantive. But I have come to think that nothing could be further from the truth. When we unpack the "closed curve" metaphor, we see that Quine is saying that synonymy and the other concepts of the theory of meaning belong to "a family of closely related notions" that are definable only in terms of one another. Such definition is not "flatly circular" here any more than it is when it is used to express the relations among logical, arithmetic, or geometric notions. The "curve" is "closed" because the concepts in the theory of meaning are not definable or explainable within some theory outside the theory of meaning. Intensional concepts form a system that is irreducible to other systems in the space of theories—in particular, the theory of reference. Ironically, what Quine was saying about the theory of meaning in summarizing his criticism of interchangeability is exactly what I am saying now: the theory is autonomous.

Of course, we do not regard autonomy in the same way. I regard it as putting the theory of meaning on a par with theories in mathematics, logic, and linguistics, and thereby giving the theory a new lease on life. Quine regards it as cutting the theory of meaning off from other theories that might be used to make objective sense of its concepts, and thereby dooming it. I see reduction as transmogrification; Quine sees it as transmutation.

Quine does not provide an argument to show that making objective sense of the theory of meaning requires reducing it to some other theory. This, I believe, is because he did not think it necessary. After all, the intensionalism he was criticizing in "Two Dogmas" is Frege/Carnap intensionalism (the notion of analyticity that Quine targets there—conversion of a sentence into a logical truth "by putting synonyms for synonyms" (22–23)—is clearly Frege's). Since reduction is at the heart of Frege/Carnap intensionalism, Quine hardly needs an argument to show that the position he is criticizing is committed to it.

Thus, Quine's mistake in "Two Dogmas of Empiricism" is the same as that of the Fregean intensionalists he is criticizing: he equates intensionalism with Fregean intensionalism. He assumes that there is only one definition of sense, Frege's, and hence only one definition of analyticity, the Frege/Carnap definition. (D) shows that this assumption is false, and, in so doing, shows (as I shall argue in detail later) that Quine's criticisms fail.

At the beginning of this section, I noted that intensionalists see Frege's reduction as desirable because it replaces what they take to be a barren and vague notion of sense with a fruitful and precise one. We have gotten a good start on our critical examination of the alleged virtue of fruitfulness. Precision is, to be sure, a genuine virtue, but logic has no monopoly on it. The formal methods that provide Fregean semantics with the precision it enjoys have been extensively applied in linguistics and are available to a linguistic semantics that represents mereological sense structure. Earlier publications of mine provide applications of such methods to an autonomous theory of sense, and, in the third part of this book, I will present some of them as illustrations. The question is not whether or not to have formal representations of semantic structure, but what kind of semantic structure to have formal representations of.

1.2. Problems with the Fregean definition of sense

The argument in this section is that the Frege/Carnap notion of semantic structure is not the correct one. I will present three problems with the Fregean definition of sense that are unsolvable within Frege/Carnap semantics and do not arise for a theory of sense based on (D). This is the first phase of my overall argument for the new intensionalism. The second and third phases consist of applications of my approach to the theory of reference and to philosophical problems.

1.2.1. The problem of too strong a constraint

The first of the three problems is that Fregean characterizations of sense—Frege's, Carnap's (1956: 239, 242), the definition of senses as functions from possible worlds to extensions in them, and others like them—constrain reference too strongly. The point is best illustrated by the case of proper names. Frege had a strong reason for taking proper names to have a sense: he could see no other way to explain the difference in cognitive significance between sentences like (1.1) and (1.2) (1952: 56–58).

(1.1)   Hesperus is Hesperus.

(1.2)   Hesperus is Phosphorus.

But if having a sense is equated with having a Fregean sense, this explanation commits us to the assumption that the sense of a name must determine its bearer(s) in counterfactual situations as well as actual ones. Yet, as John Stuart Mill observes (1862: bk. I, ch. 2, section 5), the sense of 'Dartmouth', presumably *city lying at the mouth of the river Dart*, would not pick out Dartmouth in a counterfactual situation where the river Dart changed its course so that the city is no longer located at its mouth. Wittgenstein argued (1953: sections 79–81) along similar lines, targeting Frege's semantics specifically. He pointed out that if we take the property of being the man who led the Israelites out of Egyptian captivity to be the sense of 'Moses', we are forced to deny the possibility of Moses's existing in counterfactual situations in which someone else led the Israelites out of captivity. On the basis of such examples, Wittgenstein says, clearly with Frege in mind, that "we are not equipped with rules for every possible application of [a word]."

Mill's and Wittgenstein's examples show that the cluster of properties that are most naturally taken to pick out the bearer of a name in actual situations do not pick it out in some counterfactual situations. Hence, in making senses determiners of reference, Frege makes the application of names in counterfactual situations conform to the putative criteria for picking out their bearers in actual situations, and, as a consequence, too strongly constrains the possibilities for reference in hypothetical reasoning. We want neither to exclude the possibility that Dartmouth is a bearer of 'Dartmouth' in the counterfactual situation in which the river Dart changed its course nor to exclude the possibility that Moses is a bearer of 'Moses' in the counterfactual situation in which someone else led the Israelites out of captivity.

Wittgenstein (1953: section 87) suggests that the problem extends to common nouns and adjectives as well. Putnam and Kripke take up this suggestion, extending the criticism to some members of the class of common nouns, particularly to those expressing natural kind concepts. In an early essay, Putnam (1975b) argued that taking the property of being a feline animal to be the Fregean sense of 'cat' would preclude the genuine possibility that previous uses of 'cat' referred to Martian robots that look and act like real cats. In a subsequent series of influential essays (1973a; 1975a; 1975c), Putnam presented a number of counterexamples to question whether

Fregean senses do their professed job of reference determination. In one of those essays, Putnam argues that a cluster of properties such as being a light metal, being silver in color, being durable, and being rustless gets the extension of 'aluminum' wrong, because "[f]or all [we] know, every one of these characteristics may also fit molybdenum" (1975c: 150).

Putnam uses essentially the same considerations to argue that knowledge of meaning cannot be taken to be internal to our minds (1975a). His primary target, philosophers such as Frege and Carnap, subscribe to both the principles (I) and (II):

(I)   Knowledge of the meaning of a term is just a matter of being in a certain psychological state.

(II)   The meaning of a term (in the sense of its intension) determines its extension (in the sense that sameness of intension determines sameness of extension).

Given the Twin Earth case, Fregean intensionalists have to say that references to XYZ, a substance that exemplifies all the phenomenological properties of water— for example, liquidity, odorlessness, colorlessness, tastelessness, and being thirst-quenching—but is not H_2O, are references to water. Given that (I) and (II) lead to the consequence that 'water' applies to something that is not water, they cannot both be true; Putnam concludes that (I) (internalism) is false.

Kripke's "blue gold" case (1980: 118) is parallel to Putnam's "robot cat" case. In Kripke's case, in which gold appears to us to be yellow due to an optical illusion, taking the concept *yellow metal* to be the Fregean sense (or part of the Fregean sense) of 'gold' would preclude the genuine possibility that previous uses of 'gold' referred even though gold is actually blue. Kripke's argument from his iron pyrites example (1980: 119) is the same as Putnam's argument from his molybdenum example. Kripke's tiger example (1980: 119–121) splits into two cases, one in which an optical illusion makes us think tigers have four legs when they only have three and one in which we discover tiger-like creatures that are reptiles rather than mammals. The former is parallel to the gold case with leggedness playing the role of color, and the latter is parallel to the molybdenum case, with tiger-like reptiles playing the role of molybdenum.

Kripke concludes from such cases that a wide range of common nouns, including terms for species, like 'cat', terms for substances, like 'gold', terms for phenomena, like 'heat' (and their corresponding adjectives, like 'hot') "have a greater kinship with proper names than is generally realized." Kripke goes on to say:

The modern logical tradition, as represented by Frege and Russell, disputed Mill on the issue of singular names, but endorsed him on that of general names. Thus *all* terms, both singular and general, have a 'connotation' or Fregean sense. . . . The present view, directly reversing Frege and Russell, (more or less) *endorses* Mill's view of *singular* terms, but *disputes* his view of *general* terms. (1980: 134–135)

Finally, Jerry Fodor adapts Putnam's argument as an argument against definition. He argues for the claim that

[c]oncepts can't *be* definitions because most concepts don't *have* definitions [on the grounds that] [a]t a minimum, to define a concept is to provide necessary and sufficient conditions for something to be in its extension (i.e., for being among the things that concept applies to). . . . [T]ry actually filling in the blanks in 'x is a dog iff x is a . . .' without using . . . words like 'dog' or 'canine' or the like on the right-hand side. (Fodor 1994: 104)

Since Mill's, Wittgenstein's, Putnam's, Kripke's, and Fodor's arguments share the Fregean assumption that senses are reference-determiners, Fregean intensionalists have no reply to them. They are hoist with their own petard. But, having no commitment to this assumption, an intensionalism based on (D) can reply that all such anti-intensionalist arguments are unsound. Putnam's Twin Earth argument is paradigmatic. Directed against philosophers such as Frege and Carnap, who also endorse (II), the argument does not need a defense of (II). But directed against non-Fregean intensionalists, who reject (II), the argument fails. Given that intensionalists can reject (II), the step from the falsehood of the conjunction (I) & (II) to the falsehood of (I) is fallacious.

The same difficulty is found in Putnam's aluminum/molybdenum argument. If the sense of 'aluminum' does not have to determine its referent, Putnam cannot go from the fact that a cluster of properties gets the referent of 'aluminum' wrong to the conclusion that it gets the sense wrong. Hence, what was the great strength of Putnam's arguments—the fact that they assume the same thing about the nature of sense as the Fregeans—becomes their fatal weakness.

Putnam failed to see that there could be non-Fregean intensionalism because he took the theory of sense based on (D) to be nothing more than a "translation into 'mathematical' language of precisely the traditional theory that it has been our concern to criticize" (1979c: 144–146). Thus, Putnam mistakenly argued that "[i]t follows that each counterexample to the traditional theory is at once a counterexample to Katz's theory." Putnam did not recognize how radical a departure from Frege's theory a theory of sense based on (D) is—even though the theory presented in *Semantic Theory* (Katz 1972: 1–10) and other works does not define sense as the determiner of reference.

Fodor's argument is nothing but Putnam's with a different example. Just as Putnam argued that no definition of the term 'aluminum' gets its extension right because the best we can do in the case of 'aluminum' is to cite a cluster of properties that does not provide necessary and sufficient conditions for being aluminum, so Fodor argues that no definition of the term 'dog' gets its extension right because the best we can do to fill in the blank is to cite a cluster of properties like being an animal, being a mammal and being a carnivore, but such a cluster does not provide necessary and sufficient conditions for the application of 'dog'. Hence, Fodor begs the same question as Putnam. Like Putnam's assumption of (II), Fodor's assumption that definition is Fregean definition ignores the possibility of a definition of sense as determiner of sense properties and relations.

Thus, Fodor's argument against definition is unsound, because there is an alternative to the Fregean definition of sense. At best, it shows that *if* definitions of terms in natural language are Fregean definitions, then natural kind terms do not have definitions. But since the existence of an alternative to the Fregean definition of sense shows the antecedent of this conditional to be false, the consequent cannot be detached. Hence, Fodor's conclusion that natural kind terms do not have definitions (i.e., full decompositional analyses of their senses) does not follow. The fact that senses do not provide necessary and sufficient conditions for the application of a term does not entail that they do not decompose into a set of senses that are necessary for the reference of the term and that are jointly necessary and sufficient for a full analysis of its sense.

Fodor also deployed his argument against the decompositional view of sense (the view that virtually all syntactically simple common nouns have complex senses). The view is motivated by considerations of synonymy. For example, since 'bachelor' is synonymous with 'adult human male who is single', the view says that the sense of 'bachelor' consists of the senses *human*, *male*, *adult*, and *single*. Decompositionality is the core of the traditional theory of meaning. It is found in Locke's account of trifling propositions, and forms the basis for Kant's notion that analytic judgments "merely break . . . [the subject concept] up into those constituent concepts that have all along been thought in it" (1929: 49).

Rejecting decompositionality, Fodor, Garrett, Walker, and Parkes adopt "lexical primitivism" (Pitt 1999: 143), the view that all lexical concepts are semantically simple and hence each represented independently in the language-learner's innate conceptual space (1980: 276). This position does not provide a viable semantics for nativism because it requires every lexical concept that has appeared or ever will appear in the history of natural languages to be an independent element in our innate conceptual space. This means we must suppose either that the evolutionary forces that produced our species perfectly anticipated every twist and turn in the history of science, technology, and society or that our innate conceptual space contains all of the infinitely many possible lexical concepts. Since both of these alternatives are far-fetched, to say the least, the hypothesis of decompositional sense structure, which allows senses of lexical items to be derived from a small number of highly general concepts, is a far more attractive semantics for nativism.

Kripke's influential arguments for a Millian view of names also ignore the possibility of an alternative to the Fregean definition of sense. As I shall show in the third part of this book, the arguments from counterfactual cases that Kripke uses to reject the descriptivist account of names support only the rejection of Fregean descriptivism.

The natural kind term arguments against Fregean intensionalism exploit the excessive strength of the constraint on reference imposed by Frege's definition of sense. But, since it is open to intensionalists to adopt an intensionalism based on (D), there is no pressure to sacrifice intensionalism, to limit the scope of intensionalism to a portion of the vocabulary of the language, to reject internalism, or to reject decompositional analysis and a Kantian notion of analyticity.

1.2.2. The problem of too weak a constraint

The first problem, that the Fregean definition of sense constrains reference too strongly, arises because of what that definition tells us. The second problem, that the Fregean definition does not constrain *sense* strongly enough, arises because of what that definition fails to tell us. In a nutshell, the Fregean definition of sense fails to tell us enough about *sense* to enable us to determine the senses of expressions.

I argued in section 1.1 that the Fregean definition explains sense in terms of the role it plays in an instrument/purpose structure. This makes the individuation of senses, like the individuation of tools, a matter of function, of the job they do. Once intensionalists define sense functionally, they commit themselves to saying that anything that fits the job description "determiner of the reference of the term *t*" counts as the sense of *t*. As a consequence of this commitment, they face something like the problem of multiple realization, widely discussed in the philosophy of mind.

For example, on this view, the sense of the expression 'two' and the sense of the expression 'the even prime' must be counted as the same, in virtue of the fact that they determine the same referent. But, since those expressions do *not* have the same sense (we have to *prove* that two is the even prime), we can conclude that *sense* is not a functional concept, as Fregean intensionalists claim. No such examples could arise if *sense* were a true functional concept like *screwdriver*. The differences between two tools both of which do the job of driving in screws—for instance, that one is operated manually and the other is power-driven—do not count as relevant to the question of their sameness as screwdrivers. The difference between the senses of 'two' and 'the even prime', however—viz., that the latter but not the former involves being the unique number with the properties of evenness and primality— *is* relevant to the question of their sameness as senses.

From the standpoint of Fregean intensionalism, where such differences are not relevant, we can say that the sense of 'two' is *the even prime*, and we can also say, with the same rationale, that the sense of 'two' is *the successor of one*, *the square root of four*, *the difference between fifteen and seventeen*, or anything else necessarily coextensive with the sense of 'two'.

Carnap (1956: 23–30) says as much when he equates sameness of intension with necessary co-extensiveness. And this gets him into trouble when, in effect, he characterizes synonymy as sameness of intension and, on this basis, argues (236–240) that intensionalism is preferable to extensionalism because it provides grounds for choosing the correct translation in cases of vacuous terms. Carnap argues that only intensionalism allows us to select the synonymous pairs in (1.3) and reject the nonsynonymous pairs in (1.4)

(1.3)   'Einhorn'/'unicorn' 'Kobold'/'goblin'

(1.4)   'Einhorn'/'goblin' 'Kobold'/'unicorn'

because only intensionalism can invoke possible cases. But this argument collapses because appeal to judgments about possible cases is of no avail when the question of synonymy concerns *necessarily* vacuous but non-synonymous expressions such as those in (1.5).

(1.5)   'Einhorn mit drei hornen', 'round square', 'the largest number', 'bachelor who is married', ...

Fregean intensionalism provides no way of choosing the right sense for an expression among various senses all of which necessarily determine the same referent, because any sense that does the job of determining the reference of the expression is as good as any other sense that does the job. It is arbitrary which of the senses we say is the sense or intension of the expression. This ought to come as no surprise. Since the Fregean definition of sense reduces the theory of sense to the theory of reference, the notion of sense is embedded in a system in which only extensional criteria constrain choices among semantic hypotheses. On such criteria, the intensionalist has no way to choose the right hypothesis about the sense of an expression from a set of hypotheses involving necessarily co-extensive senses. The reduction cuts us off from the intensional criteria that could determine that one hypothesis, to the exclusion of all others, is the right one.

Here we arrive by a different route at the symmetry among referentially equivalent translation hypotheses on which Quine based his thesis of the indeterminacy of translation (1960: 26–79). Quine's familiar example of extensional equivalence is as follows: "Point to a rabbit and you have pointed to a stage of a rabbit, to an integral part of a rabbit, to the rabbit fusion, and to where rabbithood is manifested. Point to an integral part of a rabbit and you have pointed again to the remaining four sorts of things; and so on around" (1960: 52–53). Referential evidence is insufficient to choose among the translations 'rabbit', 'undetached rabbit part', 'rabbit stage', and 'instantiation of rabbithood', and the radical translation situation contains no other evidence to compensate for the insufficiency of referential evidence. Similarly, referential evidence is insufficient to choose among the English translations in (1.5) or among 'the successor of one', 'the even prime', 'square root of four', 'the difference between fifteen and seventeen', and similar definitions of 'two'.

Quine argues (1960: 71–72) that symmetry among translations for the native's term 'gavagai' is a consequence of the absence of "independent controls" in the radical translation situation. In our case, too, the symmetry can be regarded as due to an absence of independent controls—that is, absence of evidence about sense properties and relations that justifies the choice of one English expression, to the exclusion of others, as the right translation for the German expression. Hence, in both Carnap's translation situation and Quine's radical translation situation, indeterminacy arises because the only evidence that can be brought to bear in choosing among intensionally distinct but extensionally equivalent hypotheses is extensional evidence.

In both the Quine and the Frege/Carnap cases, there is indeterminacy because there is evidential symmetry; there is evidential symmetry because there are no independent controls; and there are no independent controls because there is no intensional evidence—evidence about the sense properties and relations of expressions. But the restriction responsible for the absence of independent controls is different in the two cases. In Quine's case, the restriction that excludes intensional evidence is imposed from outside intensionalism. Quine sets up the radical translation situation so that only information about relations between language and the world counts as evidence for translation. In the Frege/Carnap case, the restriction is imposed from within intensionalism itself. The Fregean definition of sense reduces the theory of sense to the theory of reference, in which only referential information counts as evidence.

Thus, Fregean intensionalists are stuck with the restriction that gives rise to the fatal evidential symmetry. But non-Fregean intensionalists are not. The situation here is reminiscent of the one encountered earlier in connection with Putnam's Twin Earth argument against internalism. Just as in the latter situation Fregean intensionalists were stuck with (II) but non-Fregean intensionalists had the option of rejecting it, so, in the present situation, Fregean intensionalists are stuck with the restriction to extensional evidence, but, since the restriction is not imposed from within their position, non-Fregean intensionalists are free to reject it as something illegitimately foisted on them.

In earlier works (1988; 1990b; 1996), I argued that Quine's radical translation scenario stacks the deck against non-Fregean intensionalists. I argued that there is no reason to take radical translation as a satisfactory model of actual translation with respect to the evidence for translation. To be sure, Quine's radical translation scenario (1960: 28–29) appears innocent enough at first, being presented as the special case of actual translation dealing with "the language of a hitherto untouched people." It is advertised as an unobjectionable idealization of actual translation that merely abstracts away from "hints" provided by previous translations and shared culture. But this is misleading advertising. Since the issue between intensionalists and extensionalists is whether senses are part of natural language, restricting the evidence for translation to referential properties and relations begs the question against the intensionalist.

Quine offers no argument for the restriction. His claim that there is no intensional fact of the matter to play the role of truth maker in the theory of meaning is not backed up with argument. For everything he says in *Word and Object* (1960) and elsewhere, analytic hypotheses could be evaluated within a framework in which intensional evidence is brought to bear in choosing a translation so that the "parameters of truth" in the theory of meaning would be as stable as those in particle physics. To be sure, "Two Dogmas of Empiricism" (1953) gives an argument against the attempt to make objective sense of synonymy, which might be turned into an argument to legitimize the restriction. But, as we have already seen, that argument presupposes that the theory of sense must be reduced to another theory. This presupposition is expressed in Quine's remark that a theory of meaning that interdefines 'analyticity', 'synonymy', and its other theoretical terms is like "a closed curve in space" (1953: 30). However, in failing to consider an autonomous theory of sense constructed along non-Fregean lines, Quine provides no reason to think that reduction is obligatory for every form of intensionalism. Hence, there is nothing here to prevent us from taking the view that actual translation uses evidence about sense properties and relations to make translation decisions.

Moreover, our folk semantics encourages us to take this view. Decisions about synonymy are made on the basis of judgments about similarity and difference of sense, meaningfulness, ambiguity, synonymy, and other sense properties and relations of expressions. For example, we decide that 'disinterested' and 'uninterested' are not the same in meaning because 'disinterested' is judged similar in meaning to 'nonpartisan' and 'uninterested' as similar in meaning to 'inattentive'. 'Einhorn' is similar in sense to 'horse' and 'steed', while 'goblin' is similar in sense to 'gnome' and 'elf'; but 'horse' and 'steed' are not similar in this respect to 'gnome' and 'elf'.

Fleshing this thought out, we can sketch the role that judgments about similarity and difference in sense can play in deciding between alternative translations in Quine's 'gavagai' case. The field linguist can ask informants not only whether 'gavagai' does or does not apply to something, but also what judgments they would make about the sense properties of 'gavagai', 'rabbit', 'rabbit stage', and 'undetached rabbit part', and their sense relations to one another and to other expressions. The linguist can ask bluntly whether 'gavagai' is synonymous with 'rabbit', 'rabbit stage', or 'undetached rabbit part'. If informants provide a direct answer, positive or negative, there is some evidence. If not, there are other informants and less direct questions. The linguist can ask whether the sense of 'gavagai' bears the same part-whole relation to some expression in his or her language that 'finger' bears to 'hand' or 'handle' bears to 'knife'. Or the linguist can ask whether 'gavagai' is closer in sense to 'infancy', 'adolescence', and 'adulthood' or to 'infant', 'adolescent', and 'adult'. If some informants can make such judgments, there would be evidence relevant to distinguishing among the allegedly symmetrical translations.

Of course, bilingual informants are required. Without fluent speakers of the two languages, there is no source from which to obtain judgments about relations between expressions in them. In this respect, the study of sense relations between languages is not different from the study of sense and other grammatical relations within a language. In both cases, all our evidence comes from informants: just as the grammatical description of a single language must assume fluency in that language, so translation between languages must assume fluency in those two languages. Even Quine acknowledges what comes down to this point when he assumes a linguist who rightly "settle[s] on what to treat as native signs of assent and dissent" (1960: 29–30). Of course, the more ambitious the approach, the stronger the assumption about bilingual competence has to be. So for this approach, which aims to vindicate determinate translation between languages, however disparate, we have to assume fully bilingual informants.

Quine objects to bringing in bilinguals, urging us to resist ". . . a stubborn feeling that a true bilingual surely is in a position to make uniquely right correlations of sentences generally between languages" (1960: 74). This feeling, for Quine, is a "major cause" of the failure to perceive the indeterminacy of translation. His objection is that, whatever judgments we get from one bilingual with "his own private semantic correlation," another might have his own different private semantic correlation: ". . . another bilingual could have a semantic correlation incompatible with the first bilingual's without deviating from the first bilingual in his speech dispositions within either language, except in his dispositions to translate." This is, no doubt, a possibility—just as it is a possibility that different monolingual speakers could have incompatible sentence/sense correlations without having different speech dispositions except in dispositions to make synonymy judgments—or, for that matter, just as it is a possibility that different monolingual speakers could have incompatible sentence/pronunciation correlations without having different speech dispositions, except dispositions to make homonymy judgments. I do not deny this. They are, to be sure, all *possibilities*.

My point is that that is all they are. Hence, their negations are also possibilities. When as linguists we suppose that bilinguals will have the same, or sufficiently similar, semantic correlations, and that they will make essentially the same semantic judgments, we are supposing nothing more than the possibility that is the negation of the possibility Quine favors. We presume the existence of laws to be discovered in the same spirit as in any other study undertaking the investigation of a new domain. Thus, in presuming that there is uniformity among the semantic correlations of different bilinguals, we beg no question. We do not thereby deny the Quinean *possibility*. The presumption that bilinguals have essentially the same semantic correlations and make essentially the same semantic judgments is a working assumption—just as Quine's presumption is a working assumption. The question of which working assumption fits the facts can only be decided on the basis of an investigation of the domain of translation.

Is it, as Quine believes (1960: 73), that there is no "objective matter to be right or wrong about" in translation, or is it, as intensionalists believe, that there is? That is the question. Hence, our working assumption is just part of the methodology of an attempt to answer the question objectively. If we want to know whether there is evidence that can decide among co-extensional properties that figure in an alleged symmetry, we have no choice but to query bilingual informants about the ambiguity, antonymy, synonymy, redundancy, and other sense properties and relations of relevant examples. If Quine is right, then sufficient consistent evidence will not be forthcoming no matter how much investigating we do. If I am right, such evidence will be forthcoming. Since Quine's objection to bilinguals has no force against their use as part of an attempt to determine whether there is or is not a fact of the matter in translation, his argument for indeterminacy rests on an arbitrary exclusion of intensional evidence in the translation situation.

In both the Frege/Carnap case and the Quine case, indeterminacy arises from the exclusion of intensional evidence in the choice of translations; in the Frege/Carnap case, however, the exclusion is not imposed from the outside, but is an inherent feature of their referential semantics—something introduced by Frege's reductive definition of sense. On (D), the sense structure of an expression is the source of its meaningfulness, meaninglessness, ambiguity, synonymy, redundancy, antonymy, and other sense properties and relations. In making this connection between the sense structure of expressions and their sense properties and relations, an autonomous theory of sense supplies the required intensional evidence. This evidence constitutes the "independent controls" that enable us to characterize the notion of a right choice in translation. In short, the right choice is the simplest hypothesis that accounts for the widest range of sense properties and relations of the sentences in question.

Thus, intensionalists overcome the problem of too weak a constraint if they abandon Fregean intensionalism in favor of an intensionalism based on (D). Frege's definition of sense creates the problem of indeterminacy because it bases the explication of the notion of sense on referential considerations alone. With (D), we have an autonomous theory of sense that enables us to strengthen the constraints on sense-determination by allowing non-referential considerations—specifically, evidence about the sense properties and relations of expressions—to play a role in choosing among competing translations.

1.2.3. The problem of the wrong constraint

Frege imposed the constraint of fruitfulness on semantic theories. He used it to dismiss Kant's concept of analyticity for its sterility. Kant, he said, ". . . seems to think of concepts as defined by giving a simple list of characteristics in no special order; but of all ways of forming concepts, that is one of the least fruitful. . . . Nothing essentially new . . . emerges in the [Kantian] process [of forming concepts]" (1953: 100). But fruitfulness, as I have been arguing, is the wrong constraint to impose on semantic theories of natural language. In this subsection I will argue that it is, as it were, too much of a good thing. I will argue that making the laws of logic part of analysis so radically inflates linguistic concepts that their swollen bodies no longer bear any resemblance to senses in natural language.

The notion of analyticity in a semantic theory provides its account of semantic analysis and hence its account of the content of concepts. This is something Frege acknowledges when he says that what follows logically from a definition is "contained" in it (1953: 101). Frege's remark that logical consequences are contained "as plants are contained in their seeds" rather than "as beams are contained in a house" says that the content of concepts in his semantic theory is determined logically rather than mereologically. The point is underscored when Frege calls our attention to the logical fact that a conclusion can follow from its premises even though "[it] is not contained in any one of them alone."

For someone who puts such a premium on fruitfulness, $P \rightarrow (P \vee Q)$ should be the paradigmatic law of logic for determining the content of concepts, since it allows the introduction of completely new content. But just because this law exemplifies fruitfulness in its purest form, it shows most clearly that analyticity in Frege's sense is the wrong constraint for semantic analysis. If the content of concepts is determined on the basis of laws of logic, then there can be no concepts. The point goes back to Wittgenstein, who observed that, as a determinant of the content of concepts, $P \rightarrow (P \vee Q)$ commits us to saying that the sense of a sentence S includes the sense of the sentence S or S' where S' is any sentence whatever (1974: 248–249). Thus, Frege's account of the content of concepts produces a semantic collapse in which the sense of each sentence of the language is the disjunction of the senses of every sentence of the language. The sense of each sentence of the language includes and is included in the sense of every sentence (in the sense in which the meaning of 'spouse' includes both the meaning of 'husband' and the meaning of 'wife'). Hence, the content of every sentence is the same as that of every other sentence: all sentences are synonymous. Not only is there, in effect, one sense in the language but also, since Fregean intensionalists hold that sense determines reference, all meaningful sentences have the same reference. Since every sentence will contain a true disjunct, every sentence is true, inconsistent sentences have the same truth value, and so on. Moreover, since natural languages have infinitely many sentences, the content of each sentence is infinite. Hence, speakers of a language cannot fully understand even the simplest of its sentences.

These consequences make it necessary to abandon Fregean semantics in the study of natural language. Of course, Fregean intensionalists can try to reformulate the logical notion of analyticity without the law $P \rightarrow (P \vee Q)$ and others that lead to the same embarrassing consequences. This means reformulating Fregean analyticity so that an analytic proposition is one that is provable from definitions and a special proper subset of the laws of logic. This fallback position would represent a considerable retreat from the Fregean ideal of fruitfulness; furthermore, from the present perspective, it would be both arbitrary and pointless. It would be arbitrary because there is no principled explanation of why some laws of logic should support analytic consequences and others not. After all, logically speaking, there is no difference between the laws included in the proper subset and those excluded from it. Logically, they are all equally valid principles of inference.

Such a fallback position would be pointless because the resulting notion of analyticity still does not provide an adequate account of sense for natural language. As I have already shown, logical equivalence cannot serve as sameness of sense. Further, a version of one of the earlier problems with Fregean analyticity resurfaces: the content of every sentence will contain all the logical truths, and since there are infinitely many of them, the content of each sentence will be infinite, and, again, speakers will not be able to understand any sentence. Finally, redefinitions of analyticity based on a proper subset of the logical laws will fail to capture certain cases in which a proposition is part of another proposition. On what seems to be the best proposal along these lines, due to Ken Gemes (1994), a proposition A is part of a proposition B just in case A and B are contingent and A is the strongest consequence of B constructable with only the (essential) atomic formulas of A. But the restriction to contingent propositions is itself an admission of defeat. Moreover, as Brad Armour-Garb (in conversation) points out, such an account fails to capture the fact that the sense of P is part of the content of *Possibly P*.

The problem of the wrong constraint has the same source as the first two problems, namely, the reduction of the theory of sense to the theory of reference. The wrong constraint is imposed on the analysis of sense structure because the theory of reference sets conceptual boundaries on the basis of the laws of logic, that is, the laws of truth and reference. These laws state invariances of truth and reference in terms of model-theoretic relations among the extensions of terms in possible worlds. Those relations provide too coarse-grained an equivalence relation for sense structure: the boundaries they draw among senses are not their boundaries in natural language.

Since (D) uses the notion of sense to explain sense properties and relations of expressions, the right constraint for determining the boundaries of senses in natural language is in place from the start. If we draw these boundaries on the basis of the simplest hypotheses required to explain sense properties and relations, we guarantee that our representations of them will match the boundaries of senses in natural language. Such boundaries are intrinsic; representations of them must be based on structural invariances over senses, not on invariances over other kinds of objects. Butler's dictum "Everything is what it is, and not another thing" is as valid a protest against the twentieth-century attempt to reduce sense to reference as it was against the seventeenth-century attempt to reduce morals to psychology.

Frege's claim that "[d]efinitions show their worth by proving fruitful" (1953: 81) is, therefore, the very opposite of the truth. As I shall argue in the next two parts of this book, definitions show their worth by, in a certain sense, proving unfruitful.

1.3. The autonomous theory of sense

1.3.1. The autonomous theory of sense: what it is

(D) sets the aim for an autonomous theory of sense ("ATS") as both the description of the sense structure of expressions and the explanation of sense properties and relations of expressions in terms of features of sense structure. Since there are infinitely many expressions in a natural language, a description of the structure of senses of sentences must take the form of recursive principles. These principles explain the compositional sense structure of a language, that is, how the senses of complex expressions are a function of the senses of their syntactic constituents (together with their syntactic relations). Since the senses of syntactically complex constituents are a function of the senses of their subconstituents, compositional principles work up from the most deeply embedded constituents of a complex expression to the expression itself. Since they apply initially to syntactically atomic items, morphemes, the base for a compositional explanation is a dictionary specifying the senses of morphemes. (Idioms are the exceptions to the compositional rule and can be thought of as lexical items, appearing with morphemes in the dictionary.) The assignment of senses from the dictionary to occurrences of morphemes in a complex expression provides the starting point for the compositional construction of its sense. The syntactic structure of a complex expression directs the course of compositional construction.

The mereological structure of compositionally formed senses arises from their mode of composition. At the lowest compositional level, the parts are the senses of the morphemes combined, and the wholes are the derived senses formed from the combinations. At the next level, the parts are these morphemic senses plus the derived ones formed from their combinations at the first level, and the wholes are the derived senses formed from those derived senses. At subsequent levels, the parts and wholes sort out in the same manner.

The mereological structure of compositionally formed senses is not the only mereological sense structure in natural language. Senses of morphemes, which are not compositionally formed, have such structure, too. We reach this conclusion on the basis of an inference to the best explanation. We are committed to positing decompositional sense structure just in case the explanation of a sense property or relation of a morpheme requires us to assign it constituent senses. The posit of decompositional sense structure thus has the same basis as any scientific posit of underlying structure, namely, that the observable facts are derivable from hypotheses about underlying structure but not derivable from hypotheses about superficial structure.

The explanation of sense properties and relations of morphemes will have the same form as the explanation of sense properties and relations of syntactically structured expressions. For example, we explain the redundancy of the expression 'unmarried single man' in terms of the sense of the head 'single man' having as a part the sense of the adjective 'unmarried'. Hence, we have to explain the sense properties and relations of lexical items on the basis of the part-whole sense structure of those items. For example, to explain the redundancy of 'unmarried bachelor', 'chair that is a piece of furniture', and 'free gift', we have to represent the senses of the head nouns as having the senses of the modifiers as proper parts.

Consider two further examples. One is the synonymy of the lexical item 'bachelor' with the expression 'unmarried adult human male'. To explain this synonymy, we have to assume that the sense of 'bachelor' has a part-whole structure. Synonymy is sameness of sense, and the sense of the syntactically complex expression 'unmarried adult human male', which the sense of 'bachelor' is the same as, is complex (as even the Fregeans have to concede)—as is shown by the fact that the sense of 'unmarried adult human male' is a compositional function of the senses of 'unmarried', 'adult', 'human', and 'male'. Even such a trivial explanation commits us to decompositional structure. A more sophisticated example concerns the ambiguity of the main clauses of (1.6) and (1.7):

(1.6)   I never repeat gossip, so ask someone else.

(1.7)   I never repeat gossip, so listen carefully.

The ambiguity can be explained only on a decompositional analysis of 'gossip', because an explanation needs to make reference to its sense structure. Given that this structure has the form *information about somebody that person A tells person B*, the ambiguity can be explained as deriving from taking A to be an indefinite person other than the speaker, on the one hand, and taking A to be the speaker of the main clause, on the other. In the former case, the speaker expresses the sense that he or she will not repeat to B the gossip he or she has heard from someone else, and, in the latter, the speaker expresses the sense that he or she will not repeat the gossip that he or she is now about to pass on to B. (For other, more extensive discussions of the evidence for decompositional structure, see Katz 1987 [205–226] and Pitt and Katz 2000.)

Decompositionality says that morphemes have complex sense structure as it were *intrinsically*. The complex sense structure of 'bachelor' is as much an aspect of its grammatical nature as is its syntactic category. If senses are posited as entities over and above the expressions of a language, there is nothing about our concept of a language that tells us that the simplicity or complexity of senses must reflect the simplicity or complexity of the linguistic forms that express them. This is, I believe, the commonsense view of the matter. We normally think that nothing prevents us from introducing a syntactically simple term to stand for a complex sense, as, for example, in introducing the term 'carburetor' with the complex sense of the expression 'apparatus for combining air with an inflammable liquid for purposes of combustion'. Accordingly, definition and decompositional sense structure go hand in hand. It is hard to imagine an intensionalist account of the abbreviatory function of definition without decomposition.

As I argued in section 1.2.1, some Fregean intensionalists reject decompositional sense structure for reasons having to do with natural kind terms. An example, discussed earlier, is Fodor's claim (1994: 103–105) that there is no definition for a concept like the one 'dog' expresses because we cannot specify "necessary and sufficient conditions for something to be in its extension." We also saw that this claim begs the question against a non-Fregean intensionalist by assuming that definitions are Fregean definitions. Definitions in the decompositional sense do not have to determine extension; they only have to reveal the structure necessary to explain all relevant sense properties and relations. An intensionalism based on (D) denies that there is sense structure beyond that point.

There is a general reason for Fregean intensionalists to reject decompositional sense structure. On their referential conception of semantics, such structure plays no role in the semantic study of natural language. Fregean semantics posits the existence of expressions of a language, a domain for the extensional interpretation of the language, and Frege/Carnap-style intensions. Descriptions of natural languages thus ideally contain, for each expression and each domain, a division of the domain into the expression's extension and anti-extension, and, for each statement and domain, a set of truth conditions for the statement on the domain. Such descriptions are obtained by assigning a Frege/Carnap-style intension to each syntactically simple form of the language and, on the basis of higher-level functions, assigning intensions to syntactically complex expressions on the basis of the intensions assigned to their syntactic constituents. Given this picture of natural language semantics, complex senses of syntactically simple expressions play no role in determining the extension of syntactically simple expressions, and hence no role in the computation of extensions for syntactically complex constituents and the truth conditions of sentences. Hence, decompositional analysis is otiose.

For non-Fregean intensionalists, this picture illustrates how the sense structure of natural language is lost by the Fregean reduction of the theory of sense to the theory of reference. On an autonomous theory of sense based on (D), the picture of natural language semantics is quite different. As I have shown, on such a theory, intensionalists are forced to posit decompositional sense structure to explain the sense properties and relations of syntactically simple items. For, once sense is made the determiner of sense properties and relations, the sense properties and relations of lexical items have to be explained, and the explanation of facts such as the synonymy of 'bachelor' with 'unmarried adult human male' requires the postulation of part-whole sense structure for lexical items.

As a consequence of losing sense structure below the compositional level, Fregean intensionalism loses sense structure above the lexical level as well. This is because compositional combination typically depends on decompositional structure: compositional principles make reference to the part-whole structure of senses at the lexical level. For example, the parts of the sense of 'knife', *physical object*, *blade*, *handle*, and *instrument for cutting*, must be represented as independent components in order to obtain the right compositional meaning for 'sharp knife' because the sense of the modifier 'sharp' qualifies only the component *blade* in the sense of 'knife'. Thus, we want to say that 'The knife is sharp' analytically entails 'The blade of the knife is sharp', but not 'The handle of the knife is sharp'.

Fregean intensionalism's failure to account for sense structure at the morphemic and compositional levels is directly attributable to its taking a sense to be a function from a domain to an extension. As a consequence, a dictionary in Fregean semantics consists of pairings of morphemes with functions, and a compositional principle is a mapping of functions onto functions. Hence, the part-whole sense structure of morphemes is not analyzed at the morphemic level and the part-whole sense structure of syntactically complex constituents must correspond to syntactic structure. These restrictions on Fregean descriptions of sense structure prevent them from representing more than syntactically based sense structure at the compositional level.

In contrast, on ATS, the part-whole structure of senses does not have to correspond to syntactic structure and so is not restricted to partial representation at the compositional level. Sense is thus not only *not* something that determines reference, but, in virtue of this, is also *not* something that is determined by syntax. As a consequence, ATS descriptions of sense structure are under no restrictions limiting their scope in the representation of sense structure in natural language.

A theory of the sense structure of a natural language will thus contain: descriptions of the decompositional structure of its morphemes, a dictionary, compositional principles for forming senses of syntactically complex expressions, and definitions of sense properties and relations. These definitions are generalizations over part-whole configurations in the representations of senses of expressions. For example, the definition of meaningfulness will be 'having a semantic representation', the definition of meaninglessness 'not having a semantic representation', the definition of ambiguity 'having more than one semantic representation', the definition of synonymy 'having the same semantic representation', and the definition of redundancy 'having a head the semantic representation of which contains the semantic representation of its modifier'. Together, semantic representations and definitions of sense properties and relations entail claims about the sense properties and relations of expressions. For example, the assignment of more than one semantic representation to an expression entails that it is ambiguous. Such claims enable us to evaluate hypotheses concerning sense structure expressed in terms of semantic representations. Comparing a claim about the sense of an expression based on its semantic representations with the semantic judgments of fluent speakers about the sense properties and relations of the sentence, we can determine which of a set of hypotheses about its senses fits the facts. Having narrowed the set down to those that fit the facts, we can choose the simplest and integrate it into the theory, itself evaluated on the basis of coverage and simplicity.

1.3.2. The autonomous theory of sense: what it is not

ATS should not be confused with what is called "inferential role semantics," "conceptual role semantics," or anything similar ("IRS," as I shall refer to such semantics). Versions of IRS are sometimes construed as theories of mental concepts and sometimes as theories of linguistic concepts. In the present discussion, I am concerned only with versions of IRS as theories of linguistic concepts. So construed, IRS and ATS are both open to psychological interpretation, say, as theories of semantic competence in Chomsky's sense (1965: 3–4) (i.e., theories of the ideal speaker's knowledge of the structure of sentences), and to realist interpretation, as theories of abstract objects (i.e., theories of sentence-types). I will not bother with the issue of interpretation in this discussion, because the semantic question I am concerned with arises on either ontology. (Indeed, in my first systematic presentation of ATS [1972: 16–17], linguistic concepts are given both psychological and realist interpretations in the space of only two pages!)

The conflation of ATS and IRS arises because too much weight is put on a similarity between them, while their differences are ignored. The similarity is that, except for marginal cases like Gilbert Harman's (1987), IRS characterizations of sense (meaning or content), like the ATS characterization, eschew the Fregean principle that sense determines reference. Virtually all versions of IRS are based on a proof-theory/model-theory style distinction, on which proof-theoretic structure constrains but does not determine model-theoretic interpretation. For example, Hartry Field's version of IRS (1977) distinguishes two factors in meaning, conceptual role and truth conditions, neither of which determines the other.

This similarity occasions the quite mistaken belief that ATS is just a version of IRS in which the inference relation is analytic entailment. We can begin to see that this thought is mistaken by noting that ATS and IRS take opposite approaches to what is basic in semantic theory. Versions of IRS are like the theories Kripke criticizes (1982: 93–94) for "*inversion* of a conditional" (David Pitt, in conversation). One of Kripke's examples is the inverted logical conditional: "We do not accept the law of contradiction because it is a necessary truth; it is a necessary truth because we accept it (by convention)." IRS inverts a semantic conditional. It claims that sentences do not have the linguistic inference relations they have in virtue of the meanings they have; rather, they have their meanings in virtue of their linguistic inference relations. In contrast, ATS maintains this conditional in uninverted form: sentences have the analytic entailments they have in virtue of the meanings they have. On (D), sense structure is basic because it determines sense properties and relations. As explained at the end of the last section, definitions of sense properties and relations in ATS—in particular, analytic entailment—are generalizations over part-whole structures in representations of senses.

It is the other way around for IRS because IRS is the view that meaning is inference potential. No semantic theory is a version of IRS unless it is an instance of this claim. IRS can be thought of in the abstract as a function, $f(I) = T$, that specifies a version of IRS, T, once a particular inference relation I is specified. IRS thus encompasses a range of particular theories, each determined by the choice of an inference relation.

In contrast, ATS says that meanings are independent objects (senses) that are the source of the sense properties and relations of expressions. Senses are fundamental because sense properties and relations depend on particular structures of senses. ATS can be thought of in the abstract as a function, $f(S) = K$, where S is a system of senses and K is a set of sense properties and relations. Hence, in the case of ATS, the notion of meaning is not fixed by a choice of inference relation. To be sure, ATS postulates a unique inference relation, analytic entailment. But analytic entailment does not function in ATS in the way inference relations in IRS do. It is not a value of the variable 'I' in the schema '$f(I) = T$'. There can be no version of IRS in which the value of 'I' is analytic entailment in the ATS sense. On such a theory, analytic entailment would, *per impossibile*, be *both* an independent variable fixing the notion of meaning for the version of IRS in question *and* a dependent variable fixed by a prior system of senses (in the ATS sense). It would have to be both a basic and a derivative relation.

Rather than serving as a setting of a parameter that fixes a notion of inferential meaning, analytic entailment on ATS is just one among many sense properties and relations—meaningfulness, meaninglessness, ambiguity, synonymy, antonymy, redundancy, superordination, and so on. They are all generalizations over particular mereological structures in senses. The priority of sense puts ATS in a class by itself. Thus, when we take account of the differences between versions of IRS and ATS, it is clear that the latter is not just a version of the former on which the inference relation is analytic entailment.

Getting clear on these differences puts us in a position to see the problems with IRS. The fact that different versions of IRS arise from different inference relations means that there is a wide range of possible IRS theories. At one end of this range are theories that use some form of logical implication, such as the one in familiar systems of standard first-order logic. There are also stronger versions that use more powerful systems of logic, and there are theories that strengthen their logical inference relation further with deductive machinery from mathematics. Even stronger versions of IRS might strengthen their formal implication relations with certain types of natural knowledge, such as strongly confirmed, widely-known empirical regularities. There is obviously a wide range of options with mixed inference relations.

The inference relation for each theory in this range, being either logical implication or something stronger, is stronger than the purely mereological relation of analytic entailment. In this sense, the inference relations in versions of IRS are fruitful in Frege's sense. Indeed, Fregean semantics itself can be seen as a version of IRS—namely, one in which the sense of a sentence is its inference potential with respect to Frege's logic plus a set of ordered pairs <A, B> such that A is a function from a world to an extension and B is the expression that has A as its intension. Robert Brandom for example, takes Fregean semantics to be a version of IRS (1994: 94–97).

Now, since, as I argued in section 1.2, Fregean semantics is subject to the problems of too strong a constraint, too weak a constraint, and the wrong constraint in virtue of construing sense structure as logical structure, and since versions of IRS are at least as fruitful as Fregean semantics, the question arises which of those three problems arise for versions of IRS.

Almost all versions of IRS avoid the problem of too strong a constraint, since, like ATS, they are not committed to the Fregean principle that sense determines reference. Harman's (1987) version of IRS, which we set to one side at the beginning of this discussion, is an exception. Having that commitment, it is subject to the first problem.

Ned Block's (1986) version is not exactly in the same boat as Harman's, since Block eschews the principle that sense determines reference at the level of theories of meaning. But he adopts a metatheoretic version of the principle. He claims that the account of sense one adopts determines one's theory of reference. Block writes: "Conclusion: the conceptual role factor determines the nature of the referential factor . . . . Note the crucial difference between saying that the conceptual role factor determines the nature of the referential factor and saying that the conceptual role factor determines reference. I hold the former, but not the latter" (1986: 644). Block's reasoning is that Kripke's causal theory is a better account of names than the classical description theory, and, hence, that it determines the true theory of reference for names.

Block's metatheoretic version of the Fregean principle fails for the same reason as Fregean semantics. Block's inference is valid only if Kripke's theory and the Fregean description theory exhaust the range of theories (Armour-Garb, in conversation). Hence, the inference is valid only if intensionalism and Fregean intensionalism coincide; but, as I have shown, this is not the case. Moreover, my non-Fregean intensionalism provides a non-Fregean description theory for names that is compatible with Kripke's causal story about them but incompatible with his Millian claim that proper names do not have a sense. Hence, contrary to Block's assumption, accepting Kripke's causal account of names would still leave more than one theory of names, namely, the neo-Millian theory on which the reference of names involves no sense mediation, and my theory on which it does.

Every version of IRS is subject to the problem of too weak a constraint. The fact that they are based on a form of logical implication means that their account of sense, like Frege's, is explained entirely within the theory of reference. Hence, all versions of IRS, like Fregean semantics, impose too weak a constraint on the determination of sense and, accordingly, do not provide us with the "independent controls" necessary to make the right choice among translation hypotheses.

This is clear for versions of IRS based on formal implication, since these versions are, in effect, Fregean semantics. And it is also the case for versions that supplement a formal implication relation with empirical regularities. We do not get determinacy in radical translation by allowing field linguists to deploy reliable empirical regularities, such as that rabbits are easily frightened. If rabbits are easily frightened, so are manifestations of rabbithood. Referential structure, even necessary coreferentiality, underdetermines sense. Hence, constraints on translation based exclusively on evidence about referential structure, formal or empirical, do not permit a justified choice of an English expression with the same sense as the native 'gavagai'. Since indeterminacy is a problem about sameness of sense, constraints on sameness of sense that have the fine-grainedness of sense structure are needed.

Finally, every version of IRS is also subject to the problem of the wrong constraint. The fact that versions of IRS share the implication relation of basic logic guarantees this. Since their notion of sense (meaning or content) is based *inter alia* on the logical law $P \rightarrow (P \vee Q)$, these semantic theories have the problem that all sentences turn out to have the same sense, and the other similar problems found in connection with Fregean semantics.

Reference

2.1. Introduction

The marriage of the theory of sense to the theory of reference has been central to intensionalist thinking for so long that it is hard for intensionalists to imagine how either theory could go it alone. Accordingly, the prospect of divorce that (D) raises is apt to seem daunting to intensionalists when, in fact, they ought to see it as most welcome. The three problems with Fregean intensionalism discussed in the first part of this book show that the marriage, at least for the theory of sense, was never a good one. Only after the theory gains its independence can it expect to have a satisfactory life of its own, one in which it is no longer beset by those problems and in which it has a chance of realizing its full linguistic and philosophical potential. As far as the theory of sense is concerned, the sooner the marriage ends the better.

A divorce is also best for the theory of reference. Even though, as I shall argue, the theory of reference cannot live entirely apart from the theory of sense, a healthier relationship based on full autonomy of the theory of sense benefits the theory of reference, too. The principal reason is that an autonomous theory of sense provides a fuller account of the contribution sense makes to the relation between language and the world, which, in turn, provides a better picture of the constraints under which reference is assigned. In this part of the book, I shall argue that separation and the new relationship between the theories is good for the theory of reference.

2.2. Analyticity: logical and mereological

Nothing could be clearer than that intensionalism and extensionalism have different conceptions of the relation between language and logic. It should also be clear that Fregean intensionalism and my non-Fregean intensionalism have different conceptions of that relation as well. What is not clear is the magnitude of the difference between the two conceptions. In certain respects, the difference between the Fregean conception and the non-Fregean conception is greater than the difference between the intensionalist and extensionalist conceptions.

The earlier discussion of the Fregean definition of sense and (D) showed that the former makes language responsible for the reference of expressions and the truth conditions of sentences, whereas the latter does not. Yet as important as this difference ultimately is, it does not in itself reveal the magnitude of the difference between the Fregean and the non-Fregean perspectives. The reason is that, for everything that might be said in ATS, it is still possible to claim—outside the theory of sense, to be sure—that the sense of an expression determines its referent and the sense of a sentence its truth conditions. For what *denies* such determination, the non-Fregean account of the relation between sense and reference, is not part of ATS.

In this section, I will examine analyticity in Frege's theory of sense and in ATS. In the next sections, I will examine the non-Fregean account of the relation between sense and reference. These examinations will reveal the true magnitude of the difference.

Frege characterizes (1953: 4) analytic propositions as those that are provable from logical laws and definitions. Quine's characterization of analytic statements as belonging to two classes, those which are "logically true" and those which "can be turned into a logical truth by putting synonyms for synonyms" (1953: 22–23), is essentially the same as Frege's. Both characterizations make analyticity a species of logical truth. Thus, although extensionalists like Quine disagree with Fregean intensionalists about whether there are analytic truths over and above logical truths, they agree with Fregean intensionalists that if there are analytic truths in their sense, those truths are *au fond* a matter of logic. Indeed, it is Quine's agreement with Fregean intensionalists on this hypothetical point that motivates him to attack their notion of analyticity. As Quine sees it, acceptance of their notion would compromise the extensional purity of logic: the vocabulary of logical theory would have to contain dubious notions from the theory of meaning such as synonymy and definition.

My non-Fregean intensionalism rejects both Quinean skepticism about analyticity and the Fregean doctrine that analyticity is fundamentally a matter of logic. It sees that doctrine as another aspect of the Fregean attempt to reduce the theory of sense to the theory of reference.

The analytic/synthetic distinction in ATS, like Locke's distinction between trifling and instructive propositions (1924: 306–308), separates analytic sentences from logical truths as well as from mathematical and empirical truths. On ATS, analytic structure is nothing more or less than a kind of mereological structure. This precludes ATS's notion of analyticity from having the fruitfulness that would count what logically follows from a proposition (but is not literally contained in it) as part of its content—no insignificant matter, in light of the problem of the wrong constraint. In effect, ATS reverses Frege's logicizing of analyticity. It would return analyticity to the "beams in the house" concept that Frege took such pains to disparage.

And, of course, what applies to the treatment of analyticity in ATS also applies to the treatment of meaninglessness, meaningfulness, ambiguity, synonymy, redundancy, antonymy, and all the other sense properties and relations of natural language. The autonomy of the theory of sense allows us to embrace the generalization that sense structure is mereological structure. That is, it allows us to understand the intrinsic features of senses and their relations with other senses strictly in terms of part-whole structure.

None of this is to deny that there are instances of logical truths like 'If someone is a bachelor, then he is an unmarried man'. Rather, it is meant to deny that such complex sentences are analytic in our sense of the term, that is, in the sense of "beams-in-the-house" analyticity. My non-Fregean intensionalism says that simple sentences like 'Bachelors are unmarried men' are analytic in this sense. As I shall argue, in the case of the latter sentence but not the former, mereological sense structure suffices to account for the formal truth of the sentence.

This distinction will no doubt be questioned on the grounds that the conditional sentence is, in effect, the regimentation (in Quine's sense [1960: 157–190]) of the simple subject-predicate sentence. If the former expresses the logical form of the latter, how can the former not be analytic if the latter is? The supposition that the conditional sentence is the regimentation of the simple subject-predicate sentence is quite compatible with our saying that the former does not represent the sense of the latter. The regimentation relation expresses at best only extensional equivalence. Non-synonymous sentences like 'Two is less than seventeen' and 'The even prime is less than seventeen' have the same extensional structure, but any intensionalism worth its salt will resist the assimilation of sameness of sense structure to sameness of extensional structure here. The notion that regimentation provides logical forms that represent sense is another aspect of Frege's reduction of the theory of sense to the theory of reference.

Frege links analyticity and logical truth in characterizing analytic propositions as those that are provable from logical laws and definitions. The problem with this characterization is the unclarity of Frege's notion of definition. Frege's *Begriffsschrift* appeared prior to the *Grundlagen*, so his notion of a logical law was as clear as anyone could have wanted. But he provided no systematic explanation of his notion of definition. Had things remained as Frege left them, the concept of analyticity in Fregean intensionalism would be no clearer than his notion of definition.

But Carnap took matters in hand. He linked logical truth and analyticity without invoking the notion of definition (1956: 222–229). He proposed to state the relations among items of the extralogical vocabulary of the language for which Frege had invoked definitions in the form of a set of postulates added to the logical postulates. These "meaning postulates" are expressed with the very same formal apparatus used for expressing laws of logic. Thus, this new apparatus is in the spirit of Frege's referential semantics, since it is apparatus from the theory of reference. Like the logical postulates on which they are modeled, meaning postulates express limitations on the possible: for example, the meaning postulate '(x)(x is a bachelor $\rightarrow$ x is unmarried)' restricts the extension of 'bachelor' to the extension of 'unmarried' in model-theoretic evaluations of sentences. Given meaning postulates for a language, we can characterize its analytic sentences as the sentences of the language that are provable from its meaning postulates and the laws of logic.

Carnap's theory of meaning postulates does not have the unclarity of Frege's characterization of analyticity: we know precisely what sentences of the language belong to the class of analytic truths. Nonetheless, as Quine recognized, Carnap's theory fails to establish a substantial link between logical truth and analyticity. Quine argued (1953: 33) that, although meaning postulates tell us which sentences are called "analytic," they do not tell us what is attributed to them when they are so called.

Couldn't Carnap reply that he is simply explicating the general term 'analytic' along the same lines as logicians have explicated metalogical concepts such as logical truth? Carnap writes:

> How shall we define L-truth so as to fulfill the requirement [that a sentence be true in a system just in case it is true in the system on the basis of its rules alone]? A way is suggested by Leibniz's conception that a necessary truth must hold in all possible worlds. Since our state-descriptions represent the possible worlds, this means that a sentence is logically true if it holds in all state-descriptions. (1956: 11)

Quine responds that this

> adaptation of Leibniz's "true in all possible worlds" . . . serves its purpose only if the atomic statements of the language are, unlike 'John is a bachelor' and 'John is married', mutually independent. Otherwise there would be a state-description which assigned truth to 'John is a bachelor' and to 'John is married', and consequently 'No bachelors are married' would turn out synthetic rather than analytic under the proposed criterion. (1953: 23)

The natural response on Carnap's part is to say that he does not actually need to use intensional notions such as analyticity or synonymy to express the interdependence of 'John is a bachelor' and 'John is married'. A meaning postulate like '(x)(x is a bachelor →—(x is married))', in providing the appropriate constraint on the assignment of extensions, does the trick.

But the appeal to purely extensional constraints makes Quine's point that meaning postulates do not tell us what property is attributed to sentences when they appear on a list with the title 'analytic'. We are told that they are necessary truths, but logical and mathematical truths of all sorts are necessary truths. Appeal to the Leibnizian notion of necessary truth, in effect, concedes that meaning postulates do not capture analyticity as a property that sentences have in virtue of their meaning alone. The problem here is the problem discussed in the first part of this book: properties and relations at the level of extension are too weak to capture properties and relations at the level of sense. Recall the earlier point that it is arbitrary whether we adopt the postulate '(x)(x is the number two → x is the successor of the number one)' or the postulate '(x)(x is the number two → x is the even prime)' or the postulate '(x)(x is the number two → x is the square root of the number four)', or anything else in which the predicate in the consequent of the meaning postulate is necessarily co-extensive with 'two'. In Quinean terminology, it is indeterminate what the meaning of 'two' is, just as it is indeterminate what the translation of 'gavagai' is. The true significance of indeterminacy is not that there is no fact of the matter about meaning, but that there is no fact of the matter about Fregean meaning.

Quine was right that meaning postulates provide no insight into analyticity, but wrong that there is nothing for us to gain insight into. Meaning postulates fail, not because analyticity and other concepts in the theory of meaning cannot be made objective sense of, but because they cannot be made objective sense of in the theory of reference. Thus, Quine's criticisms do not apply to the concepts in an autonomous theory of sense; instead, they clear the decks for an approach to the explanation of synonymy and analyticity in an autonomous theory of sense.

Within such a theory, an approach to analyticity would seek to identify a mereological structure that is common to the senses of analytic sentences but absent from the senses of synthetic sentences. Here we can look to philosophers who have talked about analyticity in the appropriate sense, and to linguistic considerations. Locke's (1924: 306–308) and Kant's (1951: 14) notion of analyticity as containment of predicate concept in subject concept points us in the right direction, as do linguistic considerations. The sense structure underlying the analyticity of 'Squares are rectangles' is the same containment underlying the redundancy of 'rectangular square', the only difference being that the contained and containing senses are the sense of a predicate and the sense of a subject in the former case and the sense of a modifier and the sense of a head in the latter case. This notion of analyticity as literal containment coincides with the intuition that analyticity in the appropriate sense is redundant predication.

To be sure, Locke and Kant did not get all the details right. Their worst mistake was to leave relational analytic sentences out of the picture. Frege saw that stating containment as a relation between a predicate concept and a subject concept makes this mistake, but he took this to mean that Kant's notion of literal containment is fundamentally flawed and ought to be replaced by the notion of non-literal, logical containment. Frege does not bother to ask if there might be less extreme ways of avoiding Kant's mistakes. Nor does he pause to consider the implications of lumping his "more fruitful type of definition" (1953: 100)—for example, the mathematical definition of the continuity of a function—together with definitions like 'A bachelor is an unmarried man'. Frege seems not to have taken to heart the point Locke is making when he distinguishes propositions like 'The external angle of all triangles is bigger than either of the opposite internal angles' from trifling propositions, in virtue of the former's but not the latter's being "a real truth and convey[ing] . . . instructive real knowledge" (1924: 308).

In fact, a minimal revision of Locke and Kant's mereological account of analyticity enables it to capture analytic relational sentences. To see what this revision is, we require examples of relational sentences that *exhibit the same redundant predication as sentences that are trifling/analytic in Locke's and Kant's account*. This qualification is essential. When Kant's account is generalized on the basis of such examples, Paul Benacerraf's claim that "once the class of [analytic] propositions has been enlarged beyond the subject-predicate propositions . . . , the easy route to the a priori from the analytic is no longer available" (1981: 25) is seen to be wrong. The enlargement Benacerraf supposed, Frege's, takes us from the mereological to the logical; the one based on such examples enables us to remain mereological.

Such examples are readily at hand. Sentences like 'Henry buys books from those who sell them to him', 'Jill walks with those with whom Jill strolls' and 'Jack kills those whom Jack murders' are trifling or analytic in precisely the sense in which subject-predicate sentences like 'Squares are rectangles' and 'Bachelors are unmarried' are. Since the only difference between analytic subject-predicate sentences and relational analytic sentences is that some term other than the subject in the latter sentences is the containing term, the only revision that is necessary is to replace the containment condition in Locke's and Kant's account with the condition that the sense of some term in the sentence (subject, direct object, indirect object, and so on) contains its full predication.

Thus, we want a generalization that says that a simple sentence (one with a subject term, a main verb expressing a predicate, and n-1 other terms) is analytic if it has a sense that is literally contained in the sense of one of its n terms. I have proposed a definition based on the generalization (A) (1972: 174–177).[1]

> (A) If S is a sense of a simple sentence, consisting of a predicate $P(x_1, \ldots, x_n)$ and terms $T_1, \ldots, T_n$, such that each term T_i ($1 < i < n$) occupies the argument place x_i, then S is analytic just in case there is a term T_i that contains the predicate P and each of the terms $T_1, \ldots, T_{i-1}, T_{i+1}, \ldots, T_n$, where each T_j ($1 < T_j < T_{i-1}$ or $T_{i+1} < T_j < T_n$) occupies the argument place it occupies in $P(x_1, \ldots, x_n)$.

Corresponding to the property of analyticity, we have the relation of analytic entailment, for which I have proposed a definition based on the generalization (A') (1972: 188–191).

> (A') If S is the sense of a simple sentence, consisting of a predicate $P(x_1, \ldots, x_n)$ and terms $T_1, \ldots, T_n$, such that each term T_i ($1 < i < n$) occupies the argument place x_i, and S' is a sense of a simple sentence, consisting of a predicate $P'(x_1, \ldots, x_m)$ and terms $T'_1, \ldots, T'_n$, such that each term T'_i ($1 < i < m$) occupies the argument place x_i, then S analytically entails S' if P contains P' and each term T'_i in S' contains the corresponding term T_i in S.

(A') covers analytic entailments like 'John is a bachelor, hence, John is unmarried', as well as analytic entailments like 'Men are lonely, hence, bachelors are lonely' and 'Men wear suits, hence, bachelors wear clothing'. (A') does not, as Francis Jeffrey Pelletier claims (1982: 322), cover cases like 'A spinster is a woman, hence, a person is a woman', any more than it covers cases like 'Mary is a female, hence, Mary is a spinster'.

As I have shown, the property of analyticity that sentences like 'Squares are rectangles' and 'Bachelors are unmarried' exhibit is the sentential counterpart of the redundancy of noun phrases like 'rectangular square' and 'unmarried bachelor'. Similarly, the property of contradictoriness that sentences like 'Squares are circles' and 'Bachelors are spinsters' exhibit is the sentential counterpart of the sense structure underlying the antonymy of noun phrase pairs like 'square'/'circle' and 'bachelor'/ 'spinster'. Intuitively, antonymy is opposition in meaning, and, hence, antonymous expressions are, in some sense, negations of one another. But, on ATS, this form of negation cannot be logical negation, since logical negation is a matter of truth and reference. However, like redundancy and analyticity, antonymy and contradictoriness can be a matter of mereological structure.

Arthur Prior (1967: 458–460) and other philosophers have drawn the distinction between external and internal negation on the basis of scope. The scope of external negation is the whole sentence; the scope of internal negation is a phrase or smaller constituent. But these philosophers also define internal negation extensionally—in terms of set-theoretic relations among the objects in the domain of the language. This assimilation of the semantics of internal negation to the semantics of external negation is another instance of the influence of Fregeanism.

To obtain a definition of internal negation that does not involve logic, the definiens has to refer exclusively to aspects of sense structure. To get an idea of how this can be done, consider the antonyms 'perfect' and 'flawed'. 'Not perfect' or 'imperfect' means *flawed*, and 'not flawed' or 'unflawed' means *perfect*. In this case, internal negation functions as a "sense toggle," taking us from one sense to another, from one member of an antonymous *n*-tuple to another. In this respect, it contrasts sharply with external negation, which is a toggle, too, but a reference toggle, a toggle between truth-values. Here the difference between the two notions of negation comes into sharp focus.

Generalizing the idea of a toggle between senses, we can characterize internal negation as an operator that converts senses in its scope into certain other senses. The operator can be specified in terms of the relation between the senses to which it applies and the senses that result from its application. As the example of 'perfect' and 'flawed' and their negations suggests, the relation between these senses is otherness with respect to the members of a class of senses to which the negated sense belongs. This echoes the conception of otherness that Plato suggests in the *Sophist* (257B–193C): "So, when it is asserted that a negative signifies a contrary, we shall not agree, but admit no more than this: that the prefix 'not' indicates something different from the words that follow—or rather from the things designated by the words pronounced after the negative." This remark is preceded by the observation that saying something is not big leaves it open whether the thing is small or equal. Putting the conception of otherness together with this observation, we obtain the idea that the form of negation we want is otherness with respect to a range of conceptual options each of which differs from every other option in the range.

The members of the range are the senses of the expressions belonging to an antonymous *n*-tuple, where an antonymous *n*-tuple is *n* senses each with a common superordinate sense and standing in the otherness relation to one another. Thus, the senses of the basic color terms, 'red', 'blue', 'green', and so on form an antonymous *n*-tuple because they have the common superordinate sense *color* and are inherently other than each of their co-subordinates under 'color'. Hence, the sense of 'not red' means, roughly speaking, *some one basic color other than red, or colorless.* (See Katz 1972: 47–55, 82–88, 157–171.)

Two of the three ways antonymy relations among constituents of a simple sentence can occur give rise to types of contradictory sentence. In one of the types, the antonymy relation occurs among the components of its predicate, as illustrated by 'Mary is a married spinster'. In the other type, the antonymy relation occurs between its predicates and its terms, as illustrated by 'Spinsters are married' and 'Jack kills those whose lives Jack spares'. Accordingly, corresponding to (A) and (A'), we will have (C) and (C').

> (C)   If S is a sense of a simple sentence, consisting of a predicate $P(x_1, \ldots, x_n)$ and terms $T_1, \ldots, T_n$, such that each term T_i ($1 < i < n$) occupies the argument place x_i, then S is contradictory just in case two components of P are members of the same antonymous n-tuple, or there is a T_i the sense of which is a member of the same antonymous n-tuple as the component of P associated with x_i.

> (C')   If S and S' are the senses of simple sentences, then S analytically contradicts S' just in case a component C of the predicate P of S and a component C' of the predicate P' of S' are associated, respectively, with the same term and either C or C' has a component that analytically entails a member of the same antonymous n-tuple as a component of the other.

(A), (A'), (C), and (C') are clearly not intended as formalizations of the relations in question. First, formalizations, or even something approaching them, would not be possible at this stage because I have not provided an explanation of the formal representations of senses that would enable me to define notions like *predicate, term, contains, members of the same antonymous n-tuple, component of a predicate associated with a term,* and so on. I will say more about such formal representations in the third part of this book. Second, besides the two ways referred to in (C), there is a third way that constituents in simple sentences can stand in antonymy relations: a single term can contain members of the same antonymous n-tuple. Examples are sentences like 'Married spinsters are wise'. (C) has been written so that such sentences are not counted as contradictory. (I will say more about the reason for the special status accorded this antonymy structure when I turn to presupposition.) We mark this difference with (C''):

> (C'')   A sense of a simple sentence S consisting of an n-place predicate P with a term occupying each place is *contratermic* just in case one of the terms has components belonging to the same antonymous n-tuple.

This mereological account of analyticity avoids the problems with Frege's account of analyticity. First, Quine's criticism of Carnap's attempt to explain analyticity in terms of meaning postulates does not carry over to (A). (A) explains the property of analyticity as redundant predication and picks out analytic sentences on the basis of the property it explains—exactly what Carnap's account does not do. Second, since logical laws play no role in (A) and (A'), the problem of the wrong constraint does not arise for our semantics.

2.3. The mediation thesis

Since the vocabulary of sense theory is restricted to terms that represent an aspect of the internal structure of sentences (their decompositional and compositional sense structure), concepts expressing the relation between language and the world do not appear in representations of it. One consequence of this is that, within my non-Fregean intensionalism, hypotheses about the relation between sense and reference are unformulatable in the theory of sense.

This consequence satisfies a necessary condition for escaping the problem of too strong a constraint, since it guarantees that the theory of sense does not provide Putnam's and Kripke's arguments with the essential premise that sense determines reference. But the restriction is not itself sufficient for escaping the problem, since it does not guarantee that those arguments will not get the premise from the theory of reference. Hence, non-Fregean intensionalists must not only have an autonomous theory of sense, they must have a theory of reference containing a principle that says that the role sense plays in reference is other than determination.

In earlier works (1988; 1990a; 1992; 1994; 1997), I argued that in the case of both expression-types and expression-tokens, the relation of expressions to objects in the domain of the language is, rather than determination, mediation, in the sense of (MED).

(MED)   Sense mediates reference: sense is not sufficient for specifying the conditions for the reference of either expression-types or expression-tokens, but it is necessary for specifying the conditions for the reference of both expression-types and expression-tokens.[2]

The options in the philosophy of language heretofore have been Fregean intensionalism, which says that sense is both necessary and sufficient for reference, and extensionalism, which says that sense is neither necessary nor sufficient for reference. Once the required motivation for (MED) is provided, these options become the extremes between which my non-Fregean intensionalism, which takes sense to be necessary but not sufficient for reference, provides a middle ground.

2.3.1. (MED) and type-reference

Fregean intensionalists think that the sense of a (non-indexical) expression-type determines its reference.[3] They may take a different view about the case of token-reference, due to examples of reference under a false description, but they see themselves on firm ground in the case of type-reference. In the realm of linguistic types, there are none of the contextual factors—such as intentions of the speaker, beliefs of the audience, or salient features of the situation—that can supersede sense and give rise to reference under a false description. So Fregean intensionalists conclude that sense determines the assignment of objects to expression-types of the language. Most of them would not think that the point needs to be argued for.

To his credit, Paul Boghossian tries to provide an argument that sense determines type-reference (1994). The gist of the argument is that property exemplification delivers determination. Let us say that the sense of the English word 'bachelor' is the property of being an unmarried man. Since the set of things exemplifying this property is the set of bachelors, we have to say that the property *unmarried man—ex hypothesi* the sense of 'bachelor'—determines the type-reference of 'bachelor'.

But property exemplification does not by itself deliver determination. Something must be said about the relation between the set of objects exemplifying the property and the linguistic type that is alleged to have the set as its extension. Since it says nothing about the connection between the notions *extension of the term t* and *set of things that the sense of t picks out*, Boghossian's argument is enthymematic. It rests on the tacit premise that when a property P is the sense of a term t, the set of objects that P picks out—the exemplifiers of P—constitutes the extension of t. Since this premise is, in effect, the definition (E) for the notion 'extension',

> (E)   The extension of a term t with the sense S is the set of all the objects in the domain that fall under S.

and since (E) is just the Fregean claim that sense determines reference all over again, Boghossian's argument begs the question. It provides no reason for thinking that the set picked out by a property P is the extension of a term with the property P as its sense.

To be sure, many intensionalists will think no reason is necessary, because they mistakenly take (E) to be the trivial truth that the referent of a term is something that falls under the determiner of its referent. But once (D) is available as an alternative to the Fregean definition of sense, (E) can no longer be taken as trivial. On (D), the function of sense is only to determine the sense properties and relations of expression-types. Therefore, (E) becomes the substantive claim that what determines an expression-type's sense properties and relations also determines its referential properties and relations. Why is this supposed to be an inescapable truth? The denial of (E) coupled with the assumption, which may be accepted for the cases in question, that reference is determined, implies no more than that something other than the sense of an expression contributes to the determination of its type-reference.

We need look no further than Putnam's cases of natural kind terms such as 'aluminum' and 'molybdenum' to see what it might be other than sense that plays a role in determining type-reference. Putnam argued that we cannot get the extension of a natural kind term like 'aluminum' right if we determine it on the basis of properties like *being a metal, being light in weight, being durable in cookware, being rustless,* and so on, since, "For all [we] know, every one of these properties may also fit molybdenum" (1975c: 150). Hence, to get the "customary meaning" of 'aluminum' right, "one has to be sure one has the right extension." Now, assuming Putnam is right when he says that to be sure of the right extension we require information about the essential nature of aluminum, that information will provide a constraint on the type-reference of 'aluminum' over and above the constraint that follows from (MED) that its members have the cluster of properties comprising its sense. The further constraint will be that its members also have the appropriate essential nature.

So far, it is not clear how to state this further constraint as a general feature of the relation between sense and type-reference. Once the framework is in place for stating constraints on the assignment of extensions to expression-types, however, I will state the constraints on reference as the principle (RC3) (to appear later) that replaces (E) in our non-Fregean intensionalism.

2.3.2. Fregean sense and nonplenomic forms

The previous section showed why sense is not sufficient for the assignment of type-reference. In this section, I show why sense is necessary for the assignment of type-reference. The examples that provide the reason anticipate the more systematic discussion in section 2.4 of the role sense properties and relations play in the assignment of referential structure.

The initial distinction required in an assignment of referential structure to expression-types is between those expression-types that can have a type-extension and those expression-types that cannot. Since having a null extension—as, for example, in cases like 'unicorn' and 'the largest integer'—is having an extension, not having an extension is to be understood as not having even a null extension. Meaningless but syntactically well-formed expressions like 'crimson prime numbers' are the standard case of expressions that cannot have a type-extension, but there are also meaningful expression-types that cannot have one. The most familiar such cases are indexical expressions such as 'I', 'our car', 'your sister', and so on. Less familiar expressions the sense of which precludes the assignment of a type-extension are noun phrases like 'big ones', sentences like 'There are small ones', and similar forms with other relative adjectives such as 'fat', 'thin', and so on. Although such expressions are clearly meaningful, they cannot be assigned an extension because, unlike 'big elephant' and 'There are small cars', their head nouns lack information about the standard of comparison (see Katz 1972: 254–261). The null extension cannot be assigned to these expressions because doing so would incorrectly suggest that their senses, like those of 'unicorn' and 'the largest integer', contain information necessary for saying that everything in the domain of the language falls outside their type-extension.

Another possible case of meaningful expressions with no type-extension is, I believe, proper names. If my account of proper names (1990a; 1994; 2001) is correct, they have a sense that is an instance of the schema 'the thing which is a bearer of N'. On this account, names have two features that jointly prevent them from having type-reference. One is that they can have multiple bearers, and the other is that they are definite. Since proper names can have more than one bearer, the requirement that they refer to exactly one bearer cannot be satisfied at the type level, where there is no information available to single out any one of them. A reference-determining condition would have to specify a single individual from among the bearers of a name, but there is no way to do this because there is no context to supply the necessary information to choose among the bearers of the name.

It should be mentioned that, although no one contests the claim that proper names are definite, some philosophers, notably Kripke, have contested the claim that they can have multiple bearers. Kripke maintains that a name can have only one bearer, since "uses of phonetically the same sounds to name distinct objects count as distinct names" (1980: 8). This claim, as Kripke himself admits, "does not agree with the most common usage." It clearly does not agree with common usage, and since agreement with linguistic fact is the criterion for the truth of a linguistic thesis, Kripke's thesis, as I argue elsewhere (2001), is false. To mention a few of the linguistic facts it does not fit, note that we often speak of people as having the same name. When one John Smith is introduced to another John Smith, each can say what is the literal truth, "We have the same name." This is also illustrated in the children's song that starts, "John Jacob Jingleheimer Schmidt, his name is my name, too." If Kripke's thesis were right, we could *prove* to John Jacob Jingleheimer Schmidt that he does not have the name he has by arguing, "Premise 1: his name is 'John Jacob Jingleheimer Schmidt'; premise 2: Kripke's thesis; conclusion: your name is not 'John Jacob Jingleheimer Schmidt'."

I shall call expression-types like 'bachelor' and 'even number' that are meaningful and can have a type-extension "plenomic," and expression-types like indexical expressions, relative modifiers, and proper names that are meaningful but cannot have a type-extension "nonplenomic." There should be no doubt about the meaningfulness of nonplenomic linguistic types, since they have sense properties and relations. 'Big ones' is antonymous with 'small ones', 'light ones' is ambiguous, 'ones that are large' is synonymous with 'large ones', 'It's a heavy one' analytically entails 'It's not a light one', and so on. Clearly, indexicals have a sense, and, arguably, names do as well, since 'John Smith is a British adventurer' analytically entails 'Someone with the name "John Smith" is a British adventurer' and is analytically entailed by 'Someone with the name "John Smith" exists and everyone with that name is a British adventurer'. Moreover, the senses of nonplenomic expressions are compositional and enter into the compositional meanings of sentences containing them.

Fregeans may deny that nonplenomic expressions like 'small ones' and 'light ones' have a sense on the grounds of the context principle. Two things should be said about this. First, in section 3.5, I show that this principle itself is unacceptable because it conflicts with compositionality. Second, an appeal to the context principle does not help for nonplenomic sentences like 'It's a heavy one' or 'Your father's sister is a feminist'.

Given that nonplenomic expression-types are meaningful, they present a problem for Frege's notion of sense, because, though they have a sense, it cannot determine a reference for them. Nonplenomic forms, in principle, have no extension (not even an empty one). But, as Fregean senses are determiners of reference (either a non-empty or an empty extension) as a matter of definition, it follows both that there are meaningful expressions in natural language to which the Fregean notion of sense is in principle inapplicable, and that a large open set of senses in natural language are not Fregean senses. Hence, the Fregean notion of sense is not the right one for natural language.

2.3.3. (MED) and token-reference

In the case of token-reference, (MED) involves the claims (M1), (M2), and (M3):

(M1)   The sense of an expression-type does not determine the reference of its tokens.

(M2)   The sense of an expression-token does not determine its reference.

(M3)   The reference of an expression-token is determined by both its token-sense and the sense of the type of which it is a token.

(M4) is in the spirit of the thesis, but is not one of its claims:

(M4)   The reference of an expression-type does not determine the reference of its tokens.

A rationale for (M1) is non-literal uses of language. Given a rich enough context, the reference of a token can differ in virtually any way from what we would straightforwardly think its reference is on the basis of the sense of its type. One such context might be a debate in which the contestants are going at it hot and heavy. What matters most to them is a knock-down argument that wins the debate, and anyone who comes up with one is an instant celebrity. In the final round, such a debate-winning argument occasions the exclamation, "That's glory!" In this context, 'glory' could mean *a nice knock-down argument*, even though, as Alice quite rightly insists against Humpty Dumpty, that is not what 'glory' means in the language.

A rationale for (M2) is the phenomenon of reference under a false description. In Keith Donnellan's case (1966) of the use of 'The man drinking a martini is tall' to make the statement that a man drinking water is tall, the token of the subject of the sentence has the sense *man drinking a martini* but, due to features of the context, it refers to a man drinking water. In the days of the Salem witch trials, the term 'witch' was used with the sense of the expression-type 'woman in league with the Devil', but it nonetheless referred (under this false description) to ordinary people. (See Katz 1990a: 31–61; 1990b; 1994 for further discussion.)

The sense of an expression-type is necessary for token-reference ((M3)) because type-sense is the criterion for literal application. Literalness is, as it were, conformity to the letter of semantic law. Roughly speaking, the sense of a token is literal in case it is the sense of its type (or analytically includes it), and the referent of a token is literal in case the sense of the token is literal and the referent belongs to the extension of that sense. In literal applications, we call a spade a spade. Alice's point against Humpty Dumpty is simply that 'glory' is not the English word for a nice knock-down argument.[4]

What makes the use of a word correct is that the referent on the use fits the meaning of the word in the language. When Jacques the chef says "I made hamburger out of them," referring to the previously unpacked chunks of beef, his application of 'hamburger' is literal. This contrasts with the application of 'hamburger' on the part

of Boris, who uses another token of the type 'I made hamburger out of them' in reference to his opponents in a chess tournament. Jacques's application of 'hamburger'
is literal because 'hamburger' is the correct word for the referent in his case, because
the referent fits the meaning of 'hamburger' in English, namely, *ground beef*. Boris's
application of 'hamburger' is non-literal because 'hamburger' is not the correct word
for Boris's chess opponents, no matter how badly they lost.

In ordinary non-literal uses of language (not exceptional uses such as passwords,
codes, and so on), knowledge of the sense of an expression-type is an essential starting point for the pragmatic reasoning that traces the metaphorical route to the meaning of its token. Without knowing the sense of 'hamburger', there is no way for the
audience to know that Boris is saying that he defeated his opponents so badly that
the process can be compared to grinding hamburger. Similarly, when Virginia, referring to the dean, says to one of her colleagues, "Tyrannosaurus rex is visiting the
department today," it is their mutual, reflexive knowledge of the sense of 'Tyrannosaurus rex' that provides Virginia's colleagues with a link to her metaphorical meaning
via their recognition that her description of the dean is not intended literally.

H. P. Grice suggests an explanation of how we grasp metaphorical meaning that
underscores my claim about the primacy of linguistic meaning. On Grice's account
(1989: 34), knowledge of sense and understanding of literalness makes it obvious
that the speakers in the Boris and Virginia cases have flouted "the maxim of quality"
(supermaxim [1989: 27]: "Try to make your contribution one that is true"). As a
consequence, the hearers reason that the speaker wants them to recognize the intentional falsification as signaling that the utterance means something other than what
its words literally mean. "The most likely supposition," as Grice puts it, is that the
speaker is referring to something which resembles—"more or less fancifully"—what
a literal referent would be (1989: 34). In these cases as in other cases of metaphor,
rhetorical effect compensates for the speaker's indirectness.

2.4. A conception of the theory of type-reference

The conception of the theory of type-reference to be sketched in this section is intended to extend the contrast between Fregean intensionalism and non-Fregean
intensionalism into the area of reference, and to provide new ways of thinking about
the interpretation of natural languages. The fundamental idea underlying these ways
of thinking about interpretation is the notion of *referential correlates*. The contribution of our intensionalism to the theory of type-reference is largely a system of referential correlates.

These principles correlate a particular sense property or relation of expression-
types or their senses with a referential property or relation. There is one referential
correlate for each sense property and relation. Looked at from the perspective of the
theory of sense, such correlates spell out the referential import of sense properties
and relations. Looked at from perspective of the theory of reference, they state the
contribution that the senses of expressions make to their type-reference. Looked at
neutrally, they spell out the relation between the sense and reference of expression-

types. Assuming that the theory of type-reference is model-theoretic in form, referential correlates can be thought of as constraints on admissible models—i.e., on the assignment of collections of objects from the domain to expressions of the language.

2.4.1. Kinds of referential correlates

Referential correlates are of two kinds, because there are two kinds of sense properties and relations. Sense properties and relations are *expressional* or *non-expressional* (Katz 1990b: 62–63). Examples of expressional sense properties and relations are being meaningless, being meaningful, and being ambiguous. They are expressional because they hold of expressions *per se*. It is absurd to say of a sense of an expression that it itself is meaningful or meaningless or ambiguous. These expressional sense properties are simply a count of the number of senses an expression has. For example, the property of being meaningless is the property of having no sense, the property of being meaningful is the property of having at least one sense, and the property of being ambiguous is the property of having two or more senses. Expressional sense properties and relations hold of expressions derivatively—that is to say, in virtue of the senses they have or do not have.

Examples of non-expressional sense properties and relations are being analytic, being antonymous, analytically entailing, and analytically contradicting. In contrast to expressional sense properties and relations, non-expressional sense properties and relations apply to senses absolutely, because they are types of sense structures. Thus, they hold of senses directly and of expressions only indirectly, that is, relative to a sense. For example, the property of being analytic applies directly to a sense of the ambiguous sentence 'Dusting a surface is removing dust from it', but only indirectly to the sentence itself (since the verb 'dust' also has a sense *put dust on a surface*). In applying the notion of analyticity, we must say a sentence is "analytic on a sense," since otherwise the application itself is equivocal.

Hence, referential correlates can be correlates of expressional sense properties and relations or correlates of non-expressional sense properties and relations. (RC1) and (RC2) state referential correlates of expressional sense properties and relations:

(RC1)   If an expression-type is meaningless or nonplenomic, it has no type-extension (neither a non-null nor a null one). If an expression-type is meaningful and plenomic, it has a type-extension.

(RC2)   If an expression-type is *n*-ways ambiguous and *m* of its *n* senses are plenomic, then it has *m* type-extensions, one for each of its plenomic senses.

The fundamental referential correlate for expressional sense properties and relations is my alternative to the Fregean principle (E). It says, consistently with (MED), how the type-extension of an expression depends on its sense. (E), as we saw above, is too strong: the fact that something falls under the sense of an expression is not generally sufficient for membership in its type-extension. However, this does not mean that it is not sometimes sufficient. Hence, the wanted referential correlate is one that says when falling under the sense of an expression is sufficient and when it is not, and, furthermore, what information is required for membership in the type-extension in addition to falling under the sense.

Given that the cases of insufficiency are exclusively natural kind terms, a plausible conjecture for such a referential correlate is (RC3):

> (RC3)   If a (plenomic) sense of an expression does not contain the category *natural kind*, its type-extension is the thing(s) in the domain that fall under that sense. If a (plenomic) sense of an expression contains the category *natural kind*, its type-reference is the thing(s) in the domain that fall under both that sense and the conception of the nature of the kind.

The notion of a category in (RC3) is explained in Katz 1972 (99–100). Here I need repeat only the gist of the explanation. Senses are typically constructed from other senses hierarchically. The highest component sense is the most general one and the other component senses qualify it in one way or another. The senses of 'house', 'hotel', 'prison', and so on each consist of the sense *artifact* qualified by the sense *dwelling*, which is, in turn, qualified by senses that express the purpose of the dwelling—for example, residential use, a particular sort of transient use, use for lawful custody, and so forth. These hierarchical relations determine superordinate/subordinate relations among expressions: for example, 'artifact' is a superordinate of 'dwelling', which is a superordinate of 'house', 'hotel', 'prison', and so on. The least qualified component sense in the sense of an expression is its highest category.

On (RC3), expressions for artifactual kinds, like 'dwelling', geometrical kinds, like 'square', occupational kinds, like 'doctor', linguistic kinds, like 'anagram', and mathematical kinds, like 'prime', have type-extensions consisting of things that fall under their sense. Their senses are sufficient to determine their type-extensions. In contrast, the senses of expressions for natural kinds, such as 'aluminum', 'water', 'gold', and so on, are insufficient to determine their type-extensions. Their reference might, in analogy to reference under a false description, be described as reference under an incomplete description. According to (RC3), an explanatory conception of the nature of the kind compensates for the incompleteness. From the present perspective, Putnam was correct about what information is required for reference determination in the case of natural kind terms, but mistaken about where it comes from. It does not come from linguistic meaning. The mistake stems from his commitment to the Fregean notion that reference determination is the job of meaning.

Without this commitment, the source of some reference-determining information outside linguistic meaning can be located in the explanatory conception of the nature of the kind. The notion of an explanatory conception is a broad one. Explanatory conceptions, as I use the term, are scientific conceptions, commonsense conceptions, or protoconceptions of the referents, which take them to have the natural essence exemplified in certain paradigmatic instances of the term's application. In typical cases of natural kind terms, the conception takes the form of a scientific account of the nature of the kind. Scientific conceptions differ from linguistic concepts. A *linguistic concept* is what a term expresses in the language—that is, its sense. A linguistic concept can be thought of as specified by the analytic sentences of the language that contain the term. A *scientific conception* is the conception that a body of scientific knowledge conveys about the nature of the referent of a term. A scientific conception can be thought of as specified by the non-analytic (synthetic) sentences about the nature of the referent in the appropriate scientific theory. This distinction corresponds to the traditional distinction in philosophy between *nominal definitions* and *real definitions*: nominal definitions define linguistic concepts and real definitions define scientific conceptions.

2.4.2. Mereological analyticity and logical regimentation

In this and the next section, I shall be concerned with the referential correlates for the mereological notion of analyticity and related notions. Given the influence of the Fregean conception of semantics, the first candidate for a referential correlate for analyticity to come to mind is likely to be (F):

> (F)   If a sense of a sentence is analytic (that is, if the sentence is analytic on a sense),
> it expresses a necessary truth on that sense.

Supposing that (2.1) is analytic (on a sense),

(2.1)   Cats are animals.

(F) would require us to say that it is a necessary truth. But how can (2.1) be true in possible worlds in which there are no cats for it to be true of? If it is not true in them, how can it be true in *all* possible worlds? After so many years of indoctrination in what Quine calls "regimentation" (1960: 157–161), the answer seems so obvious as to make the question sound naive: preserving (F) in the face of catless worlds requires no more than standard regimentation. We recast sentences like (2.1) as having the logical form of complex, truth-functionally compound sentences like (2.2):

(2.2)   If something is a cat, then it is an animal.

This reveals such sentences to have the logical form $(x)(Fx \rightarrow Gx)$, and, hence, to be true in possible worlds in which their antecedents are false.

No doubt the problem can be overcome in this way. The question is whether the step of regimentation, for all its seeming obviousness, is one we should take. Mightn't this seeming obviousness only arise from decades of training in (Fregean) logic classes? Let us put aside the apparent obviousness of such a recasting, and note the *non*obviousness, from a linguistic point of view, of recasting a grammatically simple subject-predicate sentence as a compound one. Let us also remind ourselves that regimentation is not an inherent part of logic itself, which is a theory of implication, but rather a way of applying that theory to the study of inference relations among sentences in natural language. Finally, let us note that regimentation is only one proposal about the nature of inference relations in natural language. It says that they are uniformly logical. But ATS says that some of them are *non*-logical.

Hence, philosophers on both sides of the issue about regimentation are required to provide a rationale.

Regimentation begins with Frege. His rationale for the particular feature of it we are concerned with here, the recasting of simple subject-predicate sentences as compound sentences, is "perspicuity." Frege writes that recasting simple subject-predicate sentences as material conditionals unifies the diverse forms of inference in Aristotelian logic under the single rule of *modus ponens*: "In this way, an inference using any mode of inference can be reduced to our case. Accordingly, since it is possible to manage with a single mode of inference, perspicuity demands that we do so. Otherwise, there would be no reason to stop with the Aristotelian modes of inference; instead, we could go on adding new ones indefinitely. . . ." (1972: 120). We can grant what Frege says, even though it is not strictly true that he uses only *modus ponens*, since the fight in this case is between competing systems of logical rules, Frege's and Aristotle's. Aristotle is out for the count. But in the present case the fight is between competing conceptions of analyticity, Frege's logical conception and Kant's mereological conception. Frege has not laid a glove on Kant. If Frege's fruitfulness criticism of Kant's conception had succeeded, there would only be Frege's conception of analyticity, and then Frege could argue that, unless we regiment traditional cases of analyticity and analytic entailments, we have no way to explain them. For without the Fregean story about the true semantic form of subject-predicate sentences, such sentences are not derivable from laws of logic plus definitions.

The disagreement comes down to whether recasting simple subject-predicate sentences as complex conditionals or conjunctions is required in order to account for the semantics of simple sentences. Of course, given Frege's fruitfulness criticism of the traditional notion of analyticity and its replacement with his notion of analyticity as provability from logical laws and definitions, such recasting is necessary to account for the analyticity of simple subject-predicate sentences like (2.1). Without it, simple analytic sentences will not come out as analytic in Frege's sense, that is, as sentences that can be turned into logical truths by, as Quine put it, "putting synonyms for synonyms" (1953: 23). Since the fruitfulness criticism does not work, Frege's conception of analyticity is not the only conception; consequently, the analyticity of simple analytic sentences can be accounted for without regimentation, and there is no argument for recasting them.

We must entertain some suspicions about regimentation when we observe that, from a linguistic standpoint, such recasting runs roughshod over our grammatical intuition that there is a distinction between simple and compound sentences (constructions out of two or more sentences) and that sentences like (2.1) are simple sentences. Sentences like (2.1) do not have the clausal structure of a complex sentence like (2.2); nor does their structure show any relevant evidence of empty categories or movement; nor do their senses contain the notion of conditionality. Similarly, the senses of simple subject-predicate sentences like (2.3):

(2.3)   Some cats are animals.

do not contain the notion of conjunction that appears in the senses of logical recastings like (2.4):

(2.4)   There is something which is a cat and which is an animal.

These are compositionality intuitions. Given that the meaning of a sentence is a function of the meanings of its constituents, there would have to be a constituent in (2.1) the sense of which contains the notion of conditionality and there would have to be a constituent in (2.3) the sense of which contains the notion of conjunction. But there are no such constituents. Therefore, there is no compositional source for the notion of conditionality in the one case and for the notion of conjunction in the other. (See Wiggins 1980 for discussion of this point.)

Since recasting obliterates an intuitively clear grammatical distinction between simple and complex sentences, the practice of assimilating sentences like (2.1) and (2.3) to sentences like (2.2) and (2.4) is suspect from the standpoint of a linguistic study of natural language. This has led some philosophers and linguists to propose a notation involving restricted quantifiers. On this notation, (2.1) is rendered as having the form [*every x: Fx*] (*Gx*), associated with the truth condition that an instance of the form is true just in case the set of things that are *F* minus the set of things that are *G* is empty. (2.3) is rendered as of the form [*some x: Fx*] (*Gx*), associated with the truth condition that an instance of the form is true just in case the set that is the intersection of the things that are *F* and the things that are *G* has at least one member.

Note also that some philosophers and linguists, Stephen Neale (1990: 40–49), for example, further motivate this notation by arguing that it provides a way of representing "plurality quantifiers" such as 'most' "that simply resist the unary mold." But I will leave this consideration to one side, since the unsymbolizability of such unusual quantifiers in first-order notation leaves it open whether they, like the usual quantifiers in unusual sentences like 'Some critics admire only one another' (see Boolos 1998: 54–72), can be symbolized in second-order notation, and since there is no point here in getting into the relative merits of restricted quantifier notation and second-order notation.

The important point here is that restricted quantifier notation is antithetical to the Fregean account of analyticity on which simple analytic sentences like (2.1) and (2.3) are a species of logical truths. Unlike standard logical regimentation, regimentation of simple analytic sentences like (2.1) and (2.3) in restricted quantifier notation does not represent them as instances of logical truths, because it does not represent them as grammatically compound sentences with logical operators—such as the material conditional and conjunction—in them. But, since logical truth depends on such logical operators, without those operators in the representations of sentences like (2.1) and (2.3), they cannot be represented as logical truths. Even if the representations are set up on the basis of definitions or meaning postulates, so that, for example, the representation of (2.1) is '[every x: Feline Animal x] (Animal x)', they provide no basis for claiming that the represented sentences are instances of logical truths: no logical operators in the representation, no logical truth in the represented. The difficulty here is the same as the one Wittgenstein faced in trying to explain the incompatibility of color sentences like 'The spot is red' and 'The spot is green' (1961): there is no explanation of logical properties and relations without logical operators.

Restricted quantifier notation is not logical regimentation. To be sure, it displays relations among quantifiers, predicates, and terms in sentences. But although this is enough to say that it is semantic representation, it is not enough to say it is logical representation *in the Fregean sense*. This is clear from the fact that, taking simple analytic sentences to have forms in restricted quantifier notation, it is straightforward to distinguish analytic sentences from synthetic sentences on the basis of (A). Consider (2.1) represented as '[every x: Cx] (Ax)'. We interpret the expression within the brackets 'Cx' as the term of the sentence and the expression within parentheses 'Ax' as the predicate. Then we supply the appropriate decompositional structures of those expressions. Since those structures exhibit the predicate as contained within the term, an application of (A) will tell us that the sentence is analytic. Similarly, (2.3) represented as '[some x: Cx] (Ax)', interpreted in the same way and with the same decompositional analyses of the expressions, comes out as analytic with respect to (A).

The distinction I have drawn between sentences (2.1) and (2.3) and sentences (2.2) and (2.4) is, of course, not one that Frege would countenance. As he himself once put it, "The distinction of categorical, hypothetical, and disjunctive judgments appears to me to have only a grammatical significance" (1972: 114). I have long marveled at the striking irony of this remark. From the standpoint of Frege's view of natural language, the remark is, to be sure, a put-down of the first order. However, from the standpoint of my non-Fregean view of natural language, the remark expresses the simple truth of the matter. The distinction *has* grammatical significance; it is an inherent feature of the grammatical structure of natural language. There is, then, agreement between Frege and me on the grammatical nature of the distinction; the disagreement is over its philosophical import.

As Frege sees it, the distinction is another of the imperfections of natural language—further proof, if any were needed, that the sentences of natural language are an inadequate notation for rigorous thinking. When Frege said the distinction is *only* of grammatical significance, he meant, of course, that it is not of real semantic significance; and by this he meant that it is not of logical significance. Perhaps this is so; but once semantics is sharply divided into the theory of sense and the theory of reference, it is clear that the distinction is of significance for semantics in the former sense. And, given the present conception of the theory of reference as involving referential correlates, it will turn out to be of significance for semantics in the latter sense, too.

Quine is also thought to have provided a rationale for regimenting sentences. He says:

> By developing our logical theory strictly for sentences in a convenient canonical form we achieve the best division of labor: on the one hand there is theoretical deduction and on the other hand there is the work of paraphrasing ordinary language into the theory. The latter job is the less tidy of the two, but still it will usually present little difficulty to one familiar with the canonical notation. For normally

he himself is the one who has uttered, as part of some present job, the sentence of ordinary language concerned; and he can then judge outright whether his ends are served by the paraphrase. (1960: 157–161)

Such a conception of paraphrasing language bears no relation to regimentation as it is practiced. In practice, we do not let everyone do their own thing. People get both paraphrase and regimentation wrong. And they can even assign different canonical forms to different tokens of the same sentence-type. Furthermore, in *Word and Object* and everywhere else, regimentation is regimentation of sentences of a language— i.e., types, not tokens. The question in "paraphrasing ordinary language" is what semantic representation of the sentence-types gets their grammatical structure right. From this standpoint, grammatical differences like those between (2.1) and (2.2), and (2.3) and (2.4), become clear evidence that the standard practice of regimentation has gotten it wrong.

Quine cautions: ". . . *expose no more logical structure than seems useful* for the deduction or other inquiry at hand. In the immortal words of Adolf Meier, where it doesn't itch don't scratch" (1960: 160). No quarreling with Meier; but his "immortal words" are not to the point here because it cannot be assumed that logical structure is the only kind of semantic structure that sentences have. If they also have sense structure, as I have argued, then there is another "inquiry at hand"—that of representing the sense structure of the sentences in question—and this inquiry can set limits on the exposing of logical structure over and above those set by simplicity. This point is the same as the one just made in connection with Frege's rationale. The inquiry tells us that the analyticity and analytic entailments of simple sentences can be explained without assigning them "canonical forms" that represent them as having the logical structure of a material conditional, and further, that such an explanation makes more sense from a linguistic standpoint because it does not recast those sentences as compound ones.

This is not to deny logicians the use of the standard devices of regimentation for technical purposes. But, on Quine's conception, regimentation is not simply a useful notation for such purposes, having no philosophical implications. Quine makes a point of the philosophical implications of regimentation: "The quest of a simplest, clearest overall pattern of canonical notation is not to be distinguished from a quest of ultimate categories, a limning of the most general traits of reality" (1960: 161). My point is that, if philosophical capital is going to be made from the regimentation of the structure of sentences in a natural language, we had better not leave the decision of how to regiment them either to unwashed speakers or to logicians with a philosophical axe to grind. It is perhaps worth reminding ourselves that regimentation is an issue with the most serious philosophical consequences. Wittgenstein's long struggle with color incompatibility sentences (1961: section 6.3751) shows that Quine is quite wrong to claim that the job of regimenting natural language "will usually present little difficulty to one familiar with the canonical notation."

Since simple subject-predicate and relational analytic sentences can be marked as such on the basis of (A), we do not have to recast them as complex conditionals or conjunctions. Once the referential correlates for analyticity are specified, the task of

showing that recasting simple analytic sentences as logical truths is entirely unnecessary will be complete.

In the case of sentences like (2.1) and (2.3), modal interpretation does not require a truth value in all possible worlds, but only in all possible worlds in which
there is something for the sentence to be true of. (Similarly, in the case of contradictory sentences like 'Cats are not animals', modal interpretation only requires falsehood in all possible worlds in which there is something for the sentence to be false
of.) What is wanted for such sentences is, therefore, Kripke's notion of weakly necessary truth (and, for contradictory sentences, its counterpart, the notion of weakly
necessary falsehood).

Kripke characterizes the former notion in the following way: "Let us interpret
necessity here weakly. We can count statements as necessary if whenever the objects mentioned therein exist, the statement would be true" (1971: 137).

Let us flesh out Kripke's suggestion as follows:

(SW)   A possible world w is a "satisfier world" for a sense of a sentence s just in
case the extension of each term t that occurs in a referring position in s is non-empty
in w.[5]

(WNT)   A sense of a sentence s is a *weakly necessary truth* just in case there are
satisfier worlds for s and s is true in every one of its satisfier worlds.

(WNF)   A sense of a sentence s is a *weakly necessary falsehood* just in case there
are satisfier worlds for s and s is false in every one of its satisfier worlds.

Every necessary truth is a weakly necessary truth, but not every weakly necessary
truth is a necessary truth. Similarly, every necessary falsehood is a weakly necessary
falsehood, but not every weakly necessary falsehood is a necessary falsehood. Thus,
for the kinds of sentences that we have been considering, we have the referential
correlates (RC4*) and (RC5*):

(RC4*)   If a sense of a sentence is analytic in the sense of (A), then it is a weakly
necessary truth.

(RC5*)   If a sense of a sentence is contradictory in the sense of (C), then it is a
weakly necessary falsehood.

There is an inconsistency in Frege's intensionalism between his view of presupposition (1952: 68–70) and his view of the logical form of sentences. The Fregean
practice of recasting sentences like (2.1) as sentences like (2.2) treats them as expressing the same proposition, but from the standpoint of presupposition, they are
not even equivalent, since sentences like (2.2) are true in non-satisfier worlds in which
sentences like (2.1) are not. Thus, Frege's argument for presupposition (1952: 69)
(and mine in section 3.8) tell against Frege's view of the logical form of simple sentences and the practice of recasting them as sentences like (2.2).

Having shown how simple analytic sentences like (2.1) and (2.3) can be sub-
sumed under a species of necessary truth (and simple contradictory sentences as a

species of necessary falsehood), I have removed the last possible explanatory gain that might be claimed for recasting them as compound sentences. Limiting regimentation to sentences with the appropriate compound grammatical structure treats the semantics of both simple and compound sentences properly. The sentences that should come out as necessary truths come out as necessary truths, the sentences that should come out as necessary falsehoods come out as necessary falsehoods, and the sentences that should come out as neither come out as neither. (As I shall argue, a presuppositional treatment of sentences is mandatory for intensionalists.)

Further, the extensional relations between sentences like (2.1) and (2.2), and (2.3) and (2.4), are statable as well. Finally, since representations of simple analytic sentences preserve our linguistic intuitions of their grammatical simplicity, they are preferable to recastings of them that run roughshod over those intuitions. Hence, something important is gained from having a way of subsuming simple analytic sentences under a form of necessary truth without first having to recast them as compound.

2.4.3. Referential correlates for analyticity
     and contradiction

(RC4*) and (RC5*) are referential correlates for analytic sentences like (2.1) and (2.3), but not for all analytic sentences. (2.5), for example, which is analytic in the sense of (A),

(2.5)   The/that flea-bitten cat is flea-bitten.

is nonetheless not weakly necessary, since there are satisfier worlds in which it is false. Given a literal token of (2.5), Tabby, the flea-bitten cat in question, might have lived its entire life free of fleas. The difference between sentences like (2.5), literal tokens of which need not express weakly necessary truths, and sentences like (2.1) and (2.3), literal tokens of which must, is that the former can involve a referential use of their subject term whereas the latter can only involve an attributive use. Hence, I reformulate (RC4*) and (RC5*) as (RC4) and (RC5).

(RC4)   If the sense of a sentence is analytic in the sense of (A) and if its terms are used attributively, the sentence expresses a weakly necessary truth.

(RC5)   If the sense of a sentence is contradictory in the sense of (C), and if its terms are used attributively, the sentence expresses a weakly necessary falsehood.

We now need general referential correlates for analyticity and contradictoriness, that is, referential properties that hold regardless of whether the referring terms in analytic and contradictory sentences are used attributively or referentially. To provide such referential correlates, I will adopt a proposal from earlier work (Katz 1972: 179–184), taking security against falsehood and security against truth as the correlates, respectively, of analyticity and contradictoriness of (senses of) sentences.

This proposal is based on a presuppositionalist view on which the referring terms in an assertive sentence determine its presupposition, i.e., the condition under which the sense of such a sentence can have a truth value. Since inclusion of the sense of an analytic sentence in the sense of one of its terms makes its truth condition a clause of its presupposition, analytic propositions are secured against falsehood: they are either true or have no truth value. Correspondingly, contradictory propositions are secured against truth: they are either false or have no truth value. Accordingly, both attributive analytic sentences like (2.1) and referential analytic sentences like (2.5) are secured against falsehood. The assertion of an analytic proposition makes a true statement or no statement at all, but, although the assertion of an analytic proposition like (2.1) also expresses a weakly necessary truth, the assertion of an analytic proposition like (2.5) does not.

Given that security against falsehood and security against truth depend on presupposition, sentences without a presupposition do not belong to the class of sentences that have either of those referential properties. As I shall argue in section 3.19, existence sentences like (2.6a) and (2.6b) have no presupposition.

(2.6a)   Santa Claus exists.

(2.6b)   Santa Claus does not exist.

For, if they were taken to have a presupposition, they would not make the false and true statements, respectively, that they in fact make. Such existence sentences are true or false unconditionally. As (2.6a) and (2.6b) are synthetic sentences, they quite properly belong outside the class of sentences secured against falsehood and the class of sentences secured against truth. It is otherwise with analytic existence sentences such as (2.6c) and (2.6d):

(2.6c)   Existing blue roses exist.

(2.6d)   Existing round squares exist.

The former has the presupposition that there exist blue roses and the latter has the presupposition that there exist round squares. This, as will be explained later, is because the modifier 'existing' is a device for introducing a presupposition (see Katz 1979b: 118–119). Hence, an analytic existence sentence like (2.6c) is secured against falsehood and a contradictory existence sentence like (2.6d) is secured against truth.

The general referential correlates (RC4'), (RC5'), and (RC5'') can now be stated.

(RC4')   If a sense of a sentence is analytic in the sense of (A), it is secured against falsehood (i.e., it cannot be false).

(RC5')   If a sense of a sentence is contradictory in the sense of (C), it is secured against truth (i.e., it cannot be true).

(RC5'')   If a sense of a sentence is analytic in the sense of (A) and contradictory in the sense of (C), it is secured against both truth and falsehood (i.e., it cannot be true or false).

(RC5") is a consequence of (RC4') and (RC5'), and covers sentences like (2.7) and (2.8):

(2.7)   Round squares are polygons.

(2.8)   Married bachelors are unmarried.

On (RC5"), such sentences express neither weakly necessary truths nor weakly necessary falsehoods, because they can express neither truths nor falsehoods. Since (for the same basic reason) sentences like (2.9) and (2.10) cannot express truths or falsehoods either,

(2.9)   Round squares are rare.

(2.10)   Married bachelors are rich.

a broader referential correlate than (RC5") is required. Since the basic reason such sentences cannot have a truth value is that their senses are contratermic, and hence there are no satisfier worlds for them to be true or false in, (RC6) can be introduced to cover both kinds of cases:

> (RC6)   If a sense of a sentence is contratermic, the sentence is secured against both truth and falsehood.

Note that (RC6) does not express both a necessary and a sufficient condition because there are analytic sentences, such as 'The largest integer is an integer' and 'The odd square root of sixteen is odd', that are secured against both truth and falsehood, but not as a matter of sense.

This discussion of security against falsehood and security against truth anticipates the account of presupposition in the third part of this book. (RC6) comes up at this point not only because of its relation to (RC4') and (RC5'), but also because I need to discuss a further condition for security against both truth and falsehood that enters the picture with (RC3). Recall that (RC3) says that the type-reference of a natural kind term is the thing(s) falling under both the nominal definition of the term (its sense) and the real definition of the term (the explanatory conception of its referent). Since the mediation thesis (MED) says that each concept in the sense of a term serves as a necessary condition for its type-reference, the existence of this conjunctive condition opens up the possibility of a conflict between the subcondition contributed by the sense of the term and the subcondition contributed by the explanatory conception. The former could say that the sense of a term contains a concept C, while the latter could say that the extension of the term does not fall under C.

In both the case of such conflicts and the case of conflicts between subconditions contributed by the sense of a term (i.e., contratermic expressions like 'round square' and 'married bachelor'), conflict arises among the components of the condition for reference of the term. Hence, both cases should be treated in the same manner—that is, as I treat contratermic conflicts. Accordingly, I posit (RC6') and (RC6"):

(RC6')   If there is an expression with a sense that is incompatible with the explanatory conception of its type-referent, the type-extension of the expression is null on that sense.

(RC6")   If there is a term in the sense of a sentence that is incompatible with the explanatory conception of the type-referent of that term, the sentence is secured against truth and falsehood on that sense.

There are also the referential correlates (RC7), (RC7'), (RC7"), and (RC7'''):

(RC7)   If a sense S of a sentence s analytically entails a sense S' of a sentence s', then if s (on S) is true, s' (on S') is secured against falsehood.

(RC7')   If a sense S of a sentence s analytically contradicts a sense S' of a sentence s', then if one of s and s' (on S and S') is true, the other is secured against truth.

(RC7")   If a sense S of a sentence s analytically entails a sense S' of a sentence s', and the terms of s and s' are used attributively, then s' (on S') is true in all satisfier worlds in which s (on S) is true.

(RC7''')   If a sense S of a sentence s analytically contradicts a sense S' of a sentence s', and the terms of s and s' are used attributively, then s and s' (on S and S') have different truth values in all of their satisfier worlds.

2.4.4. Philosophical discussion

The term 'star' provides an illustration of (RC6'). In ancient times, this term had a sense something like *self-luminous* [*i.e., not luminous from reflected light like the moon*], *incorruptible* [*i.e., not subject to decomposition like meteors and comets*] *body seen in the heavens.* Since at that time the sense of 'star' contained the concept *incorruptible*, the term 'star' had a null type-extension—even though the term 'star' was applied to celestial bodies that decompose. This is to say, what seems nothing less than the simple fact of the matter, that stars were then referred to under a false description. When it was discovered that stars are corruptible bodies, the term 'star' was retained but its meaning changed. It lost the concept *incorruptible*. A similar thing happened in the case of the term 'atom' when it was discovered that atoms are not atomic in the sense of being ultimate, unanalyzable constituents of matter (though a vestige of the original meaning survives in expressions like 'atomic proposition').

Philosophers have sometimes taken the intuitions behind Putnam's and Kripke's natural kind cases to show that the senses of natural kind words are virtually nonexistent. The argument runs as follows. Given the strength of those conceivability intuitions, the most we can reasonably expect to say about the content of a natural kind term is that it contains general properties like being an object or a substance—since, for example, we are unable to conceive of cats that are not objects or gold that is not a substance. But, for other properties like animality, color, and so on, those intuitions show that we can conceive of the kinds without them. This line of argument might be put forth as a way of trying to trivialize the senses of natural kind terms.

Given my non-Fregean intensionalism, however, conceivability intuitions about the referents of natural kind terms cannot serve as a basis for reducing their senses to general properties like *object* and *substance*. Facts about the sense structure of expressions are what they are independently of facts about their referents. The correct conclusion to draw from such conceivability intuitions is that the sense of a natural kind term can be trivialized only if, as (RC6') says, the type-extension of the term is empty. We cannot conclude on the basis of conceivability intuitions that the linguistic intuitions that led us to say that the sense of 'cat' contains the concept *animality* are mistaken. If the linguistic intuitions are correct, and if we have reasoned properly from them to our best hypothesis about the sense of the natural kind term, then the sense contains the concepts in question, despite the fact that the term does not apply to its referent in a counterfactual situation.

Since reference under a false description typically depends on speakers' being unaware of the falsehood of their beliefs, once they discover that their beliefs are false, something has to give. In the examples of the terms 'star' and 'gold', it was a feature of the sense of the term that was changed. Hence, on the assumption that evidence about the sense properties and relations of one of the components of the term 'gold' is the sense *yellow*, (RC3) tells us that the extension of 'gold' contains only things that are yellow. In Kripke's counterfactual case, reference to gold is reference under a false description. But when we modify Kripke's counterfactual case to include the discovery that gold is really blue, the option of referring to gold under a false description of its color is no longer an innocent one, and, accordingly, there has to be a choice between two alternatives. One choice, which we have discussed, is to say that a change of meaning occurs. The other choice is to say that the extension of the term is null. This is the case with terms like 'witch' and 'warlock'. Here both the claim that the sense of the terms involves the concept of having supernatural powers and the claim that there are no such powers are preserved.

Even if we were limited to the first choice, the argument would not succeed in trivializing the senses of natural kind terms, because it falsely assumes that the only way to change meaning is to drop the component sense that does not apply to the natural kind. But another way is to drop the component sense that provides the term its status as a natural kind term. An example is the case of the term 'jade'. Science tells us that the minerals falling under the sense of 'jade'—jadeite and nephrite— have distinct molecular structures. Still, we continue to use the term 'jade' with its meaning otherwise unchanged to refer to the green and white minerals carved into rings, necklaces, statues and so on. The term 'jade' would not figure in the statement of scientific laws about the properties of minerals, but it remains in the language as a term for the class of things that exemplify the properties in question.

Furthermore, even if the conflict is resolved in favor of the scientific conception, the resolution does not have to weaken (subtract content from) the sense of the term. The resolution may in fact strengthen (add content to) it. Though we learned that the sun does not move around the earth, we still use the expression 'rising sun'.

It seems quite natural to say that the sense of 'rising sun' did not lose the concept *moving upward from the horizon*, but rather gained the qualification that the movement is merely apparent. The change of meaning strengthened the sense of 'rising sun' to something like *sun apparently moving upward from the horizon*. Hence, conceivability intuitions about the reference of a natural kind term in a case like Kripke's about the color of gold do not automatically establish a weakening of its sense. Such intuitions allow a strengthening of the sense of 'gold' similar to the case of 'rising sun', that is, a replacement of the component *yellow metal* with the component *metal appearing yellow*.

(RC6"), like (RC6'), is required as a referential correlate once the condition for the reference of a term includes an explanatory conception. (RC6") also preserves (RC4) in essentially the same way that (RC5") preserves (RC4) in the face of (2.7) and (2.8).

2.4.5. Synonymy and equivalence of sense

Two expressions are synonymous on a sense just in case they have a sense in common. I have argued that, on an autonomous theory of sense, expressions that are synonymous on a sense do not necessarily have the same type-extension on that sense, but, of course, synonymy may correlate with sameness of type-extension in the case of certain classes of non-natural kind terms. As hypothesized in (RC3), geometric terms, artifactual terms, occupational terms, linguistic terms, game terms, and so on have senses that provide complete descriptions of their referents. Thus, I posit (RC8):

(RC8)   If two non-natural kind terms have a sense in common, they have the same type-extension on that sense.

Since nonsynonymy does not correlate with difference of type-extensions, I also posit (RC9):

(RC9)   If two expressions or sentences have different senses, their type-extensions can either be the same or different.

Finally, I should mention the referential correlate for the property of redundancy exhibited by modifier-head expressions in which the sense of the modifier is contained in the sense of the head, for example, 'free gift', 'final ultimatum', and 'female spinster'. The correlate for sameness of sense is the same for all expressions, assuming, as I have, that truth values are the type-extensions of (assertive) sentences; but the correlates for redundancy of sense in the case of sentences and non-sentential expressions are sufficiently different to require the separate principle (RC10):

(RC10)   If an expression is redundant on a sense, then the type-extension of the expression on the sense is the same as the type-extension of its head on the sense.

Synonymy is the identity relation for senses: two expressions are synonymous on a sense just in case *every* sense property or relation of one (on that sense) is a sense property or relation of the other (on that sense). It is a consequence of this that a redundant expression like 'unmarried bachelor' is not synonymous with a non-redundant expression like 'bachelor'. Since the sense *unmarried* occurs once in the sense of 'bachelor' but twice in the sense of 'unmarried bachelor', the latter is redundant and the former is not. Generalizing, it seems that even if every sense-component occurring in one expression occurs in another, the two expressions may not be synonymous. Since sameness of sense requires that *every* sense property or relation be shared, repetition of sense is enough of a difference to make the expressions nonsynonymous.

What this means is that there is a further sense relation—the relation that, for example, 'bachelor' and 'unmarried bachelor' bear to one another—that needs to be considered, namely, the relation of *sense-equivalence*. Intuitively, expressions are equivalent in sense just in case they are constructed from the same set of component senses in the same way except for the repetition of a sense or senses. This relation can be defined as in (EQ):

(EQ)   The sense of one expression is equivalent to the sense of another expression just in case they analytically entail each other.

All synonymous expressions are equivalent in sense, but not all expressions equivalent in sense are synonymous. Since expressions that are sense-equivalent but not synonymous fail to be synonymous only because of the duplication of a component sense, I posit the referential correlate for sense-equivalence (RC11):

(RC11)   Sense-equivalent expressions have the same referential correlates as synonymous expressions.

Even on the basis of such a sketchy and incomplete presentation of the notion of referential correlates, it is clear that they constitute an important new source of constraints on the model-theoretic interpretation of a language. Without such further constraints on the assignment of type-reference, which explain how the type-reference of expressions depends on their sense structure, there would be no explanation of why "atomic statements" have the logical properties they have. As Quine noted:

. . . [Carnap's adaptation of Leibnizian necessity] serves its purpose only if the atomic statements of the language are, unlike 'John is a bachelor' and 'John is married', mutually independent. Otherwise there would be a state-description which assigned truth to 'John is a bachelor' and to 'John is married', and consequently 'No bachelors are married' would turn out [contingent] under the proposed criterion. (1953: 23)

Quine concluded that Carnap's criterion for determining necessary truths "serves only for languages devoid of extra-logical synonym-pairs." Given the previous discussion, the point can be put the other way around. A semantics devoid of an autonomous theory of sense and a system of referential correlates for the sense properties and relations it defines does not determine the necessary (or weakly necessary) truths for languages having the extralogical vocabulary of natural languages.

Thus, philosophers like David Lewis who dismiss autonomous theories of sense because those theories are not themselves theories of truth and reference are mistaken even from their own referentialist perspective, for surely what contributes to our understanding of truth and reference counts as semantically worthwhile from that perspective. As I have argued, an autonomous theory of sense makes a system of referential correlates possible, and such a system is indispensable to our understanding of truth and reference. Philosophers who dismiss an autonomous theory of sense as "no semantics" confuse a theory's not itself being about truth and reference with its having nothing to contribute to theories that are about truth and reference.

2.4.6. A speculation about the theory of type-reference

How close would an autonomous theory of sense together with a full system of referential correlates be to a full theory of type-reference? Although I cannot attempt a treatment of this question here, I would like to offer a speculation about the answer. The speculation is that together they would be a full theory of type-reference. That is to say, sense-compositionality and constraints on type-reference that follow from the system of referential correlates might eliminate the need for independent principles for reference-compositionality. The speculation is that sense-compositionality is the only compositionality one needs.

A compositional account of the senses of the complex expressions of a language recursively specifies the sense properties and relations of each such expression and each of its constituents. Hence, all that is required to determine the type-reference of each expression in a language, beyond an account of sense-compositionality and definitions of sense properties and relations, is a system of referential correlates. Since the type-reference for each expression would already have been specified, principles of reference-compositionality would have no work left to do. On this scenario, those principles would add nothing to the account of extensional structure.

With respect to extralogical vocabulary, this speculation is, at this stage of the argument, quite arguable. It would also be quite arguable with respect to logical vocabulary if the principles of reference assignment for logical vocabulary could be formulated as referential correlates of the senses of the logical operators. If, for example, the principle that the conjunction P and Q is true just in case P is true and Q is true could be stated in the form of a referential correlate for the sense of 'and', there would be no need to treat it as an independent principle for assigning a type-extension to conjunctions on the basis of the type-extensions of their conjuncts. If the interpretation for 'and' and all the other logical operators could be converted into referential correlates, a significant simplification of the theory of type-reference could be effected, since instead of two compositional processes—one for sense and one for reference—only the one for sense would be needed.

My answer is speculative in part because I have no argument that such a comprehensive conversion can be carried out. But even if the functions that obtain the extensions of complex expressions from the extensions of their components have to be counted as independent principles of reference-compositionality for the logical vocabulary, the worst form of duplication is still avoided. For, with the principles of sense-compositionality for the extralogical vocabulary, we avoid duplication of principles in what is by far the larger part of the vocabulary of natural languages.

Philosophy

3.1. The benefits of thinness

It is all too easy to anticipate an objection to my line of argument thus far: "Your sharp separation of the theory of sense from the theory of reference enables you to escape the three problems that beset Fregean intensionalism, but only at the price of thinning the notions of sense and analyticity down to the point where they are no longer useful in philosophy." And the objection might continue, "Perhaps an autonomous theory of sense is useful in linguistics, say, to account for thin linguistic concepts like meaningfulness, ambiguity, and synonymy, but sense and analyticity on such a theory are too thin to do philosophical work." If this objection has a familiar ring to it, it ought to. The objection is our old friend the fruitfulness criticism.

One aim in this part of the book is to silence the fruitfulness criticism once and for all. The strategy is to apply the ideas about sense and reference set out in the first two parts of this book to a large number of problems in contemporary philosophy and to show that these thin notions of sense and analyticity enable us to make significant philosophical progress toward their solution, while Frege's thick notions retard it. Thus, over and above the concern I share with other philosophers to better understand philosophical problems and make what progress can be made toward their solution, I have the special concern here of exhibiting the benefits of semantic thinness for philosophical health.

3.1.1. Frege and deflationism

Deflationism about truth, reference, and meaning have become topics of considerable interest in contemporary philosophy of language and logic. Deflationism about truth was the starting point for deflationism about reference and deflationism about meaning. And Frege was the starting point for deflationism about truth. He writes: "One might be tempted to regard the relation of the thought to the True not as that of sense to reference, but rather as that of subject to predicate. One can, indeed, say: 'The thought, that 5 is a prime number, is true.' But closer examination shows that nothing more has been said than in the simple sentence '5 is a prime number'" (1952: 64). Frege's redundancy thesis is that 'S is true' asserts nothing more than what 'S' itself asserts. Modern deflationists understand this claim to be that truth is not a substantive property in the sense of something added to the content of sentences when 'is true' is added to them as a sentential adverb. Since truth is not a substantive property, constructing theories of reference and truth in an attempt to reveal its nature is a misguided enterprise. The truth predicate is just a metalinguistic way of making statements about sentences the content of which is exhausted by the content of the "disquoted" statements in the object language. 'It is true that Socrates is wise' adds nothing to the content of 'Socrates is wise'. Since the predicate 'is true' is entirely redundant, there is no reason to think that there is a substantive property of truth that the predicate expresses, and, hence, no reason to think that there is genuine explanatory work for a theory of truth to do.

Traditionally, it is claimed that 'is true' expresses a correspondence between the proposition that a sentence expresses and what the proposition is about. In "The Thought: A Logical Inquiry," Frege denies that 'is true' expresses such a relation. He writes: "[that correspondence is a relation] is contradicted, however, by the use of the word "true," which is not a relation-word and contains no reference to anything else to which something must correspond" (1968: 509). Given that grammatically 'true' appears as a syntactically simple predicate of sentences and that the Fregean construal of the sense of an expression as a function from a referential domain to an extension does not involve decompositional sense structure, Frege can argue that 'true' is not a relation word. But here he is arguing from his own theory. On the basis of an autonomous theory of sense, on which words have decompositional sense structure, 'true' can be a relation word even though it is a syntactically simple predicate, because it can decompositionally contain a reference to something else to which the sentence must correspond. A relative adjective like 'large' in a sentence like 'The house is large' is a syntactically simple but semantically complex predicate that contains a reference to something else, namely, the size of the average house, to which the sentence compares the size of the house in question.

Frege claims that corresponding things "coincide and are, therefore, not distinct things at all" (1968: 509), and, on this basis, argues that truth cannot be correspondence because ". . . it is absolutely essential that the reality be distinct from the idea. But then there can be no complete correspondence, no complete truth" (1968: 510). One is ready to protest that correspondence is not identity, but Frege notes that correspondence might be taken as correspondence in a certain respect, and he goes on to argue that ". . . then we should be confronted by a question of the same kind and the game could begin again. . . . [T]he question would always arise whether it were true that the characteristics were present. So one goes round in a circle. Consequently, it is probable [*sic*] that the content of the word "true" is unique and indefinable." The point is not that we cannot specify the respect in which '5 is a prime number' must correspond with reality. We can. It is that 5 must exemplify the property of being prime. Frege's point is that ". . . in a definition certain characteristics would have to be stated. And in application to any particular case the question would always arise whether it were true that the characteristics were present." Again Frege is arguing from his own theory. No doubt, for Fregean definitions, which express a reference-determining sense, what he says here might be true. But since the sense of an expression can be given without giving a Fregean definition, the characteristic in question would not have to be stated in a definition. The explication will have to be schematic in that the respect in which correspondence is to obtain must come from the senses of the terms of the correspondence relation in particular cases—for example, the sense of '5' and the concept of exemplifying the property of being prime. But there is no problem about this since, as I noted, Frege fails to show that 'true' is not a relation term.

Let us now see what is wrong with Frege's redundancy account of truth. The account, as Frege gives it, is that 'The thought, that 5 is a prime number, is true' expresses the same thought as the simple sentence '5 is a prime number'. One thing that raises doubts about this account is the obvious grammatical fact that 'is true' in the sentence 'The thought, that 5 is a prime number, is true' is the predicate in the sentence and 'The thought, that 5 is a prime number', is the subject. To be sure, Frege has little patience with such a subject/predicate distinction, and, accordingly, he would recast the sentence to present it as having a different logical form. But such recasting, which was criticized in the second part of this book, is contentious here, particularly as the question at issue turns on whether such sentences are of subject/predicate form.

If the sentences are subject/predicate sentences, then recasting them eliminates a grammatical structure in the metalinguistic sentences that, when fully understood, shows that the redundancy account misses the semantic difference between such sentences and the clause in them of which truth is predicated. The distortion is seldom noticed because mental acts such as recognizing 5 to be prime and recognizing the truth of a sentence that says that 5 is prime are closely related. There is thus a slide to taking the second act to be nothing over and above the first. But if we focus on the objective sentences rather than the subjective acts of recognition, we immediately see *prima facie* differences that suggest that the senses of the sentence and its clause are not the same. The sense of the former is a compositional function of, *inter alia*, the senses of the words 'thought' and 'true', but the sense of the latter is not. It is possible for people to understand the one but not the other because they do not understand either 'thought' or 'true'. They do not have the same translations into a foreign language; and they are not about the same things. The former is about a thought, while the latter is about the number 5. Thus, a mathematical realist who is also a psychological behaviorist would have trouble with the former sentence but would accept the latter.

An autonomous theory of sense leads to the counterexamples that show that disquotation does not preserve content. Because such a theory approaches the senses of expressions from a mereological perspective, any difference in sense structure, however slight, counts as a difference in content. Thus, the fact cannot be disregarded that the sense of 'The thought, that 5 is a prime number, is true' is a compositional function *inter alia* of the senses of the words 'thought' and 'true' but the sense of '5 is a prime number' is not. The sentence (3.1) is false whereas the sentence (3.2) is true:

(3.1)   People who do not know the words 'thought' and 'true' have no trouble understanding the sentence 'The thought, that 5 is a prime number, is true'.

(3.2)   People who do not know the words 'thought' and 'true' have no trouble understanding the sentence '5 is a prime number'.

Thus, Frege is wrong to claim that "nothing more has been said [in the complex sentence 'The thought, that 5 is a prime number, is true'] than in the simple sentence '5 is a prime number'."

Perhaps it was Frege's conception of sense that led him to think that the sentences say the same thing. From the standpoint of that conception, there is no substantive difference between the content of the complex sentence 'The thought, that 5 is a prime number, is true' and the simple sentence '5 is a prime number', since both sentences express the same function from domain to truth value.[1]

3.1.2. Deflationism about meaning

These criticisms of Frege are not intended as part of a general argument against deflationism about truth. It may be that my account of the theory of reference can be expressed in deflationist terms; it may be that it cannot. This issue does not relate directly to my concern here, which is deflationism about meaning.

Given the tight relation between truth and reference, the extension of the deflationist approach from the former notion to the latter is an obligatory move (Leeds 1973; 1978). In light of the issues raised here about the relation between sense and reference, however, the extension of deflationism about truth and reference to meaning is not so clearly mandated—though it is, of course, a natural next step for a deflationist-minded philosopher of an anti-intensionalist persuasion.

Although there are a number of different contemporary proposals for understanding deflationism about meaning, I will leave my characterization loose enough to cover them all. Deflationism about meaning owes much to the treatment of meaning in the later work of Wittgenstein. (See my earlier discussion [Katz 1990b: 21–174] of his arguments on meaning.) Basically, deflationism about meaning claims that having a meaning is no more a substantive property than truth, and that constructing a theory about the nature of meaning is as misguided as constructing a theory about the nature of truth: meaning has no nature for a theory to explain. Hence, it is natural for the deflationist about meaning to treat it in the same manner in which the deflationist about truth treats truth, namely, in terms of a disquotational schema like *'s' means that m*, where *m* is a description of meaning that trivializes talk about the meaning of *s*.

I must, of course, argue against deflationism about meaning, since senses, on my view, although thin compared to Fregean and Carnapian senses, are nonetheless substantive: a theory (within linguistics) is necessary to reveal their nature. I will try to show that, even assuming that deflationists are right about truth and reference, their approach cannot be extended to sense.

Let us assume that the account of truth and reference in some version of contemporary deflationism is satisfactory, and ask whether a full account of meaning can be similarly formulated in terms of a schema like *'s' means that m*. Deflationism about meaning requires a successful disquotational account of the meaning of sentences to justify the deflationist claim that meaning is not a substantive property. The whole point of deflationism about meaning *qua* a species of deflationism is that a disquotational account of meaning is the whole story about the meaning of *s*. Only on the basis of a successful disquotational account has the deflationist justified the claim that meaning does not present us with something with a substantial nature and relations that require explanation in a theory. Hence, it is not enough for the deflationist just to be deflationist about the role of truth conditions in an account of meaning, as Field (1994) is. Such relative deflationism is compatible with a substantive notion of meaning understood, for example, in terms of a notion of conceptual role or a notion of use.

With an instance of a disquotational schema for truth, we are *ex hypothesi* left with no unanswered questions about the truth of the sentence, since the instance of the schema fully specifies the conditions under which that sentence, *s*, is true—namely, *s*. For example, having specified that the truth conditions for 'Snow is white' are that snow is white, there are *ex hypothesi* no further questions to ask about its truth conditions. Once we have an instance of the disquotational truth schema for each sentence of the language, there is nothing to explain about truth in the language.

Similarly, once we have an instance of the disquotational meaning schema for each sentence of the language, there ought to be nothing left to explain about meaning in the language. But this is not so. The parallel fails because of the fundamental difference between senses, on the one hand, and truth and reference, on the other. The former, on various approaches, are entities (like the sentences with which they are associated), while the latter are relations (between sentences and expressions of a language and things in the world). As a consequence, whereas it is plausible for the deflationist about truth to suppose that any account that provides truth conditions for each appropriate sentence is the whole story about truth in the language, it is not plausible for the deflationist about meaning to suppose that any account that specifies what senses each sentence has is the whole story about meaning in the language. There are further questions about the senses of sentences, ones that concern their intrinsic structure, their relations to other senses in virtue of their having one or another sense property or relation, and their compositional and non-compositional relations to the sentences expressing them.

To be sure, 'means' is a relational word, one connecting expressions with their senses—for example, the word 'bachelor' means (has the sense) *unmarried man*. In particular, 'means' belongs to the category of *expressional* sense relations; i.e., it is a vehicle for expressing relations of expressions to their senses in the language. Thus, instances of a disquotational meaning schema state nothing more than which sense(s) an expression has in the language. But recall that there is also a category of *non-expressional* relations, ones that relate senses directly with one another— for example, analytic entailment. The point that is decisive here is that it is primarily because sense(s) have non-expressional properties and relations that instances of a disquotational or other minimalist meaning schema, which simply state that such-and-such are the senses of a sentence, leave questions about the meaning— that is, about the sense properties and relations—of expressions unanswered.

For example, the statements (3.3a)–(3.3f) leave such questions unanswered:

(3.3a)   'The number 5 is prime' means that the number 5 is prime.

(3.3b)   'The number 5 drinks too much' means that the number 5 drinks too much.

(3.3c)   'The bank is nearby' means that the bank is nearby.

(3.3d)   'Bachelors like parties' means that bachelors like parties.

(3.3e)   'Unmarried men like parties' means that unmarried men like parties.

(3.3f)   'Bachelors are unmarried' means that bachelors are unmarried.

Why is the quoted sentence in (3.3a) meaningful, whereas the quoted sentence in (3.3b) is not? Why is the quoted sentence in (3.3c) ambiguous? Why does (3.3e) provide the same account of the meaning of the quoted sentence as (3.3d)? Why is the quoted sentence in (3.3f) trifling? Further, (3.3b) shows that an instance of the meaning schema cannot even be taken to say that the quoted sentence means something, that is, has a meaning. (Attempts to restrict instances of the meaning schema to meaningful sentences face the same problem, since such a restriction presupposes a specification of which sentences of the language are meaningful and which meaningless.) These are extremely simple examples, because compositionality plays no, or a quite small, role in forming the sense of the terms in question. The point is even clearer when the varieties of sense composition in more complex cases of the sort discussed in other sections of the book are considered. (See also Pitt and Katz 2000.) A deflationist account of meaning is thus not the whole story about meaning.

The problem of residual questions about meanings arises with Stephen Schiffer's (2000b) "Pleonastic Fregeanism" (as Schiffer explains, "... the word 'pleonastic' alludes to the deflationary, or minimalist, status of propositions and concepts"). On this form of meaning deflationism,

> [t]here's nothing more to the nature of propositions than can be read off our that-clause-involving linguistic practices. . . . [P]leonastic entities like propositions have, as Mark Johnston would put it, "no hidden and substantial nature for a theory to uncover. All we know and all we need to know about [them] in general" is determined by our hypostasizing linguistic practices.

Schiffer begins with the assumptions that the study of linguistic meanings is the study of propositions and concepts, that propositions are the referents of that-clauses of sentences expressing propositional attitudes like belief, and that concepts are components of propositions. These assumptions are not innocuous. They shift the focus from the topic of meanings to the quite different topic of referents of that-clauses. This shift obscures the fact that Schiffer's deflationism suffers from the same problem as other deflationist accounts of meaning, namely, that such accounts cannot be the whole story about meaning because they leave a host of questions about meaning unanswered.

The acknowledged task is to understand the nature of meaning. Schiffer (2000a) supposes that nothing significant about this task changes when the question of what meanings are is construed as the question of what the referents of that-clauses in sentences expressing propositional attitudes like belief are. But this construal replaces a focus on meaning with a much narrower and quite different focus. In the process, questions about the nature of meaning that are most natural to ask if the aim is the understanding of *its* nature—namely, What is meaningfulness? What is meaninglessness? What is multiplicity of meaning? What is sameness of meaning? What is opposition of meaning? What is redundancy of meaning? and so on—are lost. The loss of these questions shows that the shift introduces a new subject matter. We have replaced concern with the intensional propositions that such questions are about with concern with the extensional propositions that are the referents of that-clauses, the truths and falsehoods that function as the objects of epistemic attitudes. When we recognize that the shift is unwarranted, those questions about meaning come flooding back, and it is immediately evident that Schiffer's deflationism suffers from the same problem as other deflationisms about meaning.

The rationale for deflationism about truth can be turned against deflationism about meaning. The rationale for deflationism about truth is that truth is not a substantive property: it is not something for which a theory is required that looks beneath the surface to reveal structures that enable us to explain semantic properties and relations. Accordingly, the test of deflationism about truth is whether there is anything left to explain about truth once we have a complete disquotational treatment of the truth-apt sentences of the language. Now, the rationale for deflationism about meaning is the same: meaning is not a substantive property. Hence, the test of deflationism about meaning is whether anything is left to explain about meaning once we have an appropriately minimalist account of meaning for each meaningful sentence of the language. But, as I have argued, deflationism about meaning fails the test, since there is a great deal left to explain even after we have such an account.

Hence, an inflationist account of meaning, which can answer the questions about the nature of meanings, is the position of choice. The decompositional and compositional sense structures to which answers to those questions perforce refer explain why meaning is a substantive property: descriptions of decompositional and compositional meaning treat senses as entities, lexical senses as typically having a decompositional structure constructed from senses (in terms of mereological relations), and derived senses as resulting from combinations of lexical and non-lexical senses (on the basis of compositional principles). That meanings have a "substantial nature for a theory to uncover" is shown by the fact that the component senses and mereological relations in the syntactically "hidden" decompositional structure of lexical items are the elements on which compositional principles operate (recall the example 'sharp knife').

3.2. Indirect reference does not make sense

Frege took no interest in senses as objects of study in their own right. Senses were of interest to him only when they could be brought in to solve problems that arise for the theory of reference. Besides Frege's use (1952: 56–57) of senses as a means to solve the problem about identity that arose in the *Begriffsschrift*, the best-known example of his use of senses is his attempt to save the full generality of the logical principle that the truth value of a sentence stays the same when we replace one of its parts with something coreferential. In this section, I want to show that Frege's neglect of the study of sense leads to fatal difficulties for his own solution to the problem he raised about the generality of this logical principle.

The problem arises in connection with parts of sentences appearing in belief or other intensional contexts. In order to prevent the restriction of the principle to parts appearing just in extensional contexts, Frege points out that the truth of a belief sentence ". . . includes neither the truth nor the untruth of the subordinate clause. In such cases it is not permissible to replace one expression in the subordinate clause by another having the same customary reference, but only by one having the same indirect reference, i.e., the same customary sense" (1952: 64–67). Frege's proposal to take the reference of expressions in intensional contexts to be their customary sense prevents us from inferring (3.4) from (3.5):

(3.4)   The ancients believed that Hesperus is Phosphorus.

(3.5)   The ancients believed that Hesperus is Hesperus.

Once the reference of an expression in an intensional context is taken to be its customary sense, then, given that 'Hesperus' and 'Phosphorus' have the different senses that Frege takes them to have, their references are different, and the logical principle does not sanction substitution.

Carnap raised the difficulty that embedding within subordinate clauses involves an infinite hierarchy presupposing an infinite number of names for indirect senses (1956: 129–133). Despite the considerable effort that has been devoted to the discovery of a general method for specifying indirect senses of expressions in multiply embedded clauses in oblique contexts (see, for example, Burge 1979a; Carnap 1956; Dummett 1973, 1981; Mendelsohn 1996; Parsons 1981; Russell 1905; Searle 1968; Yourgrau 1986–1987), such a method has come to seem a will-o'-the-wisp to many. Whatever the outcome in this exploration of the technical apparatus for implementing Frege's solution, there remains an insurmountable difficulty with it.

The identification of the reference of an expression in an intensional context with its customary sense leads to trouble. In (3.6) and (3.7):

(3.6)   Americans believe, of Mikhail Gorbachev, that he liberated Russia from communism.

(3.7)   Of Mikhail Gorbachev, Americans believe that he liberated Russia from communism.

the name 'Mikhail Gorbachev' occurs in a prepositional phrase involving *de re* reference to Mikhail Gorbachev.[2] Since the pronoun 'he' in the complement clauses of (3.6) and (3.7) is anaphoric on the occurrence of 'Mikhail Gorbachev' in the prepositional phrase, it is coreferential with it. Hence, 'he' refers to Mikhail Gorbachev, too. But, since, on Frege's proposal, the pronoun refers to its customary sense, that is, to the sense of the proper name 'Mikhail Gorbachev', Frege's proposal is committed to the claim that Mikhail Gorbachev is identical to the sense of his name. The claim that a human being is identical to a sense is an absurdity on the face of it; moreover, on Frege's realism about senses, the claim implies the contradiction that a concrete object is an abstract object.

It does not help to insist on the letter of Frege's formulation, which says that the substitution condition applies to entire subordinate clauses. Essentially the same counterexample can be constructed using sentences whose verb complements are simple noun phrases. To block the substitutional inference from 'Beatrix wants to marry Dr. Jekyll' to 'Beatrix wants to marry Mr. Hyde', we would have to take the reference of the terms 'Dr. Jekyll' and 'Mr. Hyde' in these sentences to be their customary senses, but then those sentences will be understood as asserting that the relation *wants to marry* holds between Beatrix and a sense of a name.

Alonzo Church presents what looks at first like a way of escaping this problem. He writes:

According to the Fregean theory of meaning which we are advocating "Schliemann sought the site of Troy" asserts a certain relation as holding . . . between Schliemann and a certain concept, namely that of the site of Troy. This is, however, not to say that [the sentence] means the same as "Schliemann sought the concept of the site of Troy." On the contrary, the first sentence asserts the holding of a certain relation between Schliemann and the concept of the site of Troy, and is true; but the second sentence asserts the holding of a like relation between Schliemann and the concept of the concept of the site of Troy, and is very likely false. (1956: 8, fn. 20)

We can accept Church's gloss of the sentences and agree with him that the sentences are not synonymous. Still, on this view, Schliemann was engaged in semantics rather than archeology. On Frege's view, 'Schliemann sought the site of Troy' asserts that Schliemann sought a sense of 'the site of Troy' rather than its referent, the site of Troy. Frege's construal of reference in intensional contexts commits him to saying that this sentence asserts that the relation of seeking holds between Schliemann and the sense of 'the site of Troy'.

To be sure, Church is sensitive to this, remarking that the relation is ". . . not quite that of having sought, or at least it is misleading to call it that—in view of the way in which the verb *to seek* is commonly used in English." But acknowledging the problem does nothing to remove it. If Church is understood here as addressing my objection, his point would be that the relation R between a person and a sense of an expression is one in virtue of which the former Rs the latter's referent. Although the point is made in a helpful spirit, Frege cannot accept it. Its acceptance would undermine his rationale (1952: 64–67) for making the customary sense of an expression in an intensional context its referent, which, as I have suggested, is his way of preserving the logical principle that substitution of co-referential expressions does not change the truth value of sentences. Given that the site of Troy is the location where Nikos Kazantzakis wrote *Zorba the Greek*, we can go from the true sentence 'Schliemann sought the site of Troy' to the false sentence 'Schliemann sought the location where Nikos Kazantzakis wrote *Zorba the Greek*'. Accepting Church's point puts Frege back at square one.

Furthermore, it is confusing for Church to say that the relation the sentence asserts to hold between Schliemann and the site of Troy is not *x sought y*. How can it not be the sense of the verb 'sought'? The verb 'seek' means *seek*. If what we can say about English sentences is not to be constrained by the facts about English, as Church seems to be suggesting, we are in Carnap Country, where the principle of tolerance is the law of the land. Under that law, anything goes, but then what Church says about Frege's proposal has no implications for substitutional inference or any other issues in natural language.

3.3. Thinness of senses as the source of fine-grainedness

Lack of the fine-grainedness necessary for a criterion of identity for *de dicto* propositions is customarily illustrated with sentences like (3.8a) and (3.8b):

(3.8a)   Alice believes that two minus two is zero.

(3.8b)   Alice believes that the even prime minus two is zero.

Even though the propositional object of 'believe' in the premise logically implies (and is implied by) the propositional object of 'believe' in the conclusion, the inference from (3.8a) to (3.8b) is invalid. Necessary equivalence is not a fine-grained enough criterion for sameness of proposition. The difference between the beliefs in (3.8a) and (3.8b) is reflected in the fact that it is possible for Alice not to believe that the even prime minus two is zero because she does not know that the even prime is two. A criterion that is fine-grained enough must exclude all possibility of invalidity in such cases. It would be a relation R such that when A *believes that p* is true and p bears R to q, then A *believes that q* must be true, regardless of anything about A.

Only mereological containment qualifies as R. Any relation more fruitful than mereological containment opens up the possibility of invalidity in virtue of whatever principle(s) are responsible for its fruitfulness, since the believer can always be confused about the principle. Only if R is mereological containment is there no possibility for invalidity, since only in this case is the premise A *believes that p* identical to the conclusion A *believes that q*. If the sense of 'bachelor' contains the sense of 'unmarried man', then, in believing the object of the attitude in (3.9a), Alice *ipso facto* believes the object of the attitude in (3.9b):

(3.9a)   Alice believes that Tom is a bachelor.

(3.9b)   Alice believes that Tom is an unmarried man.

No ignorance or confusion on the believer's part is relevant because, the senses of the complement sentences in cases like (3.9a) and (3.9b) being one and the same, there is no sense difference (such as there is in cases like (3.8a) and (3.8b)) on the basis of which such psychological factors can make one sentence true while the other sentence is false.

While the thinness of the mereological concepts of sense and analyticity is the source of fine-grainedness, the thickness of the logical concepts of sense and analyticity is the source of coarse-grainedness. This is, of course, just another way of characterizing the difference that Frege himself was at such pains to mark between Kantian semantics and his own. He writes:

> Nothing essentially new, however, emerges in the process [of defining something with a static Kantian concept]. But the more fruitful type of definition is a matter of drawing boundary lines that were not previously given at all. What we shall be able to infer from it, cannot be inspected in advance; here, we are not simply taking out of the box again what we have just put into it. The conclusions we draw from it extend our knowledge, and ought therefore, on Kant's view, to be regarded as synthetic; and yet they can be proved by purely logical means, and are thus analytic. The truth is that they are contained in the definitions, but as plants are contained in their seeds, not as beams are contained in a house. (1953: 100–101)

As a final comment, Frege underscores the point by saying: "Often we need several definitions for the proof of some proposition, *which consequently is not contained in any one of them alone*, yet does follow purely logically from all of them together" [italics mine]. Defining the notion of analyticity in terms of a certain part-whole structure makes it a *static* notion. In defining it in terms of provability on the basis of logical laws and definitions, Frege makes it a *dynamic* one. Given the need for a fine-grained criterion of sense identity, Frege's logical semantics with its dynamic notion of analyticity is anything but desirable. It is mereological semantics, with its purely static notion of analyticity—which Frege condemned as unfruitful—that enables us to explain why inferences like that from (3.7a) to (3.7b) are invalid while ones like that from (3.8a) to (3.8b) are valid.

I have already argued that unfruitfulness in and of itself does not count against a mereological semantics. To repeat the main point of the earlier discussion: fruit-fulness is relative to a purpose, and Frege offers no reason to think that there are no legitimate purposes to which the unfruitful notion of analyticity is suited. One of these purposes in now becoming clear. If the boundaries of linguistic concepts are drawn on the basis of sameness and difference of mereological sense structure, they coincide with those in natural language. The fine-grainedness of propositional identity in the intensional constructions of natural language cannot be handled with Fregean logical sense structure.

I argued in the last section that Frege's attempt (1952: 64–67) to handle the problem of substitution into intensional contexts by identifying the reference of an expression in such contexts with its customary sense fails because such identification leads to incoherence. I now add that such an identification cannot be replaced with a substitution condition for intensional contexts based on logical consequence, since this move leads to countenancing invalid inferences involving belief sentences. Except for the extreme case where, in effect, the logical transformation maps the premise onto itself, there will be a difference between the two propositions which, however small, is enough to allow someone to believe one without believing the other. Realizing that sameness of belief requires an equivalence relation fine-grained enough to catch even the slightest difference between the sense of the substituend expression and the sense of the substituting expression, Church (1954) once proposed synonymy as the criterion for substitution into intensional contexts. Church was right that natural-language synonymy, the relation expressions bear to one another when they are different linguistic expressions of the same sense, is fine-grained enough to prevent sense differences from slipping through. But fine-grained synonymy is unavailable to Fregeans like Church. The closest a Fregean intensionalist semantics can come to the natural language notion of synonymy that Church is now proposing is some form of mutual provability. But this is not close enough, since, as I have shown, it is too fruitful. Church overlooks the fact that Frege's logicizing of sense concepts restricts them to those that are definable in the theory of reference.

Even if fine-grained synonymy were available to Church, it is the wrong relation for the criterion for substitution into intensional contexts. To be sure, synonymy is not too coarse-grained; but it is too fine-grained as a criterion. If synonymy were taken as the substitution condition, we would fail to capture certain inferences. First, certain trivial cases, like that from (3.10) to (3.11), could not be captured.

(3.10)   John believes that he is a bachelor.

(3.11)   John believes that he is an unmarried bachelor.

Since the subordinate clauses in (3.10) and (3.11) are not synonymous, (3.11) could not be obtained from (3.10). If we could capture substitutional inferences with an equivalence relation, then, as the inference from (3.10) to (3.11) indicates, the one we would want is (EQ). (EQ) would provide a sufficiently fine-grained criterion for sameness of belief because, like synonymy, it would preclude all substantive differences in the senses of the sentences but, unlike synonymy, it does not preclude differences due to redundancy.

Second, even revised on the basis of (EQ), Church's proposal does not work. (EQ) and synonymy are both too strong to be the criterion for substitution into intensional contexts. Intensionalists have to capture not only inferences like that from (3.10) to (3.11), but inferences like that from (3.10) to (3.12) as well.

(3.12)   John believes that he is unmarried.

What is required to capture the latter inference is the weaker relation of analytic entailment defined in (A').

The reduction of the theory of sense to the theory of reference puts (A') beyond the scope of Fregean semantics because, although, as I noted in section 2.1, it allows for compositionality, it does not allow for decompositionality. Since senses are world-to-extension functions associated with expressions of the language, Fregean intensionalism can provide an account of how senses of expressions in sentences can combine to form senses of other expressions; but, since the world-to-extension functions associated with lexical items are primitive, Fregean intensionalism cannot provide an account of decompositional sense structure. Since representation of such sense structure is necessary for capturing analytic entailments like that from (3.10) to (3.12), Fregean intensionalism can only deal with them on the basis of *ad hoc* devices like Carnapian meaning postulates.

Unlike synonymy and sense equivalence, analytic entailment is just fine-grained enough for inferences like that from (3.10) to (3.12). Like them, it also ensures that there is no difference in the sense content of the subordinate clauses that would allow the premise of the inference to be true and the conclusion false. Logical derivation never enters the picture. If (3.10) is true, it is because John believes himself to have the property of being a bachelor, and since the property of being a bachelor is the property of being an unmarried man, it follows that in believing that he is a bachelor, John believes that he is unmarried. The truth of (3.12) is thus already established in virtue of the truth of the premise.

Given that analytic entailment is the relation required for a criterion for substitution into intensional contexts, formulating the criterion requires a determination of which senses enter into the relation. For the sake of convenience, I have thus far been playing along with Frege's assumption that the senses in question are those of the subordinate clauses of the premise and conclusion. This is to say that the condition for substitution is imposed on the substituend and substituting expressions, the subordinate clauses in the two sentences. This assumption must now be rejected, because it allows invalid inferences (see Katz 1986a). Frege makes the assumption because he develops his approach to substitutional inference in the context of an attempt to save the principle of substitution of co-referentials in the face of intensional contexts (1952: 64). The assumption is another aspect of his reduction of the theory of sense to the theory of reference. In making the criterion for substitution in intensional contexts directly parallel to the criterion for substitution in extensional contexts, the assumption says, in effect, that the factors governing the former are parallel to those governing the latter.

This prevents an intensionalist account of inference by substitution into intensional contexts from taking significant aspects of sense compositionality into consideration. It forces the intensionalist to impose the condition of analytic entailment too low in the compositional structure of the sentences to take account of interactions between sense constituents in the matrix and subordinate clauses. The assumption, in effect, says that there are no contributions such interactions make to determining the object of the propositional attitude. This is simply mistaken. Sense interactions above the subordinate clause level of the compositional process can transform the object of the propositional attitude. For example, analytic entailment applied at the level of the subordinate clauses would sanction the inference from (3.13) to (3.14):

(3.13)   Lois Lane has come to doubt that Clark Kent is a bachelor.

(3.14)   Lois Lane has come to doubt that Clark Kent is a male.

taking us from a truth to a possible falsehood (in, for example, the case where Lois believes rumors that Clark Kent is secretly married but not rumors that he is a female cross-dresser). Frege's criterion does not allow us to take account of the fact that the sense of 'doubt' interacts with the sense of 'bachelor' to transform the propositional attitude expressed in (3.13) to the suspicion that Clark Kent is married, a child, or female.

Elsewhere (1986a) I referred to 'doubt' and similar verbs as "hyper-opaque." Such verbs differ from ordinary opaque verbs in having a sense that interacts with the sense of the subordinate clause to produce a propositional object different from the sense of the clause on its own. Given, further, that, with multiple clause embedding, hyper-opaque verbs can occur at any level in the structure of a sentence, it is safest to impose the condition at the end point of the compositional process, so that no effect of sense interactions in the compositional process can be missed. We can then account for the failure of (3.13) to imply (3.14) as the result of the operation of the negative element in the verb 'doubt'. But this is, in effect, to say that an inference by substitution goes through if the sentence into which the substitution is made analytically entails the sentence that results from the substitution. And saying this is saying that no special criterion is necessary. The definition of analytic entailment itself suffices.[3]

3.4. The paradox of analysis

I have been contrasting my intensionalism with Frege/Carnap intensionalism and with extensionalism, and contrasting its mereological notions of sense and analyticity with logical notions, namely, those in mainstream accounts of meaning such as Frege's, Russell's, Carnap's, Quine's, and Davidson's. My intention, of course, has been to stress the novelty of our intensionalism in order to overcome the knee-jerk assumptions that intensionalism is Frege/Carnap intensionalism and that semantics is logical semantics. But I do not want to create the impression that my account of meaning has no precursor in the semantically busy twentieth century. It does: G. E. Moore's account of meaning.

At bottom, the two accounts concern one and the same notion of meaning. Of course, they differ in various ways, but these mostly concern the kind, nature, and extent of their elaborations of the notion. The most significant difference is perhaps that Moore elaborated his notion of meaning within his own commonsense framework, whereas I have elaborated mine within a theoretical framework provided by developments in linguistics that occurred after Moore's time (and with which he might have had little sympathy—but then again, he might have been sympathetic, as J. L. Austin was). This difference is significant because a consequence of it is that Moore makes no attempt to define sense theoretically, to provide a methodology to explain how the senses of sentences are determined, or to locate the theory of sense within a broader grammatical study of natural language. This led to certain objections, in particular what has come to be called "the paradox of analysis," and to an unjust neglect of Moore's contribution to semantics.

A terminological difference was that Moore talked about concepts and propositions rather than senses of expressions, but he understood them to be linguistic meanings in just the way I understand senses to be linguistic meanings. Moore wrote, "'Proposition' in the sense in which, upon this theory, the object of belief is always a proposition, is *not* a name for any mere form of words. . . . It is a name for what is before your mind when you not only hear or read but *understand* a sentence. It is, in short, the *meaning* of a sentence—what is expressed or conveyed by a sentence . . ." (1953: 258–259). The meaning of an expression is neither the object it denotes, nor the form of words that it is, nor the mental image or collection of them that comes before the mind when we apprehend a concept. For Moore, "what is before your mind" is not something *in* your mind. He distinguished understanding a sentence—something subjective—from what is understood—something objective: "Concepts are possible objects of thought . . . they may come into relation with a thinker; and in order that they *may* do anything, they must *be* something. It is indifferent to their nature whether anybody thinks them or not" (1953: 57–59). This verges on my view that concepts are abstract objects (Katz 1981; 1998b).

To see how close my account of meaning is to Moore's, we need to look at what he thinks about semantic analysis. For him, the items analyzed are the concepts expressed by the words. Analysis describes a relation between concepts, not what the words expressing them refer to in the domain of the language or how speakers use them. The relation between the analysandum and analysans is, moreover, strict identity of sense. Given that Moore uses the idiom of paraphrase for analysis, his relation *is the analysis of* is my non-expressional relation *is sense equivalent to*. Finally, echoing the distinction between "trifling truth" and "real knowledge" of Locke, whose theory of meaning I have already cited as a precursor of my own, Moore distinguishes between "different cases of necessary connection":

... I say that the concept "x is a male sibling" is *identical* with the concept "x is a brother," but refuse to say that the concept "x is a cube with twelve edges" is *identical* with the concept "x is a cube," although I insist that these latter *are* "logically equivalent." To raise this question would be to raise the question how an "analytic" necessary connection is to be distinguished from a "synthetic" one—a subject upon which I am far from clear. (1942: 667)

Moore's distinction between "different cases of necessary truth," particularly his refusal to count identity of sense as the same thing as logical equivalence, and the nature of his examples of linguistic analysis, make it abundantly clear that his notions of meaning and analyticity are basically the same thin notions as ours.

John Passmore says that "Moore's uncertainties on [such] points, it would appear, did something to drive his successors in a more 'linguistic' direction" (1957: 215). It is true that subsequent philosophers of language did not follow Moore, but it is not true that Moore's "successors" went in a more linguistic direction than he. Rather, they went in the direction of logical semantics. Furthermore, it was not so much Moore's "uncertainties" and reluctance to pronounce on subjects on which he was "far from clear" that sent his "successors" in that direction as it was his failure to develop a clear linguistic direction for them to go in. Moore never undertook to define the theoretical concepts he employed, to find appropriate terms in which to explicate the analytic/synthetic distinction, or to articulate a conception of sense structure necessary to explain his distinction between the relations of identity of sense and logical equivalence. But also his commonsense presentations suffered from a confusion and a notorious problem.

The confusion was that Moore at times (1953: 205–206, 216–217, 309; 1942: 548) himself equated meaning with use. The failure to distinguish meaning in his sense of concepts and propositions from meaning in the use sense suggested to many of his "successors" that he endorsed the latter notion of meaning. But, in fact, that notion is inconsistent with his basic account of meaning. In line with his basic account, Moore says that the meaning of the sentence 'The sun is larger than the moon' is the same as the meaning of the sentence 'Le soleil est plus grand que la lune', but the two sentences do not have the same use (1944: 184–187). Worse yet, a use notion of meaning would force Moore to sacrifice strict synonymy, which is a cornerstone of his conception of meaning and analysis. For any difference in the syntax of two sentences, even quite trivial ones such as that between 'Sam looked up her name' and 'Sam looked her name up', produce a difference in use. Again, 'I always put the object in directly after the particle of the verb' has a different use from 'I always put in the object directly after the particle of the verb'. (See section 3.22 for further discussion.)

I diagnose this confusion as due to Moore's failure to elaborate an appropriate theoretical framework within which the meaning of linguistic tokens and types can be independently explained. Moore recognizes that use plays a significant role in determining the meaning of linguistic tokens, but there is no way within his commonsense framework to acknowledge this role while at the same time representing use as irrelevant to the meaning of linguistic types. My theoretical framework takes care of the problem. Within this framework, the meaning of types is not obtained, bottom-up, from the meaning of tokens, as I suspect Moore himself thinks. Conversely, the meaning of tokens is obtained, top-down, from the meaning of types. (See Katz 1990b: 88–90, 110–111.) Circumstances of use fix the meaning of linguistic tokens in cases in which they deviate from the meanings of their types, but these circumstances have nothing to do with those type-meanings.

This approach enables the meanings of tokens to be related to the meanings of types in a way that does justice to the role of use in fixing the meanings of tokens, without undermining what Moore wants to say about concepts and analysis. On the account of the semantics of tokens given in section 2.3.2, the sense of a linguistic type, which is part of its grammatical structure, serves as the criterion for the literalness of the meaning of its tokens and the starting point for speakers' and hearers' pragmatic reasoning. Here the use to which a speaker puts his or her token is the final determinant of its meaning, but use plays this role only on the basis of the meaning of the token's type. The meaning of the token does not have to be construed as a new kind of meaning based on use, but can be construed as the meaning of a type. Thus, in ironic uses of language, such as the use of 'That is a happy outcome' to express the meaning *that is a sad outcome*, the meaning of the token is the meaning of the type 'That is a sad outcome'. Use tells us that the meaning of the token is the meaning of some type other than the type of which the utterance in question is a token. (Why do we think that there will always be a suitable sentence-type available in the language? See section 3.7.)

The notorious problem is the so-called paradox of analysis. C. H. Langford argued that Moore's conception of analysis is paradoxical on the grounds that analyses based on it are either trivial or incorrect: "If the verbal expression representing the analysandum has the same meaning as the verbal expression representing the analysans, the analysis states a bare identity and is trivial; but if the two verbal expressions do not have the same meaning, the analysis is incorrect" (1942: 323). Both Moore and his critics took this problem to call into question his notion of meaning and his notion of analysis. But it is not really a problem for them at all. It is only a problem for the commonsense framework within which Moore tried to explain meaning and analysis.

The second horn of the dilemma can be disregarded, since analyses in which the analysans does not express the same concept as the analysandum are no more (correct) analyses for Moore than an equation like '2 + 2 = 17' is a truth for the mathematician. They are simply mistakes. When we turn to the first horn of the dilemma, Langford's claim that correct Moorean analyses are trivial, we encounter yet another version of Frege's fruitfulness criticism of Kant's conception of analyticity. Langford's criticism is, in effect, Frege's criticism that Kant's notion of analyticity is trivial because it "simply tak[es] out of the box again what we have just put into it." Whether or not Langford's criticism is historically connected with Frege's fruitfulness criticism, I cannot say. But it is part of the pattern of fruitfulness criticisms that I have been documenting.

Langford's charge of triviality is a straight case of overgeneralization. Certainly the particular analysis of 'brother' as 'male sibling' is unlikely to tell anyone something they do not already know. But in offering no reason to think that Moorean analysis will not be informative in other cases, Langford offers no argument to think that identity of meaning of analysandum and analysans *ipso facto* means that the analysis is uninformative about the concepts. Langford bases his whole criticism on Moore's example of the analysis of 'brother' as 'male sibling'. But there is no argument to show that other examples will be just as transparent as Moore's.

Moorean semantics is not in bad company here. Mathematics and logic sometimes tell us things we already know. To take extreme cases, mathematics tells us that one plus one is two and logic tells us that p implies p. Of course in other cases, mathematics and logic do tell us things we do not already know. But that is true of Moorean analysis as well. No one knows all the synonymy relations in his or her language; so, for each of us, there are Moorean analyses that would be informative. Indeed, if this were not so—if, that is, all cases of synonymy were as transparent as the case of 'brother' and 'male sibling'—there would be no need of dictionaries and thesauruses. The fact that they exist, are the products of considerable effort on the part of generations of lexicographers, and are widely used is itself an argument against Langford's objection that we always know the meaning of the analysans in advance.

Moreover, speakers differ in their explicit knowledge of the meanings of words. It might be hard to find a normal English speaker who does not know what the word 'brother' means, but it is easy to find one who does not know what the word 'browman' means. In the case of rare words of the language, few of us will be so knowledgeable as to find a correct analysis trivial. If we were so knowledgeable, we would not have the parlor game *Dictionary*. But even in the case of common words, there are unclear cases of all sorts, as everyone knows who has tried his or her hand at the analysis of philosophically interesting terms or the more systematic enterprise of descriptive semantics in linguistics.

Normal speakers of a natural language are something like the slave boy in Plato's *Meno*. Their implicit knowledge of the language far outstrips their explicit knowledge of it, and their explicit knowledge can increase if they make the effort. Chomsky has stressed (1965) that the linguist's systematic explicit knowledge is based on inferences from speakers' "recognitions" of what they implicitly know about the language.

In all cases of correct analysis, trivial and informative alike, the analysans explicitly presents a sense structure that is orthographically concealed by the simplicity of the syntactic structure of the analysandum. In the trivial analyses, what is hidden is nonetheless obvious (i.e., commonly known); in informative analyses, what is concealed is unobvious and sometimes may be quite obscure or misleading. Informativeness is thus a matter of degree. The more unobvious the decompositional sense structure of the analysandum that is formally exposed in the syntactic structure of the analysans, the more informative is the analysis. Thus, Moore's analysis of 'brother' as 'male sibling' is an unfortunate example on two counts. The decompositional sense structure of 'brother' is completely obvious and the structure revealed in 'male sibling' is minimal. (Moore's analysis reveals less of the decompositional sense structure of 'brother' than there is to be revealed. A more revealing analysans might be 'human male who is one of two or more children of the same parents'.) In general, the informativeness of an analysis is a matter of how much decompositional sense structure is concealed by the syntactic simplicity of the analysandum and how much is revealed in the syntactic complexity of the analysans.

In Moore's commonsense framework, analysans are paraphrases and the syntax in question is the syntax of the natural language. But the notation for analysis can also take the form of a specially constructed semantic formalism set up within a theory of sense to represent sense structure. There are two virtues of such a formalism that further undermine Langford's version of the fruitfulness criticism. The first is epistemic. It is one thing to think that an analysis is obviously correct and quite another to have appropriate semantic evidence that it is. Since analyses in the form of semantic representations enable us to marshal evidence about the sense properties and relations of the expressions that are analysanda and analysans, we do not have to be satisfied with just thinking that an analysis is correct. We can have the evidence required for knowledge that it is.

The second virtue is explanatory. Linguistic analyses in the form of formal representations can explain as well as describe synonymy relations. This means that analyses have an explanatory informativeness over and above whatever descriptive informativeness they may have. Consider the analysis of 'inflammable' as 'capable of easily being set on fire'. To many speakers, it is puzzling that this correct analysis makes 'inflammable' synonymous with 'flammable'. But a full linguistic representation of 'inflammable' will show that this adjective derives from the verb 'inflame', while the adjective 'flammable' derives from the noun 'flame'. This analysis thus clears up the puzzle by showing that the 'in' of 'inflammable' is not the negative prefix of 'ineffective' and 'infinite', but only part of the verb 'inflame'. Hence, Langford's triviality criticism, and by parity of argument, Frege's fruitfulness criticism, miss yet another way that analysis can be informative.

3.5. Frege's context principle and the linguistic turn

Frege states his famous context principle as follows: ". . . never . . . ask for the meaning of a word in isolation, but only in the context of a proposition. . . . It is enough if the proposition taken as a whole has a sense; it is this that confers on its parts also their content" (1953: x, 71). It is a measure of the importance Frege attaches to the principle that he includes it as one of his three "fundamental principles." It is thus put on a par with his distinction between the psychological and the logical and his distinction between concept and object.

Frege claimed that the importance of the context principle stems from its role as a bulwark against psychologism: "If [the context principle] is not observed, one is almost forced to take as the meanings of words mental pictures or acts of the individual mind, and so to offend against the first principle as well [the separation of the psychological from the logical, the subjective from the objective]" (1953: x). On the face of it, the claim that psychologism is "almost forced" on us if we fail to adopt the context principle is, to say the least, surprising. What connection is there between the two? What does a principle about the composition of meanings have to do with a doctrine about semantic ontology?

Moreover, Frege himself would be a counterexample to the claim. His interpretation of senses as abstract objects is not based on the context principle, but it nonetheless separates them from mental pictures or mental acts. To be sure, the context principle directs our attention to linguistic objects themselves, but, on the one hand, from certain perspectives (e.g., Chomsky's), this would be directing us to psychological objects, and, on the other hand, we do not need the context principle to direct us away from meanings as mental entities. Quite straightforward philosophical arguments of the sort Frege himself repeatedly made against psychologism provide a more satisfying rationale for taking senses to be part of an objective domain of linguistic objects.

Still, Frege's claim has won some influential supporters in contemporary philosophy. Dummett also makes a strong claim for the importance of the context principle. He makes the striking statement that the context principle is the basis for the linguistic turn in twentieth century philosophy (1991: 111–112). He locates the beginning of the linguistic turn in Frege's use of the context principle to provide a linguistic answer to Kant's problem of how numbers are given to us. Dummett writes:

> On the strength of [the context principle], Frege converts the problem into an enquiry [into] how the senses of sentences containing terms for numbers are to be fixed. *There is the linguistic turn.* . . . Plenty of philosophers—Aristotle, for example—had asked linguistic questions, and returned linguistic answers: Frege was the first to ask a *non*-linguistic question and return a linguistic answer. (1991: 111–112)

In his book *Frege* (billed as "An introduction to the founder of modern analytic philosophy"), Anthony Kenny echoes Dummett's claim: "If, therefore, analytical philosophy was born when the 'linguistic turn' was taken, its birthday must be dated to the publication of *The Foundations of Arithmetic* in 1884 when Frege decided that the way to investigate the nature of number was to analyze sentences in which numerals occurred" (1995: 211).

I agree with Dummett and Kenny that Frege initiated the linguistic turn, and I agree with Kenny that (together with Russell) Frege was the founder of modern analytic philosophy, but I think that they are mistaken to claim that what did the trick was Frege's conversion of Kant's non-linguistic question about numbers into a linguistic question about the senses of sentences. If all it took to initiate the linguistic turn was to be "the first to ask a non-linguistic question and return a linguistic answer," then the credit for initiating the linguistic turn should go to Aristotle. He asked the non-linguistic question "Are the virtues emotions?" and returned a linguistic answer. As John Passmore observes:

> [Aristotle] makes use of what it would be natural to call 'an appeal to ordinary language'. The virtues are not emotions, he argues, since '*we are not called* good or bad on the ground that we exhibit certain emotions but only in respect of our virtues and vices'; again, he argues, an emotion *is said to* 'move' us whereas a virtue or vice *is said to* 'govern' us. What 'we say', then, is the decisive factor. Arguments of this sort are everywhere to be found in Aristotle's *Nichomachean Ethics*. . . . (1957: 439)

Furthermore, the conversion of Kant's question was part of Frege's argument for logicism, in which the semantic emphasis characteristic of the linguistic turn plays a rather minor role in comparison to Frege's epistemic and ontological emphases, which, in both cases, are at odds with the prevailing epistemic and ontological thrust of the linguistic turn. Moreover, although Frege initiated the linguistic turn, it was the members of the Vienna Circle who really put it on the philosophical map. Thus, we should look at Frege's work from their perspective to see just what aspect of it counted most for them.

There was some sympathy for logicism among them, but there was more for Hilbert's formalism and Brouwer's intuitionism. To mention just one example, Carnap's *The Logical Syntax of Language* shows a far stronger debt to the antirealist, non-linguistic approach of Brouwer's constructivism. These sympathies of the logical positivists ought not, of course, to be that surprising. Frege's full "linguistic solution" to Kant's problem was only partly linguistic, involving as it did realism about senses and numbers and rationalism about knowledge of them. Clearly, Frege's philosophy of mathematics was not at all to the taste of philosophers who had set out to establish that questions about abstract objects are pseudoquestions and positions like rationalism are nonsensical metaphysics.

It is also worth noting, moreover, that Frege's conversion of Kant's question in the case of arithmetical questions was not an application of a general philosophical strategy, but an isolated aspect of his philosophy of mathematics. It does not have the status of the general philosophical strategy that became the hallmark of the linguistic turn. Frege did not accord equal treatment to geometry. He accepts the synthetic *a priori* status of geometric knowledge and he accepts an intuition-based epistemology for it. The fact that his conversion in the case of arithmetic was not something applied across the board in the manner of true linguistic philosophy, but was combined with a metaphysical treatment of geometry and a realist ontology, at best sent a mixed message to subsequent philosophers.

Furthermore, if it is plausible to think that Dummett and Kenny are right that Frege's work on arithmetic truth initiated the linguistic turn, its appeal for the logical empiricists would have had to come from the success of the enterprise of the *Grundlagen* and the *Grundgesetze*. The attractiveness to subsequent philosophers of asking "a *non*-linguistic question and return[ing] a linguistic answer" would have to have been based on success in this case being seen as encouraging the expectation of success in other cases. But Frege's enterprise was anything but a success. It was revealed as a failure even before the appearance of the second volume of the *Grundgesetze*. The inconsistency in the set theory of Frege's logical system, the so-called "Russell paradox," made it impossible for Frege's logicism to be established on that system. Moreover, the paradox arose with Basic Law V, precisely the feature of the system that is supposed to guarantee that there are objects to serve as the extension of every first-level concept. Since Basic Law V provides the condition for the extension of a concept, the paradox puts the very idea of a Fregean conversion of the question of how numbers are given to us under a cloud. It is, accordingly, hard to see how the conversion could have seemed to the logically acute philosophers of the Vienna Circle to be a philosophical paradigm on which a metaphilosophy could be based.

What aspect of Frege's work *was* responsible for initiating the linguistic turn? To answer this question, we need to see what was most important to the Vienna Circle in the pursuit of their positivist objectives. These objectives were to provide linguistic means for showing that metaphysics is linguistic nonsense. For this purpose, the logical positivists needed semantic tools that would enable them to show that metaphysical sentences are meaningless and that alleged synthetic *a priori* sentences are analytic *a priori*.

I submit that the critical aspect of Frege's work for initiating the linguistic turn was his logical semantics. Frege's initiation of the linguistic turn consisted in his supplying the early positivists with a referential notion of sense, a system of predicate logic, and, especially, a broad, logically-based notion of analyticity. These contributions afforded the logical positivists with the logicolinguistic wherewithal to mount their arguments against metaphysics.

The term 'logical' in the names 'logical positivism' and 'logical empiricism' refers to Frege's predicate logic and is thus an acknowledgment of its importance for the movement bearing those names. In particular, Frege's logical notion of analyticity was indispensable for its attempt to explain away alleged cases of synthetic *a priori* knowledge on which speculative philosophers, Husserl in particular, had based their metaphysics. Frege's notion of analyticity enabled the logical empiricists to save Humean empiricism from Kant's criticism that it failed to account for synthetic *a priori* knowledge in mathematics and science. They could answer Kant by saying that his criticism relies on an inadequate notion of analyticity and that, on an adequate—i.e., fruitful—one, this knowledge is seen to be analytic *a priori*. Hence, they could say, as Schlick explicitly did (1949: 285), that nothing requires us to follow Husserl in positing a metaphysical faculty like intuition of essences.

It was, therefore, Frege's *semantics* that set in motion the logicolinguistic approaches to philosophical problems characteristic of the first and most formative phase of the linguistic turn. Frege initiated the linguistic turn, not in "converting the problem [of mathematical knowledge] into an enquiry of how the senses of sentences containing terms for numbers are fixed," but in converting unfruitful traditional notions of sense and analyticity into fruitful logical ones based on his newly created predicate calculus. Contrary to Dummett and Kenny, the context principle is a somewhat obscure and rather minor character in the exciting drama of linguistic philosophy in the twentieth century.

What precisely does Frege's context principle assert? And is it true? By itself, the first component of Frege's statement of the principle suggests an interpretation of it on which it is merely a restatement of compositionality. On this interpretation, the principle says that the sense of a word can be seen in terms of its contribution to the senses of the sentences in which it occurs. The principle is just a way of recognizing that word meanings can be revealingly seen from the perspective of their position as components of full sentence meanings. Here, there is no denial that words have senses on their own and that those senses are the "building stones" of the senses of the sentences in which they appear. Like real building stones, the senses of words exist independently of the constructions they might be used to make, but their function can be seen in terms of their place in such constructions.

Interpreted in this way, the context principle is the converse of compositionality in just the sense in which *A is the parent of B* is the converse of *B is the child of A*, and is certainly true. But there are various reasons not to accept the interpretation. One is that it makes the context principle entirely trivial: what is the point of making so much of the converse of compositionality? But the decisive reason why this interpretation is unacceptable is that the second component of Frege's statement of the principle rules it out. It says that "it is through [the sense of the sentence] that its parts obtain their content." Here, there is a denial that words have senses on their own and that the senses of sentences are built up from them: on the contrary, senses of sentences are the source of the senses of their constituents. So construed, the context principle is inconsistent with the principle of compositionality, which asserts that the source of the sense of a sentence is the antecedently given senses of its syntactically simple constituents.

Understood in this way, Frege's context principle is not defensible. First, words have meaning in isolation. This is shown by a variety of considerations. One is that words in isolation have sense properties and relations. 'Bachelor' is ambiguous, synonymous with 'unmarried man', and antonymous with 'spinster'. The meaning of 'bachelor' explains why it has these sense properties and relations. Another consideration is that we customarily ask for the meaning of a word, in isolation, when we do not know what it means: "What does the word 'supernaculum' mean?" (Answer: "*To the last drop.*")

Second, the context principle under this interpretation conflicts with compositionality. If the sense of a sentence is built up from the senses of the words in it, as compositionality says, then words have to be independently meaningful "building stones" in order for them to contribute to the edifice of the compositional meaning of a sentence. The compositional principle is widely accepted as essential to the recursive structure of sentence meaning, and Frege himself accepts it (1984: 390).

The intuitions behind the compositional principle are so strong that no principle that conflicts with it can be acceptable.[4] No other linguistic principle is confirmed by so wide a range of clear cases—for example, the contrast between the compositional and idiomatic senses of expressions, such as the senses of 'kick the bucket' and 'eat crow'. The principle also has a secure place in theoretical thinking about language. We could not explain the lawful relations between the semantic properties and relations of sentences of natural language on the basis of the semantic properties and relations of their component vocabulary if the senses of those sentences were not a compositional function of the senses of their constituent vocabulary items. Given that the conflict between the context principle and the principle of compositionality is real, it is clearly the former that must go.

Dummett recognizes the conflict, and, accordingly, tries to show that it is only apparent, proposing what he calls "a compositional interpretation of the context principle" (1991: 202–204). Sentences are "as ordered by a relation of dependence: to grasp the thoughts expressed by certain sentences, it is necessary first to be able to grasp those expressed by other, simpler, ones." There are basic sentences, which are the simplest syntactically, have subjects that refer demonstratively to actual objects (so that their referents can be perceived), and contain "a general term carrying with it a criterion of identity." Dummett's idea is that our grasp of complex sentences depends on our grasp of simpler ones containing their component expressions, and ultimately on appropriate basic sentences. The context principle is not violated because we do not "learn the sense of [an] expression taken on its own." Learning is, *au fond*, learning of basic sentences.

This attempt at reconciliation misconstrues the issue as one about how we acquire the *knowledge* underlying our grasp of the senses of expressions. It is, rather, about the structure of those senses themselves. Dummett can be right about the psychology of acquisition without mitigating the conflict with compositionality in the slightest, for, acquisition notwithstanding, the context principle is incompatible with a compositional account of sentence meaning. Hence, Dummett provides no reason to think that the conflict between the significant context principle and sense compositionality is not a real one.

Compositionality says that the senses of syntactically complex expressions (that are not idioms) are formed from the senses of their components (in accordance with their syntactic relations)—ultimately, its morphemes. Hence, the morphemes of a sentence must have senses on their own and these must constitute the contribution of those items to the sense of the sentence. If some of those items have nothing to contribute (as in, for example, 'We saw three slithy toves'), the sentence cannot have a full sense (unless it is an idiom). Compositionality says that sentences get their content from the contents of their parts, whereas the context principle says that meaning formation goes the other way around. Since it cannot go both ways, the conflict is a real one. As I have argued, this shows that the context principle must go.

3.6. Propositions and the Epimenidean dilemma

In this section, I will present the first in a number of spurious dilemmas that follow from the assumption that intensionalism is Fregean intensionalism. These dilemmas arise because the assumption restricts their resolution to alternatives based on Fregean intensionalism and alternatives based on extensionalism, neither of which can provide a wholly satisfying resolution. The alternatives run counter to strong philosophical intuitions, and, as a consequence, none of the available resolutions of the dilemmas is persuasive, because none does justice to all of our philosophical intuitions. In the case of each of these dilemmas, I will argue that a resolution that does justice to all our philosophical intuitions is possible when my new non-Fregean intensionalism is used to expand the range of alternatives open to us.

The dilemma that I shall discuss in this section, which I will call "the Epimenidean dilemma," is supposed to show that we cannot say both that natural languages are in some sense universal or unlimited in expressive power and that they are consistent. For, if a natural language provides the means to express everything, then, in particular, it provides the means to express Epimenidean sentences and *ipso facto* counts them as significant/meaningful, and hence we are committed to asserting that something is both true and not true. But if it does not provide the means to express such sentences, then, of course, it is not universal. We are thus supposedly forced to choose between the intuition that natural languages are universal and the intuition that no sentence is true and not true.

To appreciate the force of this dilemma, we need to obtain a sense of the strength of the intuitions we have to choose between. The basic intuition that there is some appropriate sense in which natural languages are universal or unlimited in expressive power is the intuition is that sentences like those in (S) are meaningful English sentences.

(S)   The first sentence in (S) is false (not true).

This sentence is false (not true).

The third sentence in (S) is false (not true).

. . .

That they are meaningful seems clear enough, since we have no trouble saying what they mean. A sentence of (S) says that some particular sentence, the one to which the sentence makes reference, has the property of being false (not true). There is no whiff of the deviance that we find in sentences like (3.15):

(3.15)   Seventeen is titillated by pornography.

Moreover, unlike attempts to express what the sentences in (S) say, attempts to express what a sentence like (3.15) says, namely, sentences like (3.16), exhibit the same category mistake.

(3.16)   (3.15) says that seventeen is titillated by pornography.

Furthermore, unlike (3.15), the sentences in (S) have indefinitely many literal uses on which they straightforwardly make either true or false statements, for example, in a context where their subject refers to a truth like 'Snow is white' or a falsehood like 'Snow is black'. But if literal tokens of the sentences in (S) are meaningful, then the sentences in (S) of which they are tokens must themselves be meaningful. Finally, there is no problem about saying what sentences the sentences in (S) refer to. They refer to themselves. In this respect, they are not different from 'This sentence has five words'.

Given the basic intuition, the full intuition that natural languages are universal or unlimited in expressive power is as follows. If the sentences in (S) are meaningful, then so are sentences (S'), (S''), . . . :

(S')   The first sentence in (S) is false (not true), . . .

(S'')   The first sentence in (S') is false (not true), . . .

. . .

since the latter sentences present no opportunity for deviance that is not already found in the sentences in (S). That is to say, since the sentences of (S) violate no grammatical restriction in English, the sentences in the infinite sequence of sets of sentences with a referential genealogy that traces back to sentences in (S) violate no grammatical restriction in English. Since our basic intuition is that the latter sentences are meaningful, our full intuition is that the sentences (S'), (S''), . . . are meaningful, too.

The basic intuition that natural languages are consistent is that it is paradoxical to suppose they are not. Can we literally suppose that the language we speak, in which we not only conduct our daily affairs but also do logic, mathematics, and natural science and reason about consistency, is itself inconsistent? How can we consistently reason to the conclusion that the language on which our reasoning depends is inconsistent?

Consider what is involved in saying that a language is consistent (or inconsistent). We must understand these notions by analogy to what it means to speak of theories as consistent (or inconsistent). In the case of theories, consistency means that the principles for which the theory is responsible—its postulates—entail no contradiction. Since the analytic sentences of a language owe their semantic status entirely to the structure of the language, the consistency of a language is a matter of the set of its analytic sentences not entailing a contradiction. Thus, for a natural language to be inconsistent, there would have to be a derivation exhibiting a contradiction among its analytic sentences. But, as Hans Herzberger points out (1965), since the conclusion of the derivation purports to be a contradiction logically derived from statements none of which, being analytic, can be false, the conclusion must itself be false. It is a *reductio* of the claim that there is any such derivation. Thus, natural languages must be consistent.

Let us use the term 'effabilism' for the view that the sentences in (S), (S'), (S''), . . . are meaningful sentences in natural language, and the term 'ineffabilism' for the view that denies that they are. Alfred Tarski was an effabilist (1952: 19–25). He expresses his effabilism about natural language thus: "A characteristic feature of colloquial language . . . is its universality. It would not be in harmony with the spirit of this language if in some other language a word occurred which could not be translated into it; it could be claimed that 'if we can speak meaningfully about anything at all, we can also speak about it in colloquial language'" (1956a: 164).

Hence, Tarski thinks that natural languages are inconsistent: ". . . it is presumably just this universality of everyday language which is the primary source of all semantical antinomies, like the antinomies of the liar or of heterological words. These antinomies seem to provide a proof that every language which is universal in the above sense, and for which the normal laws of logic hold, must be inconsistent." He argues that a coherent notion of truth for a language depends on its metalanguage being essentially richer than the language itself: "If . . . an interpretation of the metalanguage in the object-language is possible . . . the hypothesis that a satisfactory definition of truth has been formulated in the meta-language turns out to imply the possibility of reconstructing in that language the antinomy of the liar; and this in turn forces us to reject the hypothesis in question" (1952: 23–24). Tarski's position seems to be that natural languages as they stand are inconsistent and hence have to be supplemented with an appropriate hierarchy of artificial languages. Nothing is said, however, about how a putatively inconsistent natural language can be adequate to serve mathematicians and logicians in constructing and applying the artificial languages in the hierarchy.

Tarski's view is close to Frege's view that natural languages, because of their various imperfections, are unsuitable for rigorous reasoning and have to be replaced with "logically perfect" artificial languages. But Tarski's view is based on a far more serious example of an "imperfection." Frege's examples—ambiguity, failure of well-formed expressions to refer—are small potatoes in comparison. Thus, seeing what is wrong with Tarski's view will help us to reject Frege's.

Ineffabilists accept Tarski's line of argument that if natural languages were effable they would contain their own metalanguage and, hence, would be inconsistent, but they part company with him on the universality of natural languages. Ineffabilists abandon the expressive completeness of natural languages in order to maintain their consistency. They argue that if the sentences in (S) are meaningful, they express propositions and are either true or false. But if true, they are false, and if false, they are true. Since they are either true or false, they are both true and false, thereby violating (P):

(P)   No contradictory proposition is true.

Taking this line of argument to be a *reductio* of the assumption that the language is expressively complete, ineffabilists claim that the metalinguistic apparatus for formulating meaningful Epimenidean sentences is absent from the language.

An instructive case of the effabilist/ineffabilist controversy is Graham Priest's and Timothy Smiley's exchange over the status of (P). Smiley puts the issue between them as follows: "I take the law of contradiction for granted and conclude that the Liar sentence must malfunction, without explaining the phenomenon. Priest takes for granted that grammatical sentences cannot malfunction and concludes that the Liar sentence must be both true and false, without (I say) explaining the phenomenon" (1993: 27). Priest replies: "The dialetheic solution to the Liar is, by contrast [to the complexity of a groundedness requirement] bold and simple. I cannot deny that it requires the rejection of something to which logicians are pretty firmly attached; but after that, everything falls into place" (1993: 45).

Here we have a perfect example of the Epimenidean dilemma. What will it be: effability and inconsistency or ineffability and consistency? Priest opts for effability and rejects (P) in order to escape what he calls "the silence of Cratylus" (1993: 44). Smiley opts for (P) and rejects effability in order to escape—as we might put it—the prolixity of Epimenides. Priest preserves the intuition that natural languages are in some sense universal but sacrifices their consistency, whereas Smiley preserves the intuition that they are consistent but sacrifices their full expressive power. Given the strength of the intuitions supporting effability and the intuitions supporting consistency, shouldn't we look for some way between the horns? Such an alternative would have more intuitive support than either of the alternatives requiring a sacrifice.

The criticisms Priest and Smiley make of each other are correct. Priest is right that we ought to do justice to our intuition about the meaningfulness of Epimenidean sentences. Smiley is right that we ought to do justice to our intuition that less basic principles be sacrificed before more basic ones, and, hence, that noncontradiction ought to be preserved at all costs. If Priest is right about preserving universality and Smiley is right about preserving noncontradiction, then we ought not take either horn of the dilemma, but, rather, look for the assumption of their debate that prevents them from escaping between the horns. I will show that the assumption is the assumption that Fregean intensionalism is the only form of intensionalism.

Before explaining why we are not forced to choose between universality and consistency, I want to address the fact that philosophers do not take this controversy as seriously as they should. This is, in part, because Priest's position, which rejects (P), is too quickly dismissed as unserious. (It is also in part because Fregean orthodoxy prevents philosophers from recognizing the deeper semantic issue at stake.) Even Smiley, who has invested considerable time and energy in trying to refute dialetheism, sometimes speaks of the views of Richard Routley and Robert Meyer (1976) and Priest (1987) as if they were some quaint Australian aberration (1993: 17). Some of the issues they raise are anything but that, being of the utmost importance for our understanding of language and logic. Whatever the final verdict on dialetheism, it is important for philosophers to face the unresolved dilemma between our semantic beliefs about the expressive completeness of English and our logical beliefs about the nature of truth. Priest is quite right to say that ". . . whether or not dialetheism is correct, a discussion of the questions it raises, concerning fundamental notions like negation, truth and rationality . . . can hardly fail to deepen our understanding of these notions" (1993: 35).

Let us begin our quest for a route between the horns by asking whether Smiley's and Priest's arguments are satisfactory. Smiley's denial of effability is based on a largely unexplained claim to the effect that "the Liar sentence must malfunction." Presumably, the "malfunction" is something that blocks the sentences in (S) from having a compositional meaning. Priest writes: "[Smiley] asks (p. 26) 'Can we say that [the Liar] is not true?' If '[The Liar] is not true' does not express a proposition, it is not at all clear that this makes sense; compare: 'Can we say that quadruplicity drinks procrastination?' " (1993: 42, n. 3). But if not expressing a proposition means not having a truth value, the answer to Smiley's first question can be "Yes" (the sentence is in the complement of the truths), but it can still be denied that it is clear that the sentence does not make sense in the manner of 'Quadruplicity drinks procrastination'.

What is the rationale for saying that 'The Liar is not true' does not make sense? The sentence is perfectly meaningful in English, in contrast with sentences like 'Quadruplicity drinks procrastination'. Such deviant sentences—sometimes described as exhibiting "category mistakes"—have no sense because senses of constituents of the sentence that have to combine compositionally for the sentence to have a sense cannot combine because one of them can only combine with senses belonging to a particular category to which the other does not belong. 'Quadruplicity drinks procrastination' violates such a restriction because the verb 'drinks' precludes both its subject and direct object from being an abstract noun. As I showed at the beginning of this section, Epimenidean sentences contain no such semantic violations.

Again, at what step in the compositional process for the sentences in (S) is such a malfunction supposed to occur? The lexical items in all of them are meaningful terms of the language, and no step in the compositional process violates a restriction on the compositional combination of senses. If the lexical items are meaningful and if there is no problem at any step in combining their senses, then the sentences in (S) must have compositional meanings.

Priest bases his denial of noncontradiction on the complexity of the groundedness requirement and the palliative "after that, everything falls into place." But the complexity of groundedness can be seen as a technical challenge rather than as a philosophical obstacle. Further, a strong case can be made that, on the contrary, everything falls apart with an account of negation, truth, and rationality based on a denial of the principle of noncontradiction. For example, the notion of validity as entailing and entailed by the absence of counterexample goes by the boards. Priest regards the ineffabilist's non-negotiable commitment to (P) as mulish conservatism (1993: 45). While I think this judgment may correctly reflect the attitude of some of his critics, it does not really address the intuition behind the genuine concern of others. Instant recognition of this intuition can be achieved with a well-known Sidney Morgenbesser story. In the sixties, Morgenbesser met with student protestors at Columbia University to try to express some faculty support. During the discussion, one student radical said, "Professor Morgenbesser, why do you get so upset when I don't obey the laws of logic? We Maoists believe a proposition can be true and false at the same time. Don't you?" To which Morgenbesser replied, "I do and I don't."

Arnold Koslow points out (in conversation) that Priest provides no way to tell which *prima facie* paradoxical sentences are to be treated as acceptable contradictions, like the Epimenidean sentences, and which are not. Koslow also points out that often in the history of mathematics and logic, paradox has been a warning sign that we are unknowingly basing our reasoning on a false assumption. He argues that, in the absence of a principled way of telling which cases are which, the dialetheic position runs the risk of prematurely abandoning a foundational inquiry that could reveal an undetected false assumption and bring new results to light. I will argue that in the case of the Epimenides dilemma, there is just such a false assumption.

There is a common piece of reasoning in Priest's and Smiley's arguments. Both reason from the meaningfulness of the Epimenidean sentences to the contradiction, but, of course, this reasoning plays a different role in their respective arguments. Smiley uses it as a *reductio* to deny that Epimenidean sentences are meaningful, whereas Priest uses it to deny (P). But the reasoning itself is flawed: it rests on an equation of the meaningfulness of sentences with their expressing a proposition in the sense of something that bears a truth value. It is, of course, reasonable to suppose that propositions in the sense required for meaningfulness are propositions in the sense required for sentences to be true or false if one is an extensionalist or Fregean intensionalist. The latter position guarantees that meaningfulness coincides with having a truth value, given Frege's condition that "grammatically well-constructed expressions . . . designate an object" (1952: 70) and his view that the reference of an assertive sentence is a truth value. If this condition is met, then Epimenidean sentences, being grammatically well-constructed, must designate the True or the False. For Fregean intensionalists, the meaningfulness of a sentence is either a guarantee of its having a truth value or an imperfection of language to be avoided in all serious reasoning.

The meeting of minds between extensionalists and Fregean intensionalists is a consequence of the fact that both do semantics exclusively in the theory of reference. Once the autonomous theory of sense is brought into the picture, meaningfulness is the property of having a sense, and having a sense does not imply expressing a proposition that is true or false. Hence, supposing that propositions in the sense required for meaningfulness are the same as propositions in the sense required for having a truth value requires the assumption that Fregean intensionalism is the only intensionalism.

The falsehood of this assumption enables me to say that there are two kinds of propositions, one the object of study in the theory of sense and the other the object of study in the theory of reference. The former, *intensional propositions*, are the bearers of (nonexpressional) sense properties and relations, and the latter, *extensional propositions*, are the bearers of referential properties and relations. I define 'intensional proposition' as follows:

(IP)(i)   An intensional proposition is a sense of a sentence, as understood in the definition (D);

(ii)   Two intensional propositions are the same just in case they are equivalent in the sense of (EQ).

As I have argued in my discussion of fine-grainedness, intensional propositions are the objects of *de dicto* belief and other *de dicto* propositional attitudes. How we are to understand extensional propositions, the objects of *de re* beliefs and other *de re* propositional attitudes, is not relevant here.

The existence of these two kinds of propositions invalidates the step in Smiley's and Priest's reasoning from the Epimenidean sentence's being meaningful to its having a truth value. Since a sentence can be meaningful in virtue of expressing an intensional proposition without expressing an extensional proposition, that reasoning commits a fallacy of ambiguity. On the new intensionalism I am proposing here, the only extensional property guaranteed by the meaningfulness of the Epimenidean sentence is, as the referential correlate (C1) says, its possibly having an extension. Given that the referents of (assertive) sentences are truth values, all that follows from the meaningfulness, and (even) plenomicness, of an Epimenidean sentence is that possibly it has a truth value and possibly it does not.

It is now easy to see how to go between the horns of the dilemma. First, effabilism is the claim that the sentences in (S), (S'), (S''), . . . (or their translations) are meaningful in the sense of expressing intensional propositions. This undercuts Smiley's argument for ineffabilism as a solution to the Epimenides paradox. If there were only extensional propositions, he could reason from the supposition that an Epimenidean sentence expresses a proposition to the conclusion that it is paradoxical, and hence deny effability, on the basis of his view that noncontradiction is to be preserved at all costs. But once intensional propositions are on the scene, Smiley cannot conclude that effabilism is false on the basis of that view. Since there are intensional proposi-tions in terms of which we can understand what is expressed in the effability claim, we can deny that Epimenidean sentences express extensional propositions without denying their meaningfulness.

With intensional and extensional propositions, there is no route from accepting effabilism to rejecting (P) or from accepting (P) to rejecting effabilism. We are free to treat the relation between intensional propositions and extensional propositions in whatever way does justice to our intuitions about universality and consistency. The earlier discussion of deviance in the case of sentences like 'Quadruplicity drinks pro-crastination' suggests that this deviance is a feature of sentence-types: the sentence-type 'Quadruplicity drinks procrastination' lacks a sense. In contrast, the deviance in the case of the Epimenidean sentence is not a feature of the sentence-type: the utterance or inscription of a sentence like (S) is asserted in a context in which its statementhood is necessary and sufficient for its truth or falsehood. If we treat this lat-ter deviance as parallel to the former, we can say that it too consists in the absence of a proposition—but an extensional proposition, not an intensional one. Given that there is an intensional proposition, such cases are not exceptions to universality. Since no sacrifice of effability is necessary, Priest's argument that such a sacrifice is worse than denying (P) fails—and for the same reason as Smiley's argument for sustaining (P).

The non-Fregean intensionalist thus automatically has a way of escaping through the horns of the Epimenidean dilemma. Given the absence of an exten-sional proposition in the case of tokens of Epimenidean sentences in contexts where their statementhood is necessary and sufficient for their truth or falsehood, there is nothing that bears referential properties and relations; hence nothing to be true or false; and hence no contradiction. Given intensional propositions in those cases, freedom from contradiction need not cost us effability.

Tarski's position presents a horn of the Epimenidean dilemma (now technically a *tri*lemma) different from Priest's and Smiley's. Like Priest, Tarski is an effabilist about natural languages, but, like Smiley, he places the highest priority on the ordi-nary laws of logic. Since he also takes those laws to hold for the sentences of natural languages and also takes natural languages to be semantically closed, Tarski says that natural languages are inconsistent. This alternative does not require him to de-fend the claim that the sentences in (S) "malfunction" or to reject (P), but it does require him to make an equally indefensible Frege-style commitment to recasting languages hierarchically, so that the metalanguage of each is essentially richer than it. But this solution, as observed earlier, trades one paradoxical situation for another. On Tarski's solution, interpreting a metalanguage in its object language is impos-sible; nonetheless, this is something that the language of Tarski's own papers on truth does. His solution that the language in which we reason in our theoretical and prac-tical affairs—in particular, the language in which we carry out the construction of the ideal languages themselves and on which the interpretation of those formal sys-tems depends—is inconsistent saws off the linguistic limb on which it rests.

Tarski's reasoning contains essentially the same fallacious step as Priest's and Smiley's. The fallacy in Tarski's case takes a form similar to the form it takes in Smiley's case. Tarski does not distinguish referential properties like reference deviance (inconsistency), which apply to tokens, from sense properties like sense deviance (category mistakes), which apply to types. Making this distinction, I can accept Tarski's claim that semantic closure entails inconsistency for exactly the reasons he gives without at the same time accepting his claim that natural languages are inconsistent.

There is no inconsistency, because inconsistency is a feature of reasoning with tokens of linguistic types. Tarski's definition of semantic closure contains the clause: ". . . we have also assumed that all sentences which determine the adequate usage of ['true'] can be asserted in the language" (1952: 20). This clause makes the inconsistency arising from semantic closure a property of assertive uses of language. In my view, too, the inconsistency is a property of such uses. But, on the autonomous theory of sense, reference deviance cannot be a property of natural languages, since they are (infinite) collections of sentence-types each correlated with a (finite) set of senses, and the theory of sense is a theory of the structure of senses and their relations to the sentences expressing them. The theory contains no referential vocabulary.

I noted earlier Herzberger's point that the claim that natural languages are incoherent is self-refuting. To claim that the analytic sentences contain a contradiction is itself a contradiction. Considering analyticity in the mereological sense, the point becomes more obvious still. The only properties and relations for which the language itself bears responsibility are sense properties and relations of sentences. Hence, for a natural language to be incoherent, an analytic sentence in the sense of (A) would have to be false. Since all of them are true in all their satisfier worlds, each is either a weakly necessary truth or neither a truth nor a falsehood. Here, again, my thin notion of sense and my conception of the relation between the theory of sense and the theory of reference pays off philosophically. Nothing that we do in the theory of reference in order to explicate the notion of an extensional proposition or to handle Epimenidean sentences can force us to say that natural languages are inconsistent, any more than it can force us to say that the sentences in (S) are meaningless or that (P) has to be given up. The notion that we must say one of these things is thus another consequence of the assumption that Fregean intensionalism is the only intensionalism.

My resolution of the Epimenidean dilemma is compatible with virtually any explication of the notion of an extensional proposition and of a function from contexts to extensional propositions. Nonetheless, such explications supply an important element in the full formulation of a solution to the Epimenidean paradox. In the case of functions from contexts to extensional propositions, the explication would explain why no extensional proposition is assigned in the case of tokens of sentences like (S) in contexts in which their statementhood is necessary and sufficient for their truth or falsehood, and also why an extensional proposition is assigned in the case of tokens of those sentences in contexts in which their statementhood does not imply their truth or falsehood (for example, a context in which the sentence referred to in 'The nth sentence in the set is not true' is 'Snow is white'). The prevailing explanation is the theory of groundedness in the sense of Herzberger and Katz (1967), Herzberger (1970), and Kripke (1975). This explanation makes the statementhood of assertions about assertions depend on the reference of their terms not entering a loop within which reference cycles endlessly without terminating in an unproblematic truth or falsehood. The Epimenidean paradox is thus blocked because the sentences in (S), (S'), (S"), . . . are ungrounded—which is to say, on my account, that they fail to express an extensional proposition.

Of course, to endorse the groundedness approach is not to say that any present theory of groundedness is everything we want in a satisfactory solution to the Epimenidean paradoxes. There is, as far as I can see, no reason to think that we will not at some point achieve a fully satisfactory theory, but, of course, there is no guarantee. It may turn out that every groundedness condition we formulate has undesirable consequences to the effect that statements we think we can make cannot be consistently made. In that case, it is open to us to say that it is in the nature of things that statementhood is so limited. Why shouldn't the incompleteness of statability be something we learn to live with in the way we have learned to live with the incompleteness of provability?[5] The bottom line is that, even if worse comes to worst and we are forced to accept more incompleteness than we initially bargained for, the resolution of the dilemma remains intact, since incompleteness of statability, however extensive, does not involve incompleteness of expressibility.

My non-Fregean intensionalism's sharp separation of the conditions for meaningfulness from the conditions for reference blocks such involvement. In so doing, it enables us to have a solution to the Epimenidean paradox without counterintuitively abandoning the expressive completeness of natural languages, the principle of noncontradiction, or the consistency of natural languages. The diagnosis of the paradox that took it as a sign of incompleteness was correct, but the location of the incompleteness in language was not. My new intensionalism locates it where it belongs, in our statement-making apparatus, the parts of reference and pragmatics that enable us to relate language to the world. In separating sense from referential matters like statementhood, I preserve all the intuitions about the Epimenidean sentences that are threatened by Fregean intensionalism.

3.7. A speculation about the essence of natural language

The thesis referred to as "effabilism" in the above discussion is a special case of a general thesis about the expressive power of natural languages that I referred to by the same term in earlier works (1972; 1978: 191–234). Here I will use "maximal effabilism" for the general thesis, which can be stated as (MET):

> (MET)   Natural languages are maximally effable in the sense that for every intensional proposition there is a sentence of each natural language that has it as one of its senses.

(MET) says, in effect, that the syntactic resources of a *natural* language are adequate to express what there is to express. Not everything we call a language, for example, an artificial language such as those given by the formation rules of logical calculi, has the syntactic resources for expressing every intensional proposition.

(MET) is not the trivial thesis that for every sense of a sentence there is a sentence of which it is the sense. Intensional propositions are senses of sentences, to be sure, but they comprise a realm of entities independent of the sentences in languages. Sentences are types with utterance and inscription tokens, whereas senses are not types and have no tokens. Although sentences and senses are alike abstracta, they are nonetheless different abstracta in the way that figures in pure geometry and numbers are. Languages relate senses and sentences on the basis of their dictionaries and principles of compositionality. Intensional propositions are individuated in terms of the non-expressional sense properties and relations of natural language—in particular, their analytic entailment relations. Expressional sense properties and relations of sentences are fixed automatically when intensional propositions are compositionally correlated with sentences.

In distinguishing intensional propositions from the sentences that express them, Moore once remarked: "We may thus apprehend a proposition which we desire to express before we are able to think of any sentence which would express it. We apprehend the proposition and desire to express it, but none of the words we can think of will express exactly *the* proposition we are apprehending and desiring to convey" (1953: 61). In cases like this, where we know what intensional proposition we desire to express but despair of finding the right words to express it, it is *we* who are at fault, not the language. We are at a loss for words. According to maximal effability, the sentence-type that expresses the intensional proposition we desire to express is part of the language we speak, but our command of the language and our facility in its use are imperfect. (MET) says that we can never lay the blame at the doorstep of language. To be sure, there are cases of languages lacking words. For example, English does not have a word that means *to die from lack of water* parallel to the verb 'starve'. But, as this example suggests, the words it does have suffice to plug the gap semantically, if not stylistically.

Further, (MET) does not rule out cases of failure to apprehend intensional propositions or sentences. (MET) is not a thesis about our psychological capacities, but a thesis about objective systems correlating sentence-types with sets of senses. (MET) rules out there being an intensional proposition that is not a sense of a sentence in each natural language.

Why should natural languages be such that their sentences collectively express every intensional proposition? What is it about the nature of a natural language that ensures this form of completeness? My answer is that maximal effability is the *essence* of natural language. The grammatical structures responsible for maximal effability are what make natural languages the unique symbolic systems they are. Hypothesizing that the essence of natural languages is that they are maximally effable information systems explains, on the one hand, why they differ from artificial languages and other sign systems and, on the other, why they differ from animal communication systems. Natural languages, unlike artificial languages and animal communication systems, are information systems with unrestricted expressive power. Artificial languages owe what expressive power they have to the natural language within which they are constructed and in which their signs receive interpretation. Animal communication systems (such as the bee dance), on the other hand, are not parasitic on a natural language, and their expressive power is limited to extremely narrow ranges of information. Finally, it is not easy to think of another property to serve as the essence of natural languages. Other properties, such as structure-dependence, recursiveness, infinity, and so forth, are common to various artificial languages.

Even full intertranslatability in the sense Frege put forth in criticizing the claim that words do not have exact translations is not a suitable property. Frege, it will be recalled, argued that a respect in which a word differs from its translation

> . . . does not . . . concern the sense, but only the apprehension, shading, or coloring of the thought. . . . for all the multiplicity of languages, mankind has a common stock of thoughts. If all transformation of the expression were forbidden on the plea that this would alter the content as well, logic would simply be crippled; for the task of logic can hardly be performed without trying to recognize the thought in its manifold guises. Moreover, all definitions would then have to be rejected as false. (1952: 46)

Full intertranslatability expresses a relation between languages, but nothing about the extent of the languages so related. They might be extremely limited systems, such as the propositional calculus in Polish notation and in *Principia* notation. (MET) entails full intertranslatability, but full intertranslatability does not entail (MET).

In taking the view that effability is of the essence of natural languages, my intensionalism sees the *raison d'être* of natural languages as the expression of senses. Natural languages are theory-neutral systems designed exclusively for the purpose of expression. They specifically lack the endorsement function of theories. Natural languages sanction only analytic sentences, in virtue of the fact that such sentences reflect the sense structure of the language. In contrast, natural languages sanction no synthetic sentences. Here the sanction must come from extralinguistic considerations, typically knowledge of the domain of objects with respect to which the sentences of the language are evaluated. Theories, in contrast to languages, are explicitly designed to favor one set of synthetic sentences over another—typically, the postulates of the theory. Natural languages express all propositions without favoritism.

The view is a corrective for the widespread conflation of language and theory found throughout twentieth-century philosophy. The conflation began with Frege and culminates with Quine. Frege first blurred the language/theory distinction when he abandoned the mereological notion of containment in favor of his logical notion, making principles of quantification theory linguistic truths. Carnap blurred the language/theory distinction even further when he redefined analyticity in model-theoretic terms, making the necessary truths of any theory linguistic truths, too. Quine's rejection of necessity and acceptance of semantic holism took the blurring of the language/theory distinction all the way, leaving no boundary between the analytic and the synthetic. For Quine, language and theory are so conflated that it makes perfect sense to argue, as he once did, that there can be no challenge to standard logic because "when [the deviant logician] tries to deny the doctrine he only changes the subject" (1970: 81).

My conception of the language/theory distinction runs directly counter to the conceptions underlying the various philosophical programs that arose during the linguistic turn, including Frege's logicism, the early Wittgenstein's and the logical empiricists's positivism, Quine's empiricism without dogmas, and, finally, the later Wittgenstein's attempt to show that metaphysics is "plain nonsense." Those programs sought to achieve their philosophical objectives on the basis of an account of language as having content well beyond what is required for its expressive completeness. Hence, if I am right that natural languages are without expressive limit but also without theoretical preference, the philosophical programs spawned in the linguistic turn were based on an exaggerated conception of the limits of language.

The argument for this criticism is in essence the argument of this book as a whole. Parts of the book contain specific criticisms of Frege's and Quine's (quite different) attacks on the traditional analytic/synthetic distinction. The later Wittgenstein's attack (1953: particularly, sections 65–72) on the notion that languages have an essence, which is a direct challenge to maximal effability, is not dealt with here; but I have replied to it elsewhere (1990b). One feature of this reply that deserves mention is that the criticisms of his attack continue the theme that have been repeated in the criticisms of Frege and Quine and their followers, namely, that the attack assumes that intensionalist semantics is Fregean semantics.

Many philosophers who played a role in the linguistic turn have presented alleged counterexamples to the claim that natural languages are expressively complete. It will help to explain why they do not work.

Consider J. L. Austin's example. He supposes that if ". . . we have made sure that it is a goldfinch, and a real goldfinch, and then in the future it does something outrageous (explodes, quotes Mrs. Woolf, or what not), we don't say we were wrong to say that it was a goldfinch, *we don't know what to say*. Words literally fail us . . ." (1961: 56). This case is reminiscent of Wittgenstein's example of the disappearing chair (1953: section 80, discussed at some length in Katz 1990b [114–115]). Wittgenstein denied that there is a linguistic basis for applying the term 'chair' to something that for all intents and purposes is a chair but has the disconcerting habit of disappearing and reappearing from time to time. The language, Wittgenstein claimed, does not have ". . . rules saying whether one may use the word 'chair' to include this kind of thing." In Austin's case, like Wittgenstein's, one would no doubt be initially at a loss for words. But it is far from clear that, on reflection, there is no principled decision that can be made. Philosophers like Wittgenstein and Austin suppose that there can be none because they conceive of linguistic rules as reflecting our practices of using words. Their reasoning seems to be that, since such "outrageous" objects are so far removed from anything for which those practices might have been developed, we can have no rule to tell us whether to apply the term to them. But the fact that conceiving of meaning in terms of use affords us no principled decision in such cases does not show that conceiving of meaning in other terms—in particular in terms of my notion of sense—will similarly afford us none.

Let us suppose that the best hypothesis to explain the sense properties and relations of expressions containing 'chair' is that the word means *physical artifact with a back and a seat having the function of serving as a place for someone to sit*. Given that the sense of 'chair' involves the category *artifact* rather than that of *natural kind*, (C3) says that its type-extension consists of the things that fall under that sense. The fact that Wittgenstein's chair disappears and reappears makes no difference. It is simply a disappearing and reappearing chair. We ought to have no trouble understanding this claim, since we understand fairy tales that say such things as "the witch's spell made the prince disappear and a wish of the princess made him reappear." Further, those who remember the old-time radio program *The Shadow* will recall that Lamont Cranston disappears and appears at will to foil those with evil lurking in their hearts. Disappearing princes, private detectives, and chairs are nonetheless princes, private detectives, and chairs. They just have empirically quite unexpected properties.

Austin's case is different in that it concerns a natural kind term. Here (C3) tells us that we have to fix the reference of the term in part on the basis of information about the biological nature of the kind. Thus, to determine whether the creature in Austin's case is or is not a goldfinch, we have to examine its biology. If its genetic material matches that of birds generally and goldfinches in particular, 'goldfinch' applies. In the first of Austin's examples, what we would have is an exploding goldfinch—a creature quite a bit more unusual than the electric eel, but along the same lines. In the second of Austin's examples, the creature is a novel-quoting goldfinch—perhaps some form of superparrot. And if tests show that it is not biologically a goldfinch, or even a bird, then the term 'goldfinch' does not apply.

Our modal intuitions suggest that there is nothing *linguistically* deviant about the expressions that describe things as "outrageous" as Austin's goldfinch or as "abnormal" as Wittgenstein's chair. There is nothing wrong with saying that there is a possible world in which goldfinches utter things like "Mrs. Dalloway said she would buy the flowers herself," or in which chairs behave like Lamont Cranston. Hence, we can reject the moral that Austin and Wittgenstein draw from their examples. "Outrageous" cases like Austin's goldfinch and "abnormal" cases like Wittgenstein's chair do not motivate a limitation on the expressibility of natural languages.

What makes it seems as if "words literally fail us" in cases like Wittgenstein's and Austin's is thus nothing about the cases themselves but rather the assumption that meaning is a matter of use. On this assumption, the linguistic practices that sanction the application of words presuppose that their future referents are sufficiently similar to the referents of past uses on the basis of which the practices were developed. Linguistic rules are conceived of as based on inductive projection, as Wittgenstein himself indicates when he asks (1953: sections 139 and 141) how we decide whether what comes before the mind is "the method of projection" that our teacher taught us. He underscores the point in making the frequency of occurrence of "normal cases" (for examples, chairs that stay put) and "abnormal cases" (for example, chairs that disappear and reappear) the basis of application (1953: section 142). Hence, if a hypothetical case departs too far from how things have behaved in the past, the practices formed on the basis of that behavior cannot sanction a determinate application in hypothetical cases. As Wittgenstein says, "The more abnormal the case, the more doubtful it becomes what we are to say."

From my perspective, the problem posed by "abnormal cases" arises only because use-based accounts of meaning make deviant behavior in the world do the work of deviance of sense structure in the language. The latter has nothing to do with probability or natural law; rather, it concerns the hierarchical structure of component senses in senses—in particular, the category constraints that express the limits of possible senses. Deviance here is thus not a matter of degree, of its becoming more doubtful what to say. Rather, there is a sharp line between deviant sentences like 'Goldfinches have prime square roots' and non-deviant, meaningful sentences like 'The chair disappeared and reappeared', 'Goldfinches sometimes explode', and 'Some goldfinches can quote Mrs. Woolf'.

3.8. Presupposition

Intensional propositions allow us to explain how Epimenidean sentences can be significant and natural languages effable without having to adopt Tarski's denial that natural languages are consistent or Priest's denial of noncontradiction. The compositional conditions on which the expression of intensional propositions depends explain the significance or non-significance of sentences in terms of the sense structure of the language. The groundedness conditions on which the expression of extensional propositions depends explain the extensional significance or non-significance of sentence-tokens in terms of features of the context of their utterance. Since groundedness conditions determine whether a token of an Epimenidean sentence expresses an extensional proposition (that is, is a truth or a falsehood) or expresses no extensional proposition (that is, is without a truth value), a groundedness condition is a presupposition for the assertions made in the use of Epimenidean sentences. The importance of this metalinguistic case of presupposition suggests that the general topic of presupposition should be reexamined from the standpoint of the concerns of this book.

3.8.1. Frege, Strawson, and Russell

The intensionalist owes much to Frege and Strawson for championing the cause of presupposition, but their semantic frameworks are inadequate to develop and defend the notion. The limitations of these frameworks have been responsible for the prevailing view that a Russellian conception of propositional structure is preferable to a presuppositional conception.

Frege says that "[i]f anything is asserted there is always an obvious presupposition that the simple or compound proper names used have reference" (1952: 69); he denies that the sense of the sentence

(3.17)   Kepler died in misery.

"contains the thought that the name 'Kepler' designates something." Rather than being part of the assertion that (3.17) makes, that the name 'Kepler' designates is the condition for the assertion to have a truth value. Since, in fact, the name 'Kepler' designates, (3.17) has a truth value and is true or false depending on whether or not the famous astronomer died in misery. In contrast, (3.18):

(3.18)   Hercules died in misery.

is neither true nor false, since the name 'Hercules' designates nothing. Frege thought that we had to distinguish between what is presupposed and what is asserted because otherwise the negation of (3.17) would be (3.19):

(3.19)   Kepler did not die in misery or the name 'Kepler' has no reference.

rather than what we would customarily take it to be, namely, (3.20):

(3.20)   Kepler did not die in misery.

Frege saw failure of presupposition as "an imperfection of language" (1952: 70), and recommended here, as with other "imperfections," the construction of "a logically perfect language" for scientific and other kinds of rigorous reasoning. This language had to meet the condition "that every expression grammatically well constructed as a proper name out of signs already introduced shall in fact designate an object, and that no new sign shall be introduced as a proper name without being secured a reference." Bivalence and other logical laws hold of the sentences that meet this condition.

Frege's notion of a logically perfect language has been criticized extensively, beginning with Wittgenstein (1953). We do not have to survey the criticisms of it here. It is easy to see that no language suitable for mathematics, science, or ordinary life can meet Frege's condition on the reference of signs. This is because complete knowledge of everything in the domain of the language is required to meet it. The unavoidable ignorance of many facts about mathematics, science, and ordinary life prevents the construction of a logically perfect language. If we do not know whether there is sentient life elsewhere in the universe, for example, then we cannot guarantee that Frege's condition is met in the case of a sentence like 'Sentient life elsewhere in the universe is humanoid'. If, as Frege claims, the grammatical rules of a logically perfect language require that his condition be met, then there can be no such grammatical rules.

The notion of a logically perfect language is paradoxical. We can only introduce a sign to denote something—a conjectured elementary particle, a psychological state, or an evolutionary event—if we already know that the sign has a denotation. But how could we have such knowledge? Since we cannot introduce signs without prior knowledge that their referents exist, we cannot introduce them for the purpose of acquiring knowledge of the existence of their referents. Since the requisite knowledge can only come from use of the signs in reasoning about evidence for and against the existence of the objects, logically perfect languages are an impossibility.

Of course, the Fregean notion of presupposition can be divorced from Fregean doctrines about natural languages and logically perfect languages. It can be taken, as most linguists and philosophers sympathetic to the notion have taken it, as a feature of sentences in natural languages. This is, I believe, the proper course to take; nonetheless, Frege's defense of presupposition has proven insufficient to stand up to extensionalist criticism of the notion.

Intensionalists can take a presuppositionalist view because, having a sense/reference distinction, they do not have to say that sentences are the objects for which laws of logic—in particular, the law of excluded middle—hold. Extensionalists, on the other hand, have to take sentences (or sentences under syntactic descriptions) to be the objects of which laws of logic hold, and, hence, they have to reject the presuppositionalist view. Accordingly, they need to show that Frege's argument for presupposition does not work. This is precisely what Russell's theory of descriptions (1905) does.

On that theory, definite descriptions such as 'the king of France' are "incomplete symbols," signs that are meaningless in isolation—that is, occurring outside a sentential context—but significant when they occur appropriately in a sentence. Their significance in context lies in the contribution they make to the logical forms of the sentences in which they occur. Thus, Russell analyzed the logical form of (3.21) as a conjunction of (3.22), (3.23) and (3.24):

(3.21)   The king of France is wise.

(3.22)   There is at least one thing which is king of France.

(3.23)   There is at most one thing which is king of France.

(3.24)   Whatever is king of France is wise.

On the basis of such an analysis, Russell can claim that the laws of logic hold of sentences (in virtue of their logical form) and an assertion of (3.21) is simply false.

This analysis avoids Frege's argument in connection with the negation of (3.17). Russell's account of definite descriptions can be used to make the logical form of (3.17) the denial of (3.19), that is, (3.25):

(3.25)   Kepler did die in misery and the name 'Kepler' has a referent.

So, on Russell's theory, (3.21) and (3.26) can both be false.

(3.26)   The king of France is not wise.

This, of course, means that the denial of (3.21) has to be (3.27):

(3.27)   It is not the case that the king of France is wise.

and (3.21) and (3.26) can be treated as contraries. But this will not bother philosophers who have already accepted the recasting of (3.21) as the conjunction of (3.22), (3.23), and (3.24).

Here Russell exploits Frege's own distinction between grammatical form and logical form and Frege's approach to recasting simple sentences as compound sentences to make a strong case against the doctrine of presupposition. In the spirit of my earlier criticism of that approach, I might object to Russell's analysis of simple sentences like (3.21) as complex conjunctions, but Frege is in no position to do so. Russell hoists him with his own petard.

Russell's initial rationale for his theory of descriptions was not, as many people later came to think, that it blocks a Meinongian inflation of ontology, but rather that it supports the extensionalist rejection of a notion of sense over and above the notion of reference. (See Cartwright 1987a: 97.) With the theory of descriptions, there is no pressure on extensionalists to understand the significance of sentences like (3.21)–(3.24) as a matter of their having a sense. It can be understood as a matter of their having reference. Thus, rather than avoiding inflating ontology with Meinongian subsistent objects, the initial rationale for the theory of descriptions was to avoid inflating ontology with Fregean intensional objects. In the context of the intensionalist/extensionalist controversy, Frege's argument for the presuppositionalist view was seen as insufficient when faced with the alternative of Russell's theory of descriptions and the alleged virtues of a parsimonious semantic ontology.

P. F. Strawson (1950) tried to save the notion of presupposition from Russell. Strawson is an intensionalist, but his semantic framework is a version of the use theory of meaning. On Strawson's theory, meaning is restricted to expression and sentence types: the meaning of an expression or sentence is a set of directions for how to use it to refer and make statements. Correspondingly, aboutness and truth value are restricted to expression- and sentence-tokens. Both restrictions are too severe. The latter runs into counterexamples in the case of what Quine calls "eternal sentences" (1960: 193), e.g., (3.28):

(3.28)   Seventeen is a prime number.

the truth value of which is independent of time, speaker, and circumstance. (3.28) is a sentence-type that expresses a truth about the number seventeen. The former restriction runs into trouble because utterances and inscriptions, and not just the types of which they are tokens, have meaning. For example, the tokens in the issues of *Mind* containing "On Referring" and those in the copies of the books reprinting it themselves have meaning, and must be understood as assertions about linguistic and philosophical matters. The meaning of a token cannot itself be understood as directions for *its* use.

Further, Strawson's theory explicates the significance of an expression in terms of the possibility of its being used to refer to something. This leads to trouble in the case of sentences like (3.29):

(3.29)   The largest natural number is prime.

Such sentences turn out not to be significant because their subjects cannot be used to refer to anything in any possible circumstances. On a presuppositional account of language, however, a sentence like (3.29) ought to come out significant but without a truth value. Further, Strawson's framework suffers from the standard problems with use theories of meaning (see section 3.22).

Strawson's principal argument (1950: 328) against Russell's theory of descriptions is based on the observation that someone who asserts (3.21) when France is not a monarchy would not get the response "That is untrue." Strawson points out that people would feel that the question of truth or falsehood simply does not arise, and he is probably right about this. But it does not follow that the reason that we feel this way is that we recognize the *semantic* fact that assertion of (3.21) presupposes that there is a king of France. Strawson's argument requires that this be *the* reason, but the argument fails because there could be another reason. It might well be that the reason that we feel the question does not arise is *pragmatic*, not semantic. Although, as Russell claims, semantically (3.21) asserts that there is a king of France, we recognize on pragmatic grounds that the question of the truth or falsity of the sentence arises only if there is a king of France. Russellians might take this line, arguing, as I once suggested (1979b: 93–94), that satisfaction of the most deeply embedded clause of the truth conditions of a sentence like (3.21) is the condition under which the question of the satisfaction of a less deeply embedded clause is taken to arise in a conversation.

The fact that Russellians have good replies to Frege's and Strawson's arguments for presupposition and have been able to deploy recent developments in the study of quantification and Gricean pragmatics to remove other objections has convinced the great majority of philosophers of Russell's analysis. But there are three criticisms for which, as far as I can see, Russellians do not have a satisfactory response. One follows from the general requirement on theories of natural languages that the explanation of a property or relation be uniform over the class of sentences to which the explanation applies. Thus, if the property of statementhood (having a truth value) is explained in terms of presupposition for some open class of sentences of a language, then the explanation should be extended to all the sentences for which statementhood is appropriate. As I have argued, the failure of statementhood in uses of metalinguistic sentences such as (S), (S'), (S"), and so on, is explained in terms of a violation of the groundedness requirement. But this is just the failure of the presupposition that their reference terminates in a truth or falsehood. Since non-statementhood in uses of non-metalinguistic sentences like (3.21) and (3.29) can be explained on the basis of failure of presupposition, too, it follows from the uniformity requirement that the statementhood of such sentences should also be explained on the basis of satisfaction of presupposition. Why should there be one explanation for the statementhood of sentences about Epimenidean sentences and another, quite different, explanation for the statementhood of sentences about non-linguistic objects? Or another, quite different, explanation for the statementhood of sentences about linguistic objects like 'This sentence, which has no nouns, has a verb'?

Let me sharpen the point. The Russellian account of statementhood cannot itself be uniformly applied because it cannot be applied to sentences about sentences without paradox.[6] On a Russellian analysis, the first sentence in (S) has the form (3.30):

(3.30)   There is at least one first sentence in (S) and there is at most one first sentence in (S) and if anything is the first sentence in (S), it is false.

On Russell's account of statementhood, (3.30) is either true or false, and hence, by logic, it is both. The paradox cannot be avoided by invoking the theory of types, a Tarskian language/metalanguage separation, or other devices, since they turn perfectly meaningful English sentences—including those expressing the laws of logic in general form—into meaningless ones. We do not, after all, want to "save" the law of excluded middle by making it meaningless. Hence, Russell's theory of descriptions arbitrarily forces us to distinguish between the statementhood conditions for metalinguistic sentences and those for non-metalinguistic sentences when nothing stands in the way of a uniform treatment.

The second criticism of Russell's theory of descriptions is that its assumption that expressions like 'the king of France' are meaningless in isolation is false. Here I have the same criticism I made earlier of Frege's context principle. The English noun phrase 'the king of France' has various sense properties and relations, and, moreover, ones not derivable from the contributions they make to the logical form of (3.21), in Russell's sense. For example, 'the king of France' is synonymous with 'the male monarch of France' and antonymous with 'the queen of France', 'the male king of France' is redundant, and so on. Since 'the king of France' could not have sense properties and relations if it had no sense, it follows that it has a sense.

The third criticism follows from the criticism that I made in the second part of this book of the practice of regimenting simple sentences as complex ones. Recasting the simple sentence (3.21) as a compound sentence, the conjunction of (3.22), (3.23), and (3.24), is just as counterintuitive as recasting a simple sentence like 'Cats are animals' as the compound sentence 'If something is a cat, then it is an animal'. (3.21) is not made up of two or more clauses, but is a simple copula sentence with the subject the noun phrase 'the king of France' and with the predicate the verb phrase 'is wise'. It contains no 'and' or 'if . . . then'. Given that (3.21) and its Russellian paraphrase, (3.31):

(3.31)   There is at least one king of France and there is at most one king of France and if anything is king of France, it is wise.

differ in these ways, Russell's theory of descriptions is open to the earlier complaint that its analyses require grammatically unwarranted recasting of natural language sentences.

3.8.2. Presupposition in the new intensionalism

Whereas the aim of the previous section was to provide general reasons in favor of presuppositionalism, the aim of this section is to prove that a commitment to the new intensionalism carries with it a commitment to presuppositionalism.[7]

This proof requires assuming no more than the obvious truth that there are three terms the first two of which stand in the subordinate/superordinate relation and the third of which is the antonym of the subordinate term. Given such terms, the subordinate term will be the subject of an analytic sentence like (3.32):

(3.32)   Squares are rectangles.

and its antonym will be the predicate of a contradictory sentence like (3.33):

(3.33)   Squares are circles.

Now consider the sentence (3.34):

(3.34)   Circular squares are circular.

Like the sense of the subject of (3.32), the sense of the subject of (3.34) contains the sense of its predicate, and, like the sense of the subject of (3.33), the sense of the subject of (3.34) is antonymous with the sense of its predicate. Since (3.34) has the same containment structure as (3.35):

(3.35)   Circular figures are circular.

and the same antonymy structure as (3.36):

(3.36)   Squares are circular.

(3.34) is both analytic and contradictory. Moreover, since both (3.35) and (3.36) are meaningful, so is (3.34). If syntactic well-formedness plus meaningfulness is taken to be sufficient for a sentence to have a truth value, then, since (3.34) is syntactically well-formed and meaningful, if its semantic form is not recast, a contradiction results. For, if analytic sentences have a truth value, then they are true, and if contradictory sentences have a truth value, then they are false. Accordingly, (3.34), being both analytic and contradictory, is both true and false.

   To be sure, Fregean intensionalists (and extensionalists) will recast the logical form of (3.34), taking it to be $(x)[(Cx \& (-Cx \& Tx)) \rightarrow Cx]$, where $-C$ represents the sense component of 'square' incompatible with the predicate *circular* and T represents the remaining components of the sense of 'square'. And recasting (3.34) thus certainly avoids contradiction: as a material conditional, (3.34) has a (logically) false antecedent, and, hence, is true. But my argument is directed not to Fregean intensionalists (or extensionalists), but to those who have found my arguments for a non-Fregean intensionalism persuasive, and have thus signed on to the new intensionalism. Being committed to eschewing the recasting of simple sentences as compound, they do not have the option of recasting (3.34). As a final point, note that when combined with the argument in section 2.4.2 against regimenting simple sentences, the present argument for presupposition applies to philosophers generally.

   To avoid the contradiction that (3.34) is both true and false, it must be denied that syntactic well-formedness and meaningfulness are sufficient for a sentence to bear a truth value. It is necessary to add a further condition along the lines of those that presuppositionalists from Frege on have urged, namely, a condition requiring the existence of the objects of which the predication in the sentence is made—something for it to be true or false of. I thus add the presupposition principle (PP):

(PP)(i)   The presupposition of a simple sentence is the condition that each of its terms occurring in a referential position has a non-null extension in the domain.

(ii)   An assertive sentence has a truth value with respect to a domain just in case its presupposition is satisfied in the domain.

(PP)(i) restricts the contribution to the presupposition of a sentence to those of its terms that occur in referential positions. (This feature of sense structure is discussed in Katz 1972 and 1979b, and later in this book.) Briefly, the view is this. Predicates, both referential and non-referential, have argument places. A term that occurs in a referential argument place thereby contributes a clause to the presupposition of the sentence. Each clause says, in effect, that a necessary condition for the sentence to have a truth value is that the term have a non-null extension. Terms that occur in non-referential argument places do not provide a clause for the presupposition. Examples are (3.37) and (3.38):

(3.37)   Some children dream about the tooth fairy.

(3.38)   If John has children, then all of John's children are charming.

The term 'the tooth fairy' occurs in a non-referential argument place because it occurs in an opaque context. Hence, (3.37) presupposes the existence of children but not the existence of the tooth fairy. The term 'John's children' occurs in a non-referential argument place because it occurs in the scope of a hypothesis. Hence, (3.38) presupposes John's existence but not the existence of his children. Finally, note that (PP) defines the satisfaction of the presupposition of a sentence in terms of the notion of the extension of a term. Given (C3), this means that the condition for the extension of a natural kind term includes the real definition of the term as well as its nominal definition.

Adopting (PP) enables us to do justice to our intuition that a sentence like (3.34) is both analytic and contradictory without involving us in inconsistency. Since the subject of (3.34) is itself contradictory, there can be nothing falling under it. Since (PP)'s requirement that there be objects in the domain falling under the terms in the sentence cannot be met, the statementhood condition for (3.34) is (necessarily) unsatisfied. Given (PP)(ii), (3.34) is (necessarily) without a truth value, and hence its having both the sense property of analyticity and the sense property of contradictoriness does not entail that it is both true and false.

Adopting the principle also enables us to explain the referential intuition behind the referential correlate (C4'), which says that analytic sentences are secured against falsehood, and the referential correlate (C5'), which says that contradictory sentences are secured against truth. Presupposition explains those correlates of analyticity and contradictoriness because it guarantees that analytic sentences that are not true cannot be false and that contradictory sentences that are not false cannot be true.

(PP) is not in and of itself a referential correlate, but it will become one once I say how the difference between referential and non-referential terms is expressed in the representation of sense structure (see section 3.18). It relates intensional propositions and extensional propositions by putting a constraint on what can qualify as extensional propositions, namely, they must be objects that, in virtue of their nature, are associated with an intensional proposition just in case the presupposition of that proposition is satisfied. (PP) says nothing about the nature of extensional propositions or about what the bearers of truth values are. Hence, the choice among different conceptions of extensional propositions is left open.

It is sometimes supposed that extensional propositions—in particular Russellian propositions, which are adopted in some neo-Millian views about proper names—are incompatible with intensionalism and presuppositionalism. It is true that Russellian propositions have no place in Fregean intensionalism. (The notion of an extensional proposition is that of a Fregean sense of a sentence in a logically perfect language. The significant sentences of such a language automatically denote the True or the False, and hence their senses are the bearers of truth values, the objects to which bivalence and other laws of logic apply. There is, then, no need for Russellian propositions.) But there is no conflict between Russellian propositions and our intensionalism. It is true that both have something to say about how to handle the distribution of truth values over the sentences of a language, but, seen from the perspective of my approach, what they have to say is at different levels and complementary. Each is a component of the full answer rather than a competing answer. In fact, on the autonomous theory of sense, an independent notion of extensional proposition is a necessity for intensionalism.

Furthermore, my intensionalism makes life easier for defenders of Russellian propositions because Russellian propositions can be taken to be the bearers of truth values without supposing that they can also solve Frege's puzzles about sense. When extensional propositions are used in a framework in which they are the only propositions, they are open to criticism for failing to solve those puzzles. Within the new intensionalism, however, they cannot be so criticized because intensional propositions already resolve those puzzles. Thus, the criticism is not a criticism of extensional propositions *per se*, but a criticism of semantic frameworks within which extensional propositions have to do double duty in handling intensional as well as extensional phenomena. This, as argued earlier, is an impossible task, since intensional structure requires propositions individuated on the basis of a fine-grained notion of propositional identity, while extensional structure requires propositions individuated on the basis of a coarse-grained notion.[8]

If the reflections in this section are correct, then, in different respects, Fregeans and Russellians are each right and each wrong. Fregeans are right that senses of sentences in natural language have presuppositions and that there are truth-value gaps. But Frege was wrong to hold that the existence of well-formed, meaningful expressions lacking reference is an imperfection that requires the construction of a logically perfect language. Blaming language when we reason fallaciously in connection with a referentially vacuous expression is like blaming the hammer when we miss the nail and hit our thumb. Frege himself blamed the hammer. He once criticized the language for the paradox that wrecked his set theory (1979: 269–270). Clearly, the German language did not foist Axiom V on him. Frege's view misconstrues an important feature of natural languages. The fact that natural languages contain well-formed, meaningful expressions that lack reference is a virtue, not a vice. As argued above, this feature makes it possible for us to use those languages to frame hypotheses about the unknown and reason about the future in scientific investigation and everyday life.

Russellians are right that the application of the laws of logic to the sentences of natural language requires propositions that are not subject to truth value gaps. But they are wrong that Excluded Middle forces us to introduce logical forms for simple sentences like (3.21) that radically depart from their grammatical form. As I have argued, the requirements of logic do not force us to introduce them. Logic is a theory of deduction. It does not say that its laws apply to sentences of a natural language on the basis of regimentation. Logic's requirements can be met on the basis of a notion of presupposition and a stock of extensional propositions without falsifying the grammar of sentences. It is a *philosophical* view, expressed in procedures of regimentation, that forces us to recast simple sentences as complex ones. This is the philosophical view that semantics is done exclusively in the theory of reference.

Here Frege's philosophy of language and Russell's have a common motive. Russell's motive in recasting simple sentences as compound ones was to maintain a referential semantics in the face of meaningful sentences containing referentless terms in referential positions. Frege's motive was to explicate sense and analyticity within a referential semantics. Recasting simple analytic sentences as a species of logical truths enabled Frege to capture Kantian cases of analyticity without resorting to the Kantian notion of analyticity. Regimentation allows Russell and Frege to do semantics entirely within the theory of reference.

3.9. The aboutness and confirmation dilemmas

In section 3.6, I considered the Epimenides dilemma in which the Liar Paradox is supposed to force us to choose among the universality of natural languages, their consistency, and the principle of non-contradiction. I argued that the Paradox itself was not what forced us to make this choice. It was the equation of intensionalism with Fregean intensionalism. Once an intensionalism based on an autonomous theory of sense was brought into the picture, there was a further, intuitively more satisfying way out. As I said at the beginning of section 3.6, the Epimenides dilemma is only the first of a number of similar dilemmas, to be examined in subsequent sections, that exhibit a pattern of intuitively unsatisfying choices forced on us by the equation of intensionalism with Fregean intensionalism.

In this section, I consider two further dilemmas. One is the dilemma that Carl Hempel poses in trying to explain what observations confirm a lawlike generalization, and the other is the dilemma that Nelson Goodman poses in trying to explain what a statement is about. The dilemmas are in some ways different, but they are close enough in structure and resolution to be treated together.

Hempel's dilemma (1965: 14–25) is popularly known as "the paradox of the ravens." It is a striking case in which Fregean semantics puts us in a situation where we face an unnecessary conflict between intuitions. Intuitively, (3.39a) is about ravens and confirmed by black ravens,

(3.39a)   All ravens are black.

and (3.39b) is about non-black things (and perhaps non-ravens) and is confirmed by things that are non-black and non-ravens.

(3.39b)   All non-black things are non-ravens.

These are strong intuitions and, other things being equal, an answer to the general questions of what confirms a generalization and what a statement is about should respect them. But on Hempel's and Goodman's assumption that semantics is Fregean semantics, (3.39a) and (3.39b) are logically equivalent and thus just different expressions of the same proposition. But if (3.39a) and (3.39b) express the same proposition, they are about the same things and are confirmed (disconfirmed) by the same observations. Goodman enunciates the principle (1972: 258):

(NG)   Logically equivalent statements are absolutely about exactly the same things.

Hempel enunciates the principle (1965: 13):

(PH)   Whatever confirms (disconfirms) one of two equivalent sentences also confirms (disconfirms) the other.

Now we are on a collision course with others of our intuitions. Given (NG), since (3.39b) is about *inter alia* red jelly beans, (3.39a) is also about *inter alia* red jelly beans. Given (PH), since (3.39b) is confirmed (disconfirmed) by discovering red jelly beans, (3.39a) is confirmed (disconfirmed) by discovering red jelly beans, too. This, as everyone (at least initially) recognizes, is quite counterintuitive. No philosopher would seriously think of recommending this new method of confirming ornithological and other laws to his or her science colleagues. Nor would a philosopher suggest that scientists no longer need trouble themselves with field trips since it is possible to raise the confirmation of a law quite significantly without stepping out of the house.

In connection with the aboutness dilemma, Goodman says: "The encounter in philosophy between the demands of intuition and those of logic is nowhere better illustrated than in the task of answering the general question what a statement is about" (1972: 241). Contra Goodman, I will claim that there is no conflict between "the demands of intuition" and "[the demands] of logic." The appearance of a conflict exists only because the semantics Goodman and Hempel assume is Fregean. This assumption is what underwrites (NG) and (PH).

Goodman presents (NG) as an indisputable truth not needing argument. Hempel offers an argument for (PH), but it fails to provide a reason to accept (PH). Hempel argues that, unless (PH) is accepted, two undesirable consequences will follow. One is that ". . . the question as to whether certain data confirm a given hypothesis would have to be answered by saying: 'That depends on which of the different equivalent formulations of the hypothesis is considered'—which appears absurd" (1965: 13). This argument equivocates. The term 'equivalent' can mean *expressing the same proposition*, and it can mean *logically equivalent*. In the first sense, the answer does, as Hempel says, appear absurd. But to legitimize this sense, Hempel needs the premise, use of which in the present context makes his argument circular, that identity of proposition is determined by logical equivalence. Without this premise, 'equivalent' means just *logically equivalent*, in which case there is nothing absurd in the answer. It is not at all absurd for a logician to say that a proof resting on a premise P establishes a particular theorem, but the proof does not establish the theorem when P is replaced with the logically equivalent premise Q and the proof is not expanded with further steps showing the logical relation between P and Q.

The other undesirable consequence, Hempel says, is that, if (PH) is not accepted, ". . . then it would be . . . sound scientific procedure to base a prediction on a given hypothesis if formulated in a sentence S_1; but [it would be] inadmissible to base the prediction . . . on an equivalent formulation S_2, because no confirming evidence for S_2 was available" (1965: 13). However, Hempel is wrong to say that it would be inadmissible to base predictions on S_2. If we do not know that S_2 is logically equivalent to S_1, it will be inadmissible, on anyone's story, to base predictions on it. But if we do know that S_2 is logically equivalent to S_1, we know that S_2 is true if S_1 is true; since we know on the basis of the evidence that S_1 is true, we know that S_2 is true. Given this, it will certainly be admissible to base predictions on S_2, even in the absence of directly confirming evidence.

The first objection to Hempel's paradox is this. The logical equivalence of (3.39a) and (3.39b) depends on their having, respectively, the logical forms $(x)(Rx \rightarrow Bx)$ and $(x)(-Bx \rightarrow -Rx)$. But, given the earlier discussion of regimentation, there are grounds for denying that it is proper to recast a simple sentence like (3.39a) as compound. Thus, I can challenge the claim that such simple sentences have those logical forms and hence that they are logically equivalent. Goodman's and Hempel's arguments are open to challenge even before the step from the logical equivalence of (3.39a) and (3.39b) to the conclusion that they are simply different formulations of the same proposition.

The second objection is that Goodman's and Hempel's paradoxes cannot be obtained without (NG) and (PH), which rest on the assumption that logically equivalent sentences express the same proposition. But with an alternative to the thick notion of propositional identity in Fregean semantics and no argument on Goodman's or Hempel's part to show that the thick notion applies in the case at hand, there is no basis for (PH) and (NG), and, hence, we are not forced to abandon our intuitions concerning aboutness and confirmation.

Our initial intuition that (3.39a) and (3.39b) are not about the same things is it-self a reason for saying that they do not express the same proposition. The sentences do not have the same presupposition: (3.39a) presupposes the existence of ravens, whereas (3.39b) presupposes the existence of non-ravens. In the former case, the statementhood of the proposition depends on the existence of ravens, whereas in the latter, the existence of red jelly beans will do.

In response to Hempel's argument that without (PH) we cannot explain why S_2 sanctions predictions in the absence of confirming evidence for it, I remarked that since S_2 is entailed by S_1 and S_1 is known to be true, S_2 is known to be true and, hence, sanctions predictions without directly confirming evidence. I will now sketch how this entailment can be captured without recasting (3.39a) and (3.39b).

Such simple sentences have a sense structure and a referential structure based on the system of referential correlates. The sense structure is that of a predicate associated with a term. The predicate may be a predicate of individuals, such as *is black*, or a predicate of collections, such as *is numerous*. The term may express an individual concept, such as *the thing that is a bearer of 'Socrates'*, or a set con-cept, such as *ravens*. The referential correlate is, roughly speaking, that any predi-cate $P(t)$ of individuals attributes the property P to an individual or to members of a collection t, and that any predicate $P'(t')$ of sets attributes the property P' to the set t'. Hence, we can say that $P'(t')$ is true in case there are members of t' and they have P' and false in case there are members of t' and they (or some of them) do not have P'.

Given this, it is possible to show that S_1 entails S_2 and that S_2 entails S_1 without recasting (3.39a) and (3.39b). Since (3.39a) and (3.39b) have a truth value, a model-theoretic interpretation with Venn diagrams shows that they have the same truth value. Since (3.39a) and (3.39b) are both true, R ≠ Ø and –B ≠ Ø. Since (3.39a) says that R∩–B = Ø, and (3.39b) says that –B∩R = Ø, it follows that if the former is true, so is the latter, and if the latter is true, so is the former.[9]

On my intensionalism, implication relations can be either logical or mereological. In the latter case, implications do not rest on deductive laws, since analytic entail-ments are automatically sanctioned on the basis of the structure of senses. Thus, both kinds of implication express a necessary connection between one proposition and another. But in the deductive case, it is the laws of logic that ensure freedom from counterexample, whereas in the non-deductive case, it is the containment of the sense of the conclusion in the sense of the premise that ensures freedom from counterexample. From my standpoint, logic is a theory of the relations among exten-sional propositions that preclude counterexamples to inferences, whereas the theory of sense is a theory about the sense relations among intensional propositions that pre-clude them.

Given this division of labor, (NG) and (PH) can be replaced with (ABT) and (CON).

(ABT)(i)   If a sense of a simple sentence has a presupposition, the sentence (on that sense) is about the objects that satisfy the presupposition. If the presupposition is not satisfied, the sentence is not about anything (on that sense).

(ii)   A simple positive existential sentence is about the objects of which it is true, and it is not about anything if it is false. A simple negative existential sentence is about the objects of which it is false if it is false, and it is not about anything if it is true.[10]

(CON)   An n-tuple of objects $O_1, \ldots, O_n$ confirms the sense of a simple sentence, $P(t_1, \ldots, t_n)$ just in case, for each object O_i, $i < n$, O_i satisfies the clause of the presupposition of the sense t_i, and $O_1, \ldots, O_n$ satisfy the predicate $P(x_1, \ldots, x_n)$.

Even though these principles are only first approximations, they make it clear that our pretheoretical intuitions concerning aboutness and confirmation can be maintained without a conflict with "the demands of logic." Goodman's and Hempel's problems are two more examples of the unnecessary dilemmas incurred when intensionalism is equated with Fregean intensionalism.

3.10. Names

3.10.1. The dilemma about names

Another such dilemma is found in connection with the contemporary debate about whether names have sense. The issue in that debate has been posed as the question whether names have a Fregean sense or have no sense at all, instead of as whether names have a sense or no sense at all. Given this way of framing the debate, philosophers face a dilemma in which choosing one of the horns sacrifices one or the other of two sets of strong intuitions about names in natural language. We may refer to them as "Fregean intuitions" and "Millian intuitions."

The principal Fregean intuition is the intuition that (3.40) is significant and, if true, provides real knowledge, while (3.41) is analytic or trifling and provides no real knowledge.

(3.40)   Hesperus is Phosphorus.

(3.41)   Hesperus is Hesperus.

To put it slightly differently, (3.40) cannot be saying what (3.41) is saying, since (3.41) is saying merely that Hesperus is self-identical. This intuition has functioned, virtually single-handedly, as the driving force of the contemporary debate about names. The debate can be epitomized, largely, as an attempt on the part of those who think names have no sense to explain the intuition away and an attempt on the part of those who think names do have sense to undermine such explanations. The literature is enormous—its very size serving in itself to underscore the strength of the intuition.

There is another Fregean intuition that seems even stronger than the intuition that (3.40) and (3.41) differ in cognitive value. It is the intuition that a sentence like (3.42):

(3.42)   Santa Claus does not exist.

is meaningful and that literal tokens of it are true. But (3.42) cannot be—compositionally—meaningful if its subject is bearerless and, as Millians claim, names have no meaning.

There has been far less debate on this Fregean intuition because, I believe, here philosophers who claim that names lack meaning have far less wiggle room. The only option for them is to say, as for example Nathan Salmon (1998) says, that a sentence like (3.42) is meaningful because the name 'Santa Claus' refers to an existent object. Santa Claus's existence is on a par with that of the Empire State Building. Since for those philosophers the meaningfulness of an expression consists in its having a referent, saying that 'Santa Claus' refers to an existent object enables them to escape having to deny the obvious fact that (3.42) is meaningful.

But, if anything, in taking this option they take an even more counterintuitive position. For one thing, they are now saying that (3.42) is false—that when we say "Yes, Virginia, there is a Santa Claus," we are, contrary to what we think, not telling a white lie. Moreover, since they cannot say—what seems to be obviously true—that the meaning of 'fictional' sanctions the inference from 'x is fictional' to 'x does not exist', what will they say the word 'fictional' means? These problems are not the worst of it. The position involves a demonstrably false assumption. It assumes that all names that are standardly taken to be bearerless are associated with a story that provides the information that makes it possible to talk sensibly about a fictional object. Thus, for a name with no story whatever associated with it, it makes no sense to say that it refers to a fictional object. One such counterexample is the name in the expression "As quick as you can say 'Jack Robinson'." Let us suppose that someone who used that expression replies to the question, "Is he the man who broke the color barrier in major league baseball?" by saying, "You're thinking of Jackie Robinson; Jack Robinson does not exist." Here, there is no story on which to base the supposition of a fictional object. The same is true in the case of many other names. The name 'John Jacob Jingleheimer Schmidt' in the children's song is another case. Still another is the name 'Dewey, Cheatem, and Howe', which the hosts of National Public Radio's show *Car Talk* use in their humorous acknowledgments.

These names cannot be dismissed as marginal cases. First, even if there were but one such case, it would be a counterexample, and, hence, would suffice to establish the falsehood of the view that sentences like (3.42) are meaningful because their subjects refer to something. Second, there is, in fact, an open set of such cases. This is because proper names can be formed by iterative compounding, such as in the case of 'Sergei Pablo Anthony Moshe Abdul Yuji Pierre Helmut Kai . . . Throckmorton'. Very many names in this set are bearerless, and surely all the names in subsets of the set in which the number of components of the names gets reasonably large are bearerless.

The Fregean intuitions do not settle the issue because there are also strong Millian intuitions that push us toward the opposite view that proper names have no sense. These are counterfactual intuitions such as the one we have about Mill's supposition that the name 'Dartmouth' would continue to denote Dartmouth even if the city were no longer to be located at the mouth of the river Dart. The most influential cases have been those presented by Wittgenstein (1953: section 79) and Kripke (1980) to show that the sense of a name does not determine its bearer in counterfactual situations. Intuitions in these cases, as in Mill's, show that the bearer of a name in another possible world need not fall under the description that we take to be the best candidate for its reference-determiner in the actual world.

If we give the neo-Millian answer, we sacrifice our semantic intuitions that names must have sense, and if we give the Fregean answer, we sacrifice our modal intuitions. Faced with this situation, philosophers have adopted the natural strategy of choosing the intuitions that seem, on balance, the strongest. The problem with this strategy is that the intuitions judged the weaker are still strong enough to remain troublesome. Thus, John Searle's rejection of Millian modal intuitions about proper names on the basis of his liberalization of Fregean descriptivism (1958) did not make those intuitions go away. Kripke's new versions of Mill's counterfactual argument (1980) showed that Searle's descriptivism is as problematic as Frege's original descriptivism. Moreover, Kripke's (1971) rejection of Fregean semantic intuitions about proper names on the basis of his Millian anti-descriptivism did not make those intuitions go away, either. They remain to haunt the neo-Millian position, as is clear from the difficulty it has explaining the meaningfulness of negative existence sentences like (3.42) and resolving the puzzle about belief Kripke formulates with his Pierre case (1988).

Since we cannot do justice to all of our intuitions, we are faced with a dilemma like the ones we encountered in connection with truth, confirmation, and aboutness. Hence, we should try the same method of resolution, namely, looking for a way to go between the horns of the dilemma.

Rejecting the assumption that sense is Fregean sense exposes a flaw in the reasoning on the part of both sides in the debate. Fregean descriptivists use the assumption to argue from (F1) to (F2):

(F1)   Fregean intuitions force us to say that names have sense.

(F2)   Hence, for every name, there is a description that determines its reference (if it has a bearer).

and Millian anti-descriptivists use it to argue from (M1) to (M2):

(M1)   Millian intuitions force us to say that there is no description that determines the reference of a name.

(M2)   Hence, names do not have sense.

Thus, once there is a non-Fregean intensionalism, Fregeans can no longer argue from the fact that names must have senses to the conclusion that they must have Fregean senses, and Millians can no longer argue from the fact that proper names do not have Fregean senses to the conclusion that proper names do not have senses. Neither the Fregean conclusion (F2) nor the Millian conclusion (M2) can be drawn from its respective premise (F1) or (M1).

Given that there is no argument for thinking that names do not have sense or that their sense is a description that determines their reference (if they have a bearer), we have found the way of going between the horns of the dilemma. Since, on (D), sense is only required to be the determiner of sense properties and relations, the senses of names are not required to be reference-fixers, which enables us to do justice to the intuitions concerning the Millian counterfactual examples. Since senses in accord with (D), thin as they are, are still senses, we can do justice to the intuitions concerning the Fregean puzzles. All that is required to solve those puzzles are senses, not thick ones. How can (3.42) be compositionally meaningful if its subject is beaerless and, as the Millians say, names have no sense? Easy: names have non-Fregean sense. A non-Fregean sense for the subject of (3.42) will allow us to say that the sentence has a compositional meaning. Is (3.40) saying only what (3.41) is saying, that Hesperus is self-identical? No; not if 'Hesperus' and 'Phosphorus' have senses and their senses are different.

So now I have to explain what my conception of a non-Fregean sense is, and why it is that when two names are different their senses are different, too. (D) tells us that what we say about the nature of the sense of a word depends on inference to the best explanation of the sense properties and relations of expressions in which the word occurs. Thus, consider (3.43a) and its contradictory (3.43b):

(3.43a)   Socrates is a bearer of 'Socrates'.

(3.43b)   Socrates is not a bearer of 'Socrates'.

The former is analytic and the latter contradictory. Here analyticity depends on the subject containing the predicate; so the name 'Socrates' ought to have a sense with the content of the metalinguistic predicate *bearer of 'Socrates'*. Only if this is so can the compositional meaning of (3.43a) be analytic and the compositional meaning of (3.43b) be contradictory.

The analyticity of (3.43a) does not depend on 'Socrates' being Socrates's name in the Athenian community in which he lived. (3.43a) is a sentence of English, and hence 'Socrates' only has to be the name of Socrates in English. The predicate *is a bearer of* is automatically satisfied in literal uses of names, since the name in such uses applies to something having the name. Thus, Kripke's objection to the metalinguistic account of names does not apply to my account. If I say "Socrates is wise," the referent of 'Socrates' does not have to have had that name in the Athenian community, but, of course, as the truth of 'Socrates is wise' shows, the referent of 'Socrates' is a bearer of the name 'Socrates' in the English-speaking community to which I and my audience belong.

Something like this explanation of the analyticity of (3.43a) was William Kneale's motivation for proposing that the sense of a name is metalinguistic (1962). His account of the sense of 'Socrates' was *the individual called 'Socrates'*. However, this account adds the further condition that the bearer of 'Socrates' be called by that name (presumably by his compatriots). Working within the Fregean framework, Kneale required such a further condition to ensure that the sense of 'Socrates' would determine its bearer. But this quite small addition was enough to open Kneale's proposal up to Kripke's objection that "it is dubious that the Greeks *did* call him 'Socrates'"

(1980: 69) (and even if the Greeks did call him 'Socrates', there are possible worlds in which they did not). Kripke's objection is effective against Kneale's particular implementation of the metalinguistic idea, but it does not address the general idea that the sense of a name is metalinguistic or the idea that the motivation for such a sense can come from the trifling character of sentences like (3.42).

The moral is obvious. A metalinguistic theory of names, unlike Kneale's, must be a *pure* metalinguistic description theory in the sense that no predicate other than *bearer of 'N'* occurs in the sense of '*N*'. Thus, my theory is that the sense of a name '*N*' is an instance of the schema (3.44):

(3.44)   the thing that is a bearer of '*N*'.

where bearing is the relation that something has to a name '*N*' when its name is '*N*'. Since the senses of names have no content beyond what they have as instances of (3.44), they contain nothing that could make them vulnerable to the counterfactual counterexamples Kripke uses against Kneale's theory.

My theory also avoids Kripke's "main reason" for rejecting Kneale's proposal, namely, that it is circular: "Taking [such an account as genuinely trifling] it seems to be no theory of reference at all. We ask, 'To whom does he refer by "Socrates"?' And then the answer is given, 'Well, he refers to the man to whom he refers'. If this were all there was to the meaning of a proper name, then no reference would get off the ground at all" (1980: 70). This consideration cannot be directed at an account of names within my new intensionalism because it is not intended to explain how reference is fixed. Since Kripke's circularity criticism depends on a theory of meaning's being put forth as a theory of reference, it is only a criticism of theories of meaning within Fregean intensionalism.

The indefinite article in (3.44) represents the possibility that a name can have multiple bearers. The name 'John Smith' is the name of each John Smith. The definite article in (3.44) expresses the condition that the referent in a literal use of a name must be exactly one of its bearers. Together the indefinite and definite aspects of names present speakers with the problem of ensuring that the referent of their use of a name is contextually definite. The problem may be solved automatically because the context itself makes the use of the name definite. If not, the speaker has to provide descriptions that discriminate between the intended bearer and the other bearers. Since such descriptions fix the reference of a name-token just for the one context, they have no implications for other tokens of the name-type in other contexts, and hence cannot give rise to counterfactual counterexamples.

(3.44) does justice to Fregean intuitions because, even though such senses lack the content to fix reference, they do have metalinguistic content. This is all that is required to do justice to Fregean intuitions, since, if names have metalinguistic senses in the manner of (3.44), then whenever two names are different, their senses are different, too.[11] Consider the intuition that (3.40a) and (3.40b) differ in cognitive significance. Since, on (3.44), the sense of the name 'Hesperus' is *the thing that is a bearer of 'Hesperus'* and the sense of the name 'Phosphorus' is *the thing that is a bearer of 'Phosphorus'*, we automatically explain the intuition that (3.40a) is significant, and, if true, provides real knowledge, whereas (3.40b) is trifling and provides no real knowledge.

Further, as I have argued elsewhere (Katz 1994; 2001), (3.44) solves Kripke's Pierre problem (1988). Since the sense of a name contains a representation of the name, the sense of the subject of the sentence expressing the belief that Pierre acquired in Paris is *the thing that is a bearer of 'Londres'* and the sense of the subject of the sentence expressing the belief that he subsequently acquired in London is *the thing that is a bearer of 'London'*. Since Pierre's beliefs are, therefore, that the thing that is a bearer of 'Londres' is pretty and that the thing that is a bearer of 'London' is not pretty, there is no inconsistency, and no threat to Pierre's rationality.

As indicated above, this Pure Metalinguistic Theory of proper names also does justice to the Millian intuitions. This is because, in accordance with (D), the senses of names are not required to fix their reference, and, in accordance with (3.44), they are too thin to be vulnerable to Millian counterexamples. Moreover, the problem that Millians have with sentences like (3.42)—that their subjects have neither sense nor reference to contribute to their compositional meaning—does not arise for us because, thin as they are, instances of (3.44) are still senses.

Neo-Millians have made much of the fact that something's having the name that it has is one of its contingent properties: Socrates, for example, might not have been named 'Socrates'. This fact, they claim, rules out metalinguistic theories of names, because it implies that (3.43a) is not analytic and that (3.43b) is not contradictory. But, on my new intensionalism, this fact alone does not rule out such theories. That Socrates might not have been a bearer of 'Socrates' does not imply that (3.43a) is not analytic or that (3.43b) is not contradictory. Without the further assumption that analyticity and contradiction are defined in the Fregean way, these implications fail.

First, on my new intensionalism, analyticity is the purely mereological property explicated in (A). Second, when the containing term of an analytic sentence is a proper name, it is used referentially, and hence, as explained in the second part of this book, the referential correlate of the sense of the sentence is security against falsehood—not necessary truth or weakly necessary truth. Hence, my new intensionalism does not claim that (3.43a) expresses even a weakly necessary truth, but only that it is secured against falsehood. Literal tokens of (3.43a) make a true statement, since the object picked out as the bearer of 'Socrates' is a bearer of 'Socrates', even though he might not have been. This is the case in spite of the fact that the statement these tokens make—that the object in question bears the name 'Socrates'—is not a weakly necessary truth, since there are satisfier worlds in which Socrates does not bear the name 'Socrates'. (For further discussion, see Armour-Garb and Katz 1998 and Katz 2001. Thanks to David Pitt for helping me to work this out.)

To recap: Fregean definitions of sense and analyticity automatically commit intensionalism to saying that literal uses of analytic sentences express necessary truths or weakly necessary truths. This puts the claim of a metalinguistic description theory that there are analytic sentences that turn on the meaning of the names in them in conflict with the fact that bearer relations are contingent. But my new intensionalism's

definitions of sense and analyticity provide the option of having a referential correlate for analyticity that makes this claim consistent with the contingency of bearer
relations.

Let us now return to the dilemma about names with which we began. Choosing the Fregean solution sacrifices our intuitions about the reference of names in
counterfactual situations, while choosing the Millian solution sacrifices our intuitions about Fregean puzzles. I have argued that, as with the other dilemmas I have
considered, this one too rests on the assumption that intensionalism is Fregean
intensionalism, and hence that dropping the assumption enables us to go between
the horns and do justice to all of our intuitions. Since a theory that preserves all
our intuitions is preferable to a theory that preserves some and sacrifices others,
again, I contend that Fregean semantics has kept us from having the preferable
theory.

3.10.2. Names and rigid designation

One of the most influential theses in contemporary philosophy is Kripke's claim
that "proper names are rigid designators," where "something [is] a *rigid designa-
tor* if in every possible world it designates the same object" (1980: 49). Kripke
justifies this statement by saying that "although the man (Nixon) might not have
been the president, it is not the case that he might not have been Nixon." There is
surely no disagreeing here. Nixon had to be Nixon. But the thesis that proper names
are rigid designators goes beyond this modal truth, insofar as it constitutes a thesis
about names in the language while the truth confines itself to *de re* possibility.
Hence, there is room to drive a wedge between the two formulations, which are
usually taken to amount to much the same thing. The wedge is the fact of multiple
bearerhood.

I take it that the discussion on multiple bearerhood in 3.10.1 (and at much greater
length in Katz 2001) has shown that names in natural language have multiple bearers. To see how the wedge is inserted, I ask, to what are we referring when we are
talking about proper names in the thesis that names are rigid designators? There are
two possibilities. One is that we are referring to types—abstract objects. The other is
that we are referring to tokens—concrete occurrences of utterances or inscriptions.

It is easy to see that the thesis makes no sense if we take proper names to be
types, and this is for two reasons. The first reason is that proper names are definite,
requiring reference to a particular bearer of the name to the exclusion of the others.
Such exclusion requires contextual information that has no status at the abstract level
of word types. The second reason is that if we decide to try to avoid definiteness by
simply assigning to a name in a possible world a reference consisting of all and only
its bearers, there will be no rigidity, since the name will have radically different sets
of bearers in different possible worlds.

If, then, the thesis that names are rigid designators is to be formulatable, the term
'proper names' must refer to proper name tokens, particular and concrete utterances
or inscriptions. But if the general thesis is about proper name tokens it is surely false.

Very many name tokens designate nothing, as the earlier examples 'Jack Robinson' and 'John Jacob Jingleheimer Schmidt' show. Similarly, the names in common popular love songs have no reference. This is also true for the occurrences of names in copies of books with titles like *What to Name the Baby*.

An interesting example of how rigidity fails in the case of natural language, where multiple bearerhood is the rule, is the following. Someone sets up a lottery so that his brother-in-law, Hubert Jones, will win. He calls the name 'Hubert Jones' and, sure enough, the brother-in-law, who meets the condition for winning that he be present at the drawing, wins the rigged lottery. But there are other possible worlds in which the brother-in-law missed his train and another Hubert Jones was present at the lottery. In those worlds, the reference is different from the reference to the brother-in-law in the actual world. The range of examples makes it clear that multiple bearerhood defeats the general claim that name tokens are rigid designators.

It is nevertheless the case that when Kripke says that "for although the man (Nixon) might not have been president, it is not the case that he might not have been Nixon," what he is saying is that the self-same Nixon, who might not have been president, could not but be Nixon. But this is a fact about how we as speakers use the token of 'Nixon' in the particular circumstances in question. It is not in virtue of the use's being the use of a name token but of our establishing an intention to refer to the self-same individual in every possible world.

Thus, identities like 'Aristotle is Aristotle', as tokens, are incomplete without further information about communicative intention. There is, therefore, no way to assign them a referential interpretation under which they come out as necessary truths. Why shouldn't such an incomplete identity express a false claim about a great philosopher and some other bearer of the same name (as Searle once suggested)?

The conclusion I draw is that the thesis that proper names in natural language are rigid designators is mistaken. This is not to say that the phenomenon of rigid designation is not a real one, but it is to say that it is not a feature of names; rather, it is essentially a feature of how speakers use words.

Nor is it to say that names in artificial languages, such as Kripke's language for quantified modal logic, cannot be taken as rigid designators. Such artificial languages belong to the Fregean tradition of attempting to construct a logically perfect language within which to formulate principles of logic. The concern in such systems is with a consistent and revealing account of a class of logical inferences. The only condition on linguistic rules in such systems is that they meet this constraint.

There is no independent question in such systems of whether linguistic rules comport with the facts of a language because the artificial language is whatever its linguistic rules say it is. In natural language, however, things are otherwise. In natural language, there are independent linguistic facts that our rules have to square with. It is this further constraint that is ignored when philosophers directly transport constructions from artificial languages into their account of natural language. It is an aspect of what Wittgenstein referred to as "subliming our language."

3.11. The natural kind term dilemma and the epistemology of semantics

The assumption that intensionalism is Fregean intensionalism creates a dilemma about natural kind terms. Like the other dilemmas discussed thus far, this one also forces us to sacrifice one or the other of a set of strong intuitions. In the first subsection below, I will examine this dilemma. In the next, I will look at related questions concerning the epistemology of semantic knowledge.

3.11.1. The dilemma

Putnam once put forth the modal intuition that "[i]t might not be the case that all cats are animals; they might be automata" (1975b: 238). On the basis of this intuition, he argued that sentences like (2.1),

(2.1)   Cats are animals.

even if they are analytic in *some* sense, are not necessary in the absolute Leibnizian sense. Putnam's own view of the matter was that such sentences are only *more or less* necessary, depending on the role their subject terms play in scientific laws and theories.

Donnellan once put forth the following linguistic intuition: ". . . if one knows what cats are and what animals are, I believe he must see that cats are animals. If a child seriously asks us whether cats are animals, I think he automatically raises doubt about his understanding of the two words 'cat' and 'animal'" (1962: 653). Adding "Another truth in the same category is: Blue is a color," Donnellan made it clear that his is a general point, not one dependent on the particular example (2.1).

Donnellan's intuition might be fleshed out in something like the following way. One cannot grasp the meaning of 'blue' without grasping its internal relation to the superordinate concept *color* because the relation is constitutive of the meaning of 'blue'. Hence, it makes no sense to suppose that we can somehow subtract the superordinate concept *color* from the meaning of 'blue' and still have that meaning. Hence, someone with no grasp of this internal relation does not understand the word 'blue'. Since 'cat' is related to 'animal' in the same way that 'blue' is related to 'color', someone with no grasp of the internal relation does not understand the word 'cat'. Thus, (2.1) is analytic, and hence, we can infer that what is not an animal, such as Putnam's cat-simulating robots, is not a cat. On the basis of his linguistic intuitions, Donnellan argued that such sentences express necessary truths in the absolute Leibnizian sense.

Faced with this apparent conflict between modal intuitions and linguistic intuitions, philosophers have followed the same strategy they followed in the previous dilemmas of choosing the set of intuitions that seemed to them to be the strongest. As in the previous dilemmas, this strategy does not satisfactorily resolve the conflict, because, again, the intuitions in the other set do not go away. Most philosophers have chosen to side with the modal intuitions, especially as beefed up by

Putnam's elaborations of them with various other natural kind terms and various other scenarios, for example, the Twin Earth case. But the pull of Donnellan-style linguistic intuitions should still be felt—if not in cases like (2.1), then at least in cases like 'Blue is a color' and 'Squares are rectangles'. From the perspective of Donnellan's general point, Putnam's claim that analytic truths are not necessary in the Leibnizian sense—a claim, we should note, that he does not weaken to a claim about only natural kind cases—is a hasty generalization. Even if we concede such, perhaps bad, examples of analytic truth as (2.1), there are still good examples, like 'Blue is a color' and 'Squares are rectangles'.

The strategy of going between the horns taken in the previous dilemmas is plausible here, too. I suggest that the cause of the dilemma in the present case is also that the reasoning from intuition to dilemma is unsound because the arguments on both sides depend on the Fregean notions of sense and analyticity. Once the dependency is exhibited, we can show how to preserve both our modal intuitions and our linguistic intuitions.

Donnellan's argument from linguistic intuitions about how we understand words like 'cat' and 'animal' to the conclusion that an analytic sentence like (2.1) is necessarily true assumes Fregean analyticity. Given that intuition tells us that 'cat' and 'feline animal' are synonymous, Donnellan still requires that notion of analyticity to get the further conclusion that (2.1) is necessarily true. Only on the assumption that analyticity is Fregean analyticity can he say that the analyticity of (2.1) is a matter of putting 'cat' for its synonym 'feline animal' in the logical *truth* 'All feline animals are animals', and hence necessarily true.

The assumption that sense determines reference is particularly evident in Putnam's reasoning. His conclusion that (2.1) is only *more or less* analytic, and not necessarily true, depends on assuming Fregean senses. The conclusion does not follow just from the modal intuition that the referents of our uses of 'cat' might have been, not cats, but automata. That intuition remains intact on a scenario in which there are no cats, and cat-simulating automata were referred to under the false description 'feline animal'. Putnam's conclusion requires the further premise that we continue to use 'cat' to refer to automata *with no change of Fregean sense*. For if we continue to use 'cat' to refer to the same things but with a change of meaning—e.g., from *feline animal* to *cat-simulating automaton*, then (2.1) can express a necessary truth.

Putnam's "own feeling," as he puts it, is that "to say that cats turned out not to be animals is to keep the meaning of both words unchanged" (1975b: 239). Now, he does not give an argument to show that this is the case. But the only way for him to establish the required premise that 'cat' continues to refer to automata without a change of sense is to assume that senses are Fregean senses—functions from worlds to referents—since, on Putnam's counterfactual scenario that cats have always been Martian robots, the continued use of 'cat' to refer to automata would involve no change of sense.

Instead of trying to defend his feeling, Putnam claims that "[t]oday it doesn't seem to make much difference what we say," since there is no "developed linguistic theory" to determine which decision about what to say is correct. We might wonder here why Putnam should think that absence of a developed linguistic theory at present means that it makes no difference what we say. It made a difference what the ancients said about matter even though there was no developed theory of matter at the time. Things that some of them said were true and things that others of them said were false. Be this as it may, Putnam's real point is that a developed linguistic theory, if and when we have one, will make no difference either. This, as Putnam says, is because ". . . then 'meaning' will itself have become a technical term, and presumably our question now is not which decision is changing the meaning in some future technical sense of 'meaning', but what we can say in our present language" (1975b: 239).

This is a non sequitur. True enough, a developed linguistic theory will have a technical notion of meaning; but if that theory is a good theory of "our present language," its technical—or theoretical—notion of meaning cannot be irrelevant to the question of which decision is changing the meaning of 'cat'. This point is obscured by Putnam's talk about "some future technical sense of 'meaning'"—as if a developed linguistic theory would impose one or another technical sense of the term quite arbitrarily. On the contrary, the technical concept of meaning in the theory will be an explication of meaning in the pretheoretical sense, in the same sense in which the linguist's technical concept of a sentence is an explication of sentencehood in the pretheoretical sense. As such, the linguist's technical notion of meaning will be chosen on the principled basis of its ability to provide the best explanation of sense structure in the language. Hence, Putnam is mistaken to dismiss "some future technical sense of 'meaning'" as irrelevant to the issue. He might as well argue that decisions about what consequences to draw from a set of premises that arose before there was a developed logical theory cannot be settled on the basis of the technical sense of logical consequence in the logical theory we have now.

The assumption that senses are Fregean comes to play an explicit role in Putnam's arguments when he moves from criticizing the traditional concept of analyticity to criticizing the traditional theory of meaning (1973a; 1973b; 1975a; 1975c). The criticism that knowledge of meaning is not in the head, which is based on a modal intuition about the Twin Earth example, is typical of these later arguments. Grant that references to XYZ are not references to water because, even though that substance exemplifies what Putnam calls the phenomenal concept expressed by our word 'water', XYZ is not H_2O. Grant also, as Putnam claims, that this shows that (I) and (II) cannot both be true.

> (I)   Knowledge of the meaning of a term is just a matter of being in a certain psychological state.

> (II)   The meaning of a term (in the sense of its intension) determines its extension (in the sense that sameness of intension determines sameness of extension).

Even so, unless we also grant (II), Putnam cannot conclude that (I) is false. Of course, Frege's and Carnap's intensionalism, against which the Twin Earth argument was in part directed, accepts (II). But once there is an intensionalism that rejects (II), Putnam's argument is unsound. There is no more reason to argue from –((I) & (II)) and (II) to –(I) than there is to argue from –((I) & (II)) and (I) to –(II). As I argued in the second part of this book, this difficulty is found in all of Putnam's and Kripke's reasoning from modal intuitions about the reference of natural kind terms.

In the natural kind dilemma as well, blocking such reasoning removes the pressure to sacrifice our modal or linguistic intuitions. To be sure, Putnam and Kripke might be right that the nature of kinds determines the reference of natural kind terms. But this does not entail what it has been assumed it entails, that the senses of natural kind terms are incomplete accounts of their meanings. It would be incomplete if completeness were a matter of the sense of a term having the content to determine its reference. But this sort of completeness is no longer obligatory. Completeness can be a matter of the sense of a term having the content to explain its sense properties and relations. For example, the meaning of 'blue' is incomplete only if it fails to explain such things as the redundancy of 'a blue coat that is not colorless', the analyticity of 'Blue is a color', the ambiguity of 'blue movie frames', the synonymy of the English 'blue' and the French 'bleu', the antonymy of 'blue' and 'red', and so on.

Hence, the analyticity of (2.1) depends on whether or not the sense properties and relations of 'cat' remain the same after we discover that the referents of our applications of it have been automata. The question whether or not the reference remains the same is beside the point. As we noted, the sense of 'cat' can remain the same even though its extension changes—from a set of automata to the null set—after the discovery.

Since the domain of sense is independent of the domain of reference, the modal intuitions and the linguistic intuitions are about different things. The former are about what determines the *reference* of terms, while the latter are about what determines their *sense*. Moreover, as I argued in section 2.4.1, the Fregean notion of the extension of a term must be rejected because it entails the false claim that what determines the sense properties and relations of expressions also determines their reference. *This* is precisely what examples like Putnam's own Twin Earth case show to be false. As I also argued in section 2.4.1, what determines sense properties and relations in the case of a non-natural kind term like 'bachelor' does determine its reference. The moral is clear. This difference among types of words requires a flexible definition of 'the extension of a term' on which falling under the sense of a term is the referential condition for some kinds of terms but not others.

This moral is in itself a serious problem for Fregean intensionalism, since it is unable to state such a flexible definition. On Fregean intensionalism, all senses, by definition, automatically determine the reference of the terms of which they are the senses. Alternatively, (D) makes it possible to formulate the flexible definition (C3). With (C3), our modal intuitions and linguistic intuitions cannot conflict, and, hence, we no longer have to choose between them.

3.11.2. Burge's argument for externalism

Externalism has implications for issues in areas other than philosophical semantics. In epistemology, it threatens the rationalist view of knowledge. If Putnam's and Kripke's arguments for semantic externalism were sound, it could be argued that knowledge of the senses of natural kind terms would rest on experience, and hence

such knowledge could not be *a priori*.[12] Rationalism would lose out in an area traditionally important for its proponents. But if I am right that Putnam's and Kripke's
arguments depend on assuming that senses are Fregean, then no challenge to rationalism in this area could arise.

In the present connection, the significance of Tyler Burge's argument for externalism is that it does not assume that senses are Fregean. This means that Burge's
argument breathes new life into the challenge. Furthermore, Burge's argument for
externalism applies to a far wider range of vocabulary, so the challenge does not rest
on the special class of natural kind terms. Hence, Burge's argument constitutes an
independent and, in terms of scope, broader threat to a rationalist account of semantic knowledge.

Burge argues (1979b: 77–79) that the meanings of terms reflect the social envi-
ronment of language users. He argues for this conclusion on the basis of thought
experiments, of which the following is the most celebrated. Burge asks us to consider two cases in which a man thinks that he has arthritis in his thigh and reports
what he thinks about his medical condition to his doctor. In one case, the disease has
been defined as a painful inflammation of the joints in the language community,
and, in the other, the disease has not been so defined. Burge construes the former
as a case in which the patient has the false belief that he has arthritis in his thigh;
he construes the latter as a case in which the patient has no arthritis-belief at all.
The difference in the cases on Burge's construals reflects the difference in the social environments. Hence, the meaning of the term is externally determined.

In an earlier discussion, I argued (1990: 230–232) that Burge's thought experi-
ment is unconvincing because his construal of the former case is open to question on
the grounds that there is an alternative construal that is at least as plausible. Burge
supposes that the patient's belief contains the full dictionary concept of arthritis; but
why can't we suppose rather that the belief contains only a part of the dictionary
concept? Such a supposition is one we make quite confidently in similar cases. For
example, we make it in the case of the very young child who calls all adult males
"Daddy." The cases are similar in that the patient and the very young child can be
expected not to have a complete concept, the former because of medical ignorance
and the latter because of linguistic immaturity. Thus, we can say that the patient's
belief contains only part of the dictionary concept of arthritis, leaving out the restriction to inflammation of the joints, in much the way that the child's belief expressed
by 'daddy is home' leaves out the restriction to the adult male who is its parent. The
child's belief is only an adult-male-belief, and, similarly, the patient's belief is only
a painful-inflammation-belief.

Burge would no doubt defend his construal of the patient's belief as based on
the view that our interpretive practices do not revise an ascription of beliefs based on
the meaning of a word in the language when we learn that the speakers themselves
do not fully understand it. I find this view dubious. We would certainly revise our
view that the Smiths' very young child is expressing the belief that its father is home
when it says "Daddy is home" if we discover that it says the same thing when the
television repairman, the milkman, the plumber, or a traveling salesman comes to

the door. Our interpretive practice here is to say that the Smiths' child has not yet acquired a complete grasp of the sense of 'daddy'.

Fodor (1982) and Pitt (in preparation) have argued more generally that Burge's construal of the case is blocked by pragmatic principles for interpreting utterances. Fodor says that the principle of charity, which "operates to prohibit accusing one's fellows of inconsistency in [a] flagrant and inflammatory way" (1982: 108), tells against Burge's construal. If we take the patient's belief to contain that concept of arthritis, then we have to say that the patient's statement to the doctor is a flat contradiction. The statement would be that the patient has a condition in his thigh that cannot, as a matter of definition, occur in the thigh. If, as seems clearly to be so, our interpretive practice rests on some such principle of charity, Fodor's observation is a good *prima facie* reason for thinking that Burge's patient lacks the full dictionary concept of arthritis.

That principle prevents us from construing someone's statement as a flat contradiction unless the circumstances are so special that we are left with no alternative to adopting this most uncharitable interpretation. For example, theologians like Tertullian, Kierkegaard, and Luther, who explicitly put theology above logic, sometimes give us no choice but to construe certain of their statements as flat contradictions (Luther said, "Whoever wants to be a Christian should tear the eyes out of his reason"). But no such special circumstances obtain in the case of Burge's patient. In fact, the circumstances are special in a way that works against Burge's construal. Since the patient is medically uneducated and is making the sort of mistake that can easily occur among such people, it seems uncharitable in the extreme for us to convict him of contradiction. Hence, rather than supporting Burge's construal of the patient's statement, our practice of interpreting speech undermines it.

A fully convincing argument against Burge's externalism would combine our semantic point that the patient has only part of the concept *arthritis* with Fodor's point about the principle of charity to block Burge's construal. Both points are essential. Without the former, we have no way of arguing against Burge's interpretation on the grounds that standard interpretation precludes us from construing the patient's statement as asserting that he has a condition in his thigh that cannot occur in the thigh. Without the latter, we have no way of understanding the patient's statement as involving a consistent use of 'arthritis'. Pitt (in preparation) has given such an argument.

Fodor, however, cannot combine his objection to Burge with my construal because, as we have seen, he rejects decompositionality. Since this rejection is a central principle of his semantics, he cannot say that the sense of the lexical item 'arthritis' can be factored into the concepts *painful*, *inflammation*, and *located in a joint*. His position is that the senses of lexical items are invariably atomic. So, unless Fodor wants to say that the patient's utterance is meaningless, which presumably he would not, he has to say that the patient's utterance is meaningful in virtue of expressing this atomic property. But this means that Fodor ought to take the Burgean position against which he has made such a forceful pragmatic objection.

Before concluding this discussion of externalism, I ought to take account of some benefits of a defense against it that go beyond the issue of whether knowledge of

meaning in natural language is *a priori*. I will briefly discuss two other general philosophical concerns that are threatened by arguments for externalism.

One is the concern to preserve first-person privileged access—the direct access
we have to many of our own mental states. It is argued that externalism makes such
privileged access problematic.[13] Since externalism says that the content of our intentional state attributions is wide, knowledge of our own mental states must be based
in part on information from the external world. Hence, our access to such mental
states must in part be as indirect as, and on a par with, the access other persons have
to them. If you are on either Earth or Twin Earth but do not know which, you will
not know whether your thoughts about the stuff you are drinking are water-thoughts
or twater-thoughts. You have to investigate the external world to see if the stuff you
are thinking about is H_2O or XYZ. But then your knowledge of your own thoughts is
based on evidence from the external world, and, hence, is indirect.

The other concern is that thoughts construed on the basis of wide content are
otiose in causal accounts of behavior. Since the causes of behavior are events in the
central nervous system that produce muscular contractions and glandular secretions,
the conditions in the external world that are represented in the wide content of thoughts
(and other intentional state attributions) can play no role in the causation of behavior. Since people on Earth and their molecule-for-molecule duplicates on Twin Earth
have the very same psychological make-up, the causal conditions for their behavior
in the same situations are the same. The problem that externalism raises is, therefore, that it demands a psychology that explains intentional state attributions on the
basis of wide content, whereas such explanations are an unnecessary complication
for psychological theory, since the explanation of behavior requires no more than
narrow content.[14]

If, as I have argued, Putnam's, Kripke's, and Burge's arguments for externalism
are inadequate, accounting for semantic knowledge does not present my intensionalism
with a problem about privileged access. No such problem arises for it. If we understand
the content of intentional state attributions in terms of the intensional propositions in
the sense of my autonomous theory of sense, where the content of such propositions is
exclusively a matter of grammatical structure, then there is no conflict between the
semantics of such attributions and the fact that we have first-person direct access to
many of our mental states. Also, my account of semantic knowledge does not face
the problem of explaining how properties that play no causal role in behavior can
nonetheless turn out to figure in psychological theory. There is no problem of justi-
fying causally inert mental states with wide content because there are no mental states
with wide content.

3.11.3. Rationalist semantics

There is another argument against a rationalist view of semantic knowledge that has
been kicking around for some time. It, like Burge's, does not rest on the principle
that sense determines reference. This is Gilbert Harman's argument against the idea
that analyticity is a basis for *a priori* semantic truth: ". . . what is to prevent us from
saying that the truth expressed by 'Copper is copper' depends in part on a general

feature of the way the world is, namely, that everything is self-identical?" (1967: 128). The argument is that if the truth of even an analytic sentence like 'Copper is copper' depends on the way the world is, then our knowledge of truth is never independent of experience.

Of course, on my autonomous theory of sense, meaning *per se* cannot guarantee truth: analyticity is not truth by virtue of meaning. Furthermore, in an example like Harman's involving natural kind terms, my intensionalism does not say that knowledge of their truth is *a priori*. Still, there is a need to answer Harman's argument. For, on my account of the relation between sense and reference, knowledge of the truth of a wide variety of other analytic sentences is *a priori* knowledge of weakly necessary truth. Since presumably Harman would offer the same argument in the case of any analytic sentence of the form $a=a$, his claim that such statements are *a posteriori* truths is inconsistent with my position.

Harman's claim is based on two contentions: first, that the truth of so-called analytic sentences depends upon "a general feature of the way the world is," and second, the (implicit) contention that the way the world is is something that can only be known on the basis of *a posteriori* information. There are various difficulties with this basis for claiming that analytic truth is not *a priori* truth. One is that Harman's argument assumes that our knowledge of the logical law that everything is self-identical is *a posteriori* knowledge. This begs the question against rationalists, who hold that knowledge of logical laws is *a priori*. Of course, Quineans and others have taken an empiricist view of logic; but that is beside the point here. Harman is not arguing that the statement 'Copper is copper' is an *a posteriori* truth because Quine is right.

Another difficulty is that it is not the truth of analytic sentences that needs to be explained, but their necessary (or weakly necessary) truth. Hence, we are not concerned just with the way the world is, as Harman says, but with the way all possible worlds are (or at least the way all satisfier worlds are). Accordingly, the "general feature" in question is not that everything in the actual world is self-identical, but rather that everything *in every possible world* is self-identical. That *that* is the case, however, is not plausibly taken to be an empirical matter, since we cannot have knowledge about how things stand with the sentence in question in all possible worlds on the basis of *a posteriori* information about how they stand in the actual world. Again, Quinean doctrines—in this case, Quine's views on necessity—are not available to Harman here, since presumably he is attempting to provide an independent argument for empiricism.

I now want to explain how analytic statements that are weakly necessary can be known to be such *a priori* without taking them to be instances of logical laws. This explanation requires showing that knowledge of the analyticity of sentences is *a priori* knowledge and that knowledge of the referential principle that connects analyticity to necessity in these cases is also *a priori*. Showing this is showing that the analyticity of statements is independent of the way things change across possible worlds, in the sense that whatever the facts are in a possible world, if the statement has a truth value, it is true. This is because, however things are in a possible world, the truth conditions of the proposition are contained in the referential conditions of its terms so that the referents of those terms must satisfy those truth conditions. As explained in section 2.4, we know *a priori* the inclusion relation between the truth conditions and the referential conditions of terms, and we also know *a priori* that weak necessary truth is a referential correlate of analyticity in the cases under consideration. Since no *a posteriori* information about a satisfier world is required for us to know whether an analytic statement is true in it, we know *a priori* that the sentence is a weakly necessary truth.

The rationale for claiming that knowledge of sense structure, and of analyticity in particular, is *a priori* is based on the methodology for acquiring knowledge of sense structure. According to this methodology, we infer sense structure from our knowledge of sense properties and relations of expressions. This knowledge is based on the facts we obtain from linguistic intuition. For example, linguistic intuition tells us that the sentence 'Sherlock Holmes loves his mother' is meaningful, that the sentence 'The number seventeen loves its mother' is not, that the sentence 'Sherlock Holmes dusted the table' is ambiguous, that the expressions 'sister' and 'female sibling' are synonymous, that the words 'open' and 'closed' are antonymous, that the expression 'unmarried bachelor' is redundant, that the sentence 'Squares are rectangles' is analytic, and that the sentence 'Squares are circles' is contradictory.[15]

Further, knowledge from such intuitions is *a priori*. Linguistic intuition is not sense perception or introspection, and the information it provides is not empirical evidence from the observation of concrete utterances or inscriptions. Like the mathematical intuition that four is composite, the intuition that 'Sherlock Holmes dusted the table' is ambiguous is an immediate grasp of a structural fact about a sentence-type—that is, an abstract object. It is not a fact about a sentence-token, as can be seen from the fact that, generally speaking, tokens of the type unambiguously mean either that Holmes put dust on the table (e.g., to detect fingerprints) or that he removed dust from the table (e.g., to clean up his rooms). (See Katz 1998: 160–163 for a discussion of tokens.)

It does not matter that many cases will not be clear enough for us to decide them on the basis of linguistic intuition, since knowledge of them can be obtained from the principles that provide a rational systematization of the facts obtained from intuitions about clear cases. That is, we can infer sense properties and relations in unclear cases from the laws and theories constructed on the basis of the use of reason to systematize the clear cases. Since the construction of such laws and theories is entirely a matter of *a priori* reasoning, we can have *a priori* knowledge of the senses of sentences, and since analyticity is simply a particular kind of sense structure, we can have *a priori* knowledge of which sentences are analytic.

Suppose we know *a priori* that a particular sentence *s* is analytic in the sense of (A). Given our sharp sense/reference distinction, this, by itself, tells us nothing about the referential status of *s* or about the referential status of literal uses of its tokens. The conclusion to draw from this limitation, however, is not that knowledge of the referential status of *s* is *a posteriori*, but that it cannot be *purely* grammatical knowledge. Knowledge of the referential status of analytic sentences and their literal tokens can be wholly *a priori*, but it has to be partly extragrammatical.

We can show that such knowledge is *a priori* if we can establish *a priori* that the referential correlate for the cases of analyticity in question is weakly necessary truth.

Establishing this is, in effect, establishing the correlate (RC4). Here, then, is an *a priori* argument that connects analyticity in the cases in question to weakly necessary truth. Consider an arbitrary sentence, *s*, with a sense *P* that is analytic in the sense of (A) and that contains no inconsistent term. In determining weakly necessary truth, the worlds with which we are concerned are all and only the satisfier worlds for *P*. Since the extension of all terms T_i of *P* is non-empty in all the satisfier worlds for *P* and *P*'s terms are all consistent, *P* has a truth value in them. Since the sense *P* contains a term T_n that has the entire sense content of *P*, and, hence, the conditions for T_n having a non-empty extension include the truth conditions of *P*, it follows that *P* is true in all of its satisfier worlds. Thus, by (WNT), *P* is a weakly necessary truth. Since this argument is based on reason alone, we have *a priori* knowledge that analytic propositions in the cases in question are weakly necessary truths.

3.12. Fregean sense in the philosophy of mathematics

The equation of intensionalism with Fregean intensionalism has restricted debate not only in the philosophy of language and logic, but also in areas more removed from semantics. In section 3.9, I presented an example from the philosophy of science. In this section, I shall present two examples from the philosophy of mathematics.

3.12.1. Are number predicates second-order?

As is well known, Frege (1953) construed number predications as second-level predications about first-level concepts. To say that there is no round square is to say that the concept *round square* has no instances; to say that there is one God is to say that the concept *God* has one instance; and to say that there are two dancers in a tango is to say that instances of the concept *dancers in a tango* are pairs of dancers. This construal seems to conflict with our ordinary reflections about number predications. For example, when we say "It takes two to tango," we take ourselves to be specifying how many dancers it takes to tango. Given the truth of this specification together with the fact that there is but one team of tango dancers on the floor of the ballroom, we can infer that the dancers on the floor are two in number. This is a conclusion about the people on the dance floor. It says nothing about concepts. Moreover, numerically distinguishing the dancers in a tango from those in square dances or ballet solos is distinguishing one multiplicity from another in terms of size—not, as Frege would have it, distinguishing one concept from another in terms of number of instances.

Despite the intuitive plausibility of these ordinary reflections, Frege will argue that his view about number predications is the right one, on the grounds that there is nothing at the first level—for example, the level at which the dancers are doing the tango—to serve as the object of the predication. There is only each dancer him- or herself, the set of them, and the mereological sum of them, all of which are one. Frege thinks that we mistakenly treat numerical predications in the same manner as, for example, color predications:

Is it not in totally different senses that we speak of a tree as having 1000 leaves and again as having green leaves? The green color we ascribe to each single leaf, but not the number 1000. If we call all the leaves of a tree taken together its foliage, then the foliage too is green, but it is not 1000. To what then does the property 1000 really belong? It almost looks as though it belongs neither to any single one of the leaves nor to the totality of them all; is it possible that it does not really belong to things in the external world at all? (1953: 28)

This, of course, is a rhetorical question. Frege thinks that numerical properties cannot belong to things in the external world in the manner of colors, so we are forced to make a semantic ascent to the concepts under which objects at the first level fall.

But why think the alternatives Frege considers are exhaustive? Why can't the object of the predication of *two in number* be the dancers in the team of Fred Astaire and Ginger Rogers? As David Bell argues (1990: 66–69), Frege overlooks the possibility set out by Husserl in *The Philosophy of Arithmetic* that what is two is "the aggregate designated by [the] indirect plural term"—in our case, the aggregate designated by 'the dance team of Fred Astaire and Ginger Rogers'. The predication expresses the fact that the team has two members.

On Bell's reconstruction of Husserl (1990: 68–69), the predication of *is two* (also: *is numerous*) to such an aggregate is the predication of a *collective* property like *are a dance team*. Such properties do not apply to the members of an aggregate in the way that distributive properties like *is ceramic* apply to collections like tea sets and their members. Bell claims that collective properties can always be cashed out in terms of specifiable conditions on the members as individuals. In the case of *are a dance team*, these conditions, "retrieval conditions" as Bell calls them, might be something like the condition of being someone who gets together with others for the purpose of dancing together in public performances. Thus, the predicate *are a dance team*, applied to Fred Astaire and Ginger Rogers, can be cashed out on the basis of those of their properties that are necessary and sufficient for their being a dance team. This requires saying no more than that Fred Astaire and Ginger Rogers are each the other's partner in the appropriate performances.

Frege's only way of dealing with this sort of case would be to assign sentences like (3.45) the semantic form of sentences that refer to the concepts and their instances.

(3.45)   There are two dancers on the ballroom floor.

But, given the new intensionalism's criticism of the Fregean practice of recasting simple sentences as complex ones, recasting (3.45) as a sentence expressing no plural reference is hardly an uncontentious move. Further, there is no compositional justification for recasting such sentences as referring to concepts. Compositionality makes it plausible to say that the predication in a sentence like (3.45) is that there are n such and suches—e.g., there are two dancers on the ballroom floor.

Moreover, on this conception of their semantic form, analytic sentences of this kind, such as 'A tango team has two dancers', 'A string trio has three string players', and so on, are handled by (A) straightforwardly, since the predicates 'two', 'three', and so on, are contained in their respective subjects. Finally, such sentences are weakly necessary truths since, in all worlds where there are tango teams, string trios, and so on, they have two members, three members, and so on, respectively (for the same reason that, in all worlds where there are bachelors, there are single people). No recasting is necessary to account for the analyticity or weakly necessary truth of such sentences.

This criticism is similar to a point Bell makes in defending Husserl's account of number predications against Frege's: "[for a Fregean to invoke quantification theory] . . . would beg the very question at issue. Quantification theory, that is, is itself yet another device for de-pluralization, for eliminating plurally referring terms: variables of quantification are *individual* variables, and predicate-letters are all *singular*" (1990: 242, n. 57). Bell's point can, in fact, be seen as part of my more general criticism of the Fregean practice of regimenting simple sentences. The more general criticism is, then, that to decide a philosophical issue by invoking the practice of recasting sentences on the basis of a Frege-style logical form begs the question because that practice itself is a large part of what is at issue. Husserl's account of number predication in *The Philosophy of Arithmetic*, *modulo* the details of his theory of aggregates, is the one I have been urging as the most intuitively plausible. Hence, from my perspective, Bell is right in his protest on Husserl's behalf that it is illegitimate for Frege to base his criticism of such an account on a recasting of the critical sentences into the idiom of his quantification theory. This protest is, therefore, a special case of the earlier criticism of regimenting simple sentences as compound sentences.

This is not a protest against the idea that the surface form of sentences often disguises a more semantically revealing underlying form. The question is generally understood in Fregean terms, that is, as a grammatical form/logical form distinction, but this is an oversimplification. The basic question is whether there is a semantic form of some sort underlying the surface form. On this question twentieth-century philosophers differ sharply. Those like Frege and Russell think that significant semantic facts are disguised by aspects of surface form; those like Wittgenstein (1953: sections 92 and 109) think that all such facts "lie open to view." Here I side with Frege and Russell and against Wittgenstein. But, for the former philosophers, there is a further question about the nature of the underlying semantic facts. Frege and Russell think that it is in the main logical, while I do not. I think that such underlying semantic facts are just facts about syntactic structure and decompositional sense structure. If I am right, then given the previous point about regimentation, sentences like (3.45) do not make second-order assertions about concepts.

3.12.2. Are numbers determinate objects?

Frege writes:

> We can, of course, by using . . . [our] definitions . . . say what is meant by "the number 1 + 1 belongs to the concept F" and then, using this, give the sense of the expression "the number 1 + 1 + 1 belongs to the concept F" and so on; but we can never—to take a crude example—decide by means of our definitions whether any concept has the number JULIUS CAESAR belonging to it, or whether that same familiar conqueror of Gaul is a number or is not. (1953: 68)

This "crude example" of the failure of the sense of number terms to determine their reference is only the tip of the iceberg. As we learn from recent philosophy, deviant interpretations of all sorts can be cooked up for Peano arithmetic, and all of them would have to be excluded for numbers to be determinate objects. Daniel Isaacson puts the point succinctly: "The compelling and immediate reason for rejecting the idea that mathematics is about particular objects is that for any mathematical theory the domain of objects which that theory is taken to be about can always be replaced by a domain consisting of different objects, so long as the second domain has a structure isomorphic to that of the first" (1994: 123). I want to suggest that taking Frege's conception of the relation between sense and reference as our basis for understanding the relation between mathematical definitions and numbers makes it impossible to solve the problem of excluding deviant interpretations of Peano arithmetic. The resulting indeterminacy undermines our natural conception of numbers as objects and initiates an unnecessary flight to mathematical structuralism.

Paul Benacerraf argues for this indeterminacy and for mathematical structuralism in his celebrated essay "What Numbers Could Not Be" (1983). He claims that the intended interpretation of Peano arithmetic, the numbers themselves, cannot be distinguished from deviant interpretations that also have the structure of a progression. This is because the objects in such interpretations play the same role in the abstract arithmetic structure of a progression as the numbers. Hence, Benacerraf writes that "[t]he search for which independently identifiable particular objects the numbers really are (sets? Julius Caesars?) is a misguided one." The moral Benacerraf draws from the inevitable failure of this quest for determinate mathematical objects is mathematical structuralism: "Arithmetic is . . . the science that elaborates the abstract structure that all progressions have in common merely in virtue of being progressions. It is not a science concerned with particular objects—the numbers." In a subsequent reflection on the argument in "What Numbers Could Not Be," Benacerraf himself notes its dependency on the Fregean principle that the sense of a term determines its reference:

["What Numbers Could Not Be"] . . . can be read as arguing that either the definitions of the mathematical terms do not preserve their meaning, or their meaning does not determine their reference, since different and equally adequate definitions assign different referents to the mathematical vocabulary. . . . [Frege] and I speak with one voice. Definitions adequate to *his* purposes need not preserve reference. (1981: 18–19)

Later, Benacerraf draws an antirealist conclusion from the failure of mathematical terms to preserve reference: ". . . I hope that these examples make it clear that a straightforwardly 'realist' construal of Frege's intentions or accomplishments will fail to do justice to [the mathematician's] practice" (1981: 31). Given Fregean semantics, Benacerraf's argument is irresistible. If the definition of a number term determines its reference and if the definitions of number terms characterize objects as the numbers on the basis of their forming a progression, then deviant models of arithmetic count as the numbers every bit as much as the objects in the intended model, and, hence, the definitions radically change the reference of number terms. Thus, the Fregean concepts of numbers, as captured in Fregean definitions of number terms, together with Fregean semantics, force us to abandon the realist view that arithmetic is a science of particular objects—the numbers. The symmetry of intended and deviant interpretations, as Benacerraf once put it, establishes that "there is no unique set of objects that are the numbers" (1983: 291).

To be sure, Frege and Benacerraf "speak with one voice." But it is the voice of Fregean intensionalism. Given my non-Fregean intensionalism, I am not obliged to follow Benacerraf in concluding that definitions of number terms "need not preserve reference." In light of the fact that intensionalists can deny that sense determines reference, Benacerraf's argument for mathematical structuralism has the same form, and, hence, the same difficulty, as Putnam's argument for semantic externalism. Benacerraf's argument affirms the Fregean principle that sense determines reference and concludes that definitions of number terms do not preserve reference, but it is possible to deny the principle and conclude that definitions of number terms do preserve reference. All that follows from turning the argument around in this way is that the definitions of number terms in pure mathematics, since they do not preserve reference, are, however serviceable as definitions within pure mathematics, incomplete as definitions from an ontological standpoint.

It follows further that a complete definition must make use of properties that go beyond those required to specify a progression. The mathematical definitions, which characterize the numbers in terms of their structural properties, are adequate for the mathematician's task of proving theorems about the numbers, but they are too restricted to specify the domain of arithmetic. Hence, the definitions must include non-structural properties that do precisely what the symmetry shows the mathematical definitions do not do, namely, distinguish the intended domain of arithmetic from the various deviant isomorphic domains that the mathematical definitions allow.

We can illustrate the use of non-structural properties for this purpose with Frege's question of whether Julius Caesar is a number, say, the number seventeen. Since the number seventeen has the non-structural property of being an abstract object (in having no spatial or temporal location) and Julius Caesar has the property of being a concrete object (having lived at a certain time and place), deviant interpretations on which the conqueror of Gaul stands in for the number seventeen can be ruled out if the definition of seventeen includes the condition that seventeen is an abstract object.

The use of non-structural properties to break the symmetry between intended and deviant models for arithmetic is reminiscent of the use of sense properties to break the symmetry between the various translations of 'gavagai' in radical translation. In both cases, indeterminacy is an artifact of constructing the situation so as to exclude just the set of properties required to distinguish the intended interpretation from deviant ones. Just as the exclusion of non-referential properties produces symmetry of intended and deviant translation, so the exclusion of non-structural properties produces symmetry of intended and deviant model. What is required to develop this comparison into a full response to Benacerraf's indeterminacy thesis is a way of guaranteeing that we can always identify an appropriate property to distinguish the intended interpretation from any deviant interpretation that might be cooked up.

Elsewhere I have argued that there is such a way because the alleged symmetries on which arguments for indeterminacy rest themselves exhibit a paradoxical feature that provides the symmetry-breaking property (1996; 1998b: 85–116).[16] For example, the symmetry puzzle in Quine's indeterminacy argument had a paradoxical feature: translations of 'gavagai' like 'rabbit', 'undetached rabbit part', 'rabbit stage', and so on have to be both equivalent and incompatible. They have to be equivalent in order for them to be symmetrical and incompatible in order for them to be rivals. The status of the translations as rivals seems to conflict with their status as equivalent, but they have to be both equivalent and competing to pose the challenge to determinate translation.

An example of such a paradoxical feature that provides the property that breaks the symmetry between an intended and deviant model of arithmetic is the following. The alleged symmetry between the intended model in which the numbers zero, one, two, and so on are assigned to the terms 'zero', 'one', 'two', and so on and the deviant model that involves the same assignments except that Julius Caesar is assigned to the term 'seventeen' is paradoxical because they are equivalent (structurally) and competing (extra-structurally). Thus, the properties of being a concrete object, of being a human being, a Roman, of no longer existing, and so on which are what make the models incompatible with the intended model in the case of the term 'seventeen', are the properties we require to break the symmetry. The fact that Julius Caesar has them but numbers do not shows that the deviant model does not assign a number to the term 'seventeen' even though it assigns something with the same position in a progression.

Although I cannot here provide the full discussion necessary to substantiate the claim that there will always be such a symmetry-breaking property (see Katz 1998b: 85–116), I can indicate the basic reason. On the skeptic's own account of the symmetry puzzle, the hypotheses in question must be competing interpretations. Otherwise, there is nothing to stop us from saying that the objects involved in the deviant interpretation are just the objects involved in the intended interpretation under a deviant description. If, in the case of the alleged indeterminacy of numbers, skepticism is not to be lost for lack of a response to the claim that the objects in the allegedly deviant model are just the numbers under a deviant description, then it must be clear in what respects those objects differ from the numbers (e.g., the number seventeen is abstract while Julius Caesar is concrete). But given such respects, we can resist Benacerraf's argument against the determinacy of numbers on the grounds that the features the skeptic employs to show that a deviant interpretation of Peano arithmetic competes with the intended interpretation are the very features required to break the symmetry. Since such features always occur as part of a well-defined symmetry problem, either there is no well-defined symmetry problem or there is a solvable one.

3.13. The irony of indeterminacy

Quine's arguments for the indeterminacy of translation and inscrutability of reference (1960: 26–79; 1969: 26–45) have convinced many philosophers that there is no fact of the matter about the sense and reference of expressions. This has caused less consternation than might have been expected because comfort is taken in the thought that there is a fact of the matter about the meaning and reference of their tokens. The loss of determinacy at the semantic level seems acceptable because determinacy seems alive and well at the pragmatic level.

In this section, I will argue that the true picture is the very opposite. There is no reason to think that we are faced with semantic indeterminacy, but there is reason to think that we are faced with pragmatic indeterminacy. I defended the first half of this claim in the first part of this book where I argued that Quine's case for semantic indeterminacy has force only against Fregean intensionalism. In this section, I will defend the second half of the claim. I will argue that for an indefinite number of cases at the pragmatic level, there is no fact of the matter about the meaning of linguistic tokens. The situation is this: there is no indeterminacy where received wisdom tells us it exists, and there is indeterminacy where received wisdom tells us it does not.

Doubts about determinacy at the pragmatic level arise from reflection on a familiar feature of communication. Given determinacy at the semantic level, determinacy at the pragmatic level would follow if words were always used with exactly their sense in the language. But, typically, language use involves tokens the sense of which differs, to a greater or lesser extent, from the sense of their types. Sometimes the sense of the token differs from the sense of its type in a way that the context makes entirely evident. When I say to my neighbor at a James Galway concert, "He plays marvelously," the sense of my utterance is evident. Its sense is *James Galway plays the flute marvelously*. At other times, however, things are not so simple.

Jane Gardam's novel *A Long Way from Verona* presents an amusing case of someone flat-footedly misconstruing the speaker by putting an absurdity in his or her mouth. The irrepressible teen-age heroine reports:

> Lady Pap-Musher said, "But Boo-Boo (yes) you couldn't send them to a local school *anyway*. I mean they're so *crowded* and nobody *does*." I could see the mother looking at me and pretending to be embarrassed but really rather enjoying it (she's the ghastliest and she hates me) so I suddenly said, "How can they be so crowded if nobody does?" and there was the most terrible, horrible silence all around the room. (1971: 108).

Yogi Berra is reported to have said: "Nobody goes there anymore, it's too popular." The claim of the song title (3.46a):

(3.46a)   Everybody loves Saturday night.

is absurdly denied on the grounds that there are splenetic people who love nothing and unfortunate people who work at unpleasant Saturday night jobs; and (3.46b):

(3.46b)   The burglars took everything!

is absurdly denied on the grounds that the burglars left a smelly old tennis sock.

To avoid construing the quantifier in utterances like Lady Pap-Musher's and Yogi Berra's as literally ranging over everyone, it is necessary to say that the senses of such quantifier tokens are contextually expanded so that their reference is restricted to a proper subset of the people in the world. It seems quite plausible to say that the sense of Lady Pap-Musher's utterance of 'nobody' is contextually expanded to mean something like 'nobody in our circle of friends and acquaintances'. Of course, not any expansion will do. The expansion must correctly represent the relevant content of the speaker's communicative intention. Lady Pap-Musher's utterance of 'nobody' cannot be expanded to say the hoi polloi do not send their children to the local school. The question with which we are concerned is, then, whether there is generally a fact of the matter about such content for proposed contextual expansions to get right or wrong.

Donnellan once expressed doubts about whether the process of contextual expansion can always be counted on to provide "one unique 'amended' statement to be assessed for truth value" (1966: fn. 10). His point was that the amended statement can contain "any description that does correctly pick out what the speaker intended to refer to." I think that Donnellan's doubts are well placed, but that the indeterminacy we find here goes even deeper than a plethora of co-extensive descriptions. There is indeterminacy in connection with the *de re* proposition as well as the *de dicto* proposition. I will present a case, typical of the use of numerical expressions, in which the utterance is not a slip of the tongue or in some other way defective, but in which there is no fact of the matter about the speaker's communicative intentions. The case presents a symmetry problem in which there are indefinitely many contextual expansions for the speaker's utterance that are consistent with the total pragmatic evidence but fix different intensions and extensions.

On returning to her London flat, Lady Pap-Musher notices that her Corot painting is missing from the living room wall. Then she notices that her Ming vase, her Meissenware figures, and her Japanese scroll painting are also missing. On her way to the dining room, she notes that the antique suit of armor that stood in the hall is no longer there, and, in the dining room, she sees that the silver tea service has been taken, too. She exclaims, "The burglars took everything!" It goes without saying that 'everything' in this utterance is not the universal quantifier, but it is also clear that it is not the restricted quantifier 'everything in the flat'. Her gardening book is still on the table, as are her old gardening gloves. More plausibly, therefore, 'everything' in Lady Pap-Musher's utterance might, for example, be taken to mean (1) 'everything in the flat worth stealing', (2) 'everything valuable in the flat', (3) 'everything in the flat that is expensive', (4) 'everything in the flat that is irreplaceable', or (5) 'everything in the flat that Lady Pap-Musher cherishes'. Since, besides (1)–(5), there is an open set of other descriptions that Lady Pap-Musher's use of 'everything' might be taken to mean, the problem is that of choosing a hypothesis that best describes what she did mean when she uttered the token of (3.46b).

But what makes us think there is such a hypothesis? Since she had no notion of the true extent of her loss at the time, there need be nothing definite that she did mean. She saw that the Corot was missing, the Ming vase was missing, the Meissen figures were missing, the Japanese scroll painting was missing, the antique suit of armor was missing, and the silver tea service was missing. She had not searched the first floor and had not looked upstairs, but no doubt things were missing there, too. Generalizing, in some sense, Lady Pap-Musher says "everything." As an expression of the extent of the loss, this exclamation seems to be an induction of some sort, where the conclusion expresses the class of burglarized items, one which contains more than those thus far noted, but less than literally everything in the flat.

But her conclusion is not really an inductive generalization. Unlike a true induction, her conclusion about what has been taken is not based on projecting a property that the members of the sample have in common. What is missing is some characterization of the class in question beyond a number of examples of items belonging to it. Choosing between the hypotheses (1), (2), (3), (4), (5), and so on requires determining which hypothesis expresses her characterization of this class; but she herself has none. Since there is nothing in her mental state at the moment that reflects the way in which one of the hypotheses differs from the others, there is no fact of the matter about Lady Pap-Musher's mental state on which to ground one hypothesis as the right expansion of 'everything' in her utterance. The evidence necessary to break the symmetry simply is not there.

Someone might be tempted to say that Lady Pap-Musher's use of 'everything' means 'everything worth stealing or valuable or expensive or cherished or something of the sort'. But restricting the quantifier in this way is no more helpful than saying that the translation of 'gavagai' is 'rabbit or undetached rabbit part or rabbit stage or rabbithood manifestation or something of that sort'. Moreover, while there is at least something in the context to which each translation applies, there is nothing in Lady Pap-Musher's communicative intention to which any of the hypotheses in question applies.

Given that we do not have determinacy for token-sense, the question arises of whether there might nonetheless be determinacy for token-reference. Perhaps we can avoid the problem of having to determine which of the various expansions of the sense of the sentence-type captures the intended sense of the token if extensions are assigned directly to utterances. Such direct assignment would restrict the reference of occurrences of the universal quantifier to the particular objects to which a speaker makes reference.

The trouble here is that the problem resurfaces as an indeterminacy in the choice among competing hypotheses for specifying the objects to which a speaker makes reference. Hypotheses (1)–(5) and so on now play the role of competing hypotheses for specifying the conditions that entities must meet to qualify for inclusion in the extension. The Corot painting belongs to the extension of (2) but not to the extension of (1) because the painting is too well known to be disposed of. The cherished doily that Aunt Martha knitted belongs to the extension of (4) but not to the extension of (1) or of (2) because it has no monetary value. The cast iron Art Nouveau staircase belongs to the extension of (2) and (3) but not to the extension of (1) because the burglars could not remove it. The point about the dependence of extensional determinacy on intensional determinacy is, of course, one first made by Quine to argue that "[r]eference itself proves behaviorally inscrutable" (1969: 35). Further, since none of the concepts in question figures in Lady Pap-Musher's communicative intention, we cannot specify the objects for the extension of her use of 'every-thing'. There is essentially the same reason for indeterminacy in choosing a particu-lar reference for the token of 'everything' as there was in choosing a particular sense for the token of 'everything'.

3.14. Wittgenstein's family resemblance criticism

The most influential of Wittgenstein's arguments against theories that construe mean-ings as objects such as essences, concepts, forms, attributes, and the like is his fam-ily resemblance argument (1953: sections 66–70). Wittgenstein argues that such theories assume that there is something common to the things to which we apply a general term, but that ". . . if you look at [the proceedings to which we apply such a term], you will not see something that is common to *all*, but similarities, relation-ships, and a whole series of them at that" (1953: section 66). He presents various examples of what we call 'games' to show there is nothing common to them, but only ". . . a complicated network of similarities overlapping and criss-crossing: some-times overall similarities, sometimes similarities of detail." The examples are "re-minders" the purpose of which is to establish that meaning derives from the practices on which the normative aspect of language use rests (1953: section 127).

On this view, the problem of indeterminacy discussed in the last section has a more general solution—or rather dissolution. The problem arises only because we construe meanings as concepts. Since there are no such things as concepts in this sense, it was a mistake to expect Lady Pap-Musher's exclamation to reflect more than a family resemblance among the items observed to be missing and to take (1)–(5) and similar descriptions to be hypotheses among which we have to choose. Hence, according to Wittgenstein, we manufacture a problem for ourselves when we adopt a theory of meaning and look at uses of language through its distorting lens.

In general, Wittgenstein believes that intensionalists are in the grip of a "pic-ture" on which general terms express essences that serve as norms operating inde-pendently of us, and, as a consequence, they lack a "clear view" of their use of language (1953: sections 114, 115, and 122). He thus sees the issue as one that can be settled by reminding such philosophers of how their language is actually used, that is, by "bring[ing] words back from their metaphysical to their everyday use" (1953: section 116). This construal of the issue is not only widely accepted in some quarters, but it is sometimes even taken as unassailable by philosophical argument. Rob-ert Fogelin writes that it is not ". . . possible to offer an *a priori* critique of Wittgenstein's notion of family resemblance for, after all, the question is essentially factual . . . we can only look and see [whether we see] what Wittgenstein says he sees" (1976: 121). But for us to see what Wittgenstein says he sees is not enough to establish his notion of family resemblance. The facts as Wittgenstein reports them do not in and of them-selves constitute counterexamples to theories that take meanings to be objects such as essences or concepts. It is necessary to show that the facts are incompatible with such theories. But the argument Wittgenstein uses to show incompatibility, the fam-ily resemblance argument, as I am calling it, requires the premise that theories of meaning are Fregean theories of meaning. It is only on this further premise that intensionalism implies that the activities to which the term 'game' applies share a common essence. Hence, it is only on this further premise that Wittgenstein's observation that what we call games have nothing in common is a counterexample to intensionalism.

Wittgenstein's counterexamples apply only to those theories of meaning that equate the meaningfulness of a term, its having a sense, with its referent's (or referents') falling under a concept. Since, on my theory, the *raison d'être* for senses is the determination of sense properties and relations, a word can have a sense without there being anything common to the things to which it applies. The case of names is a convenient illustration of this. On the metalinguistic description theory of names set out in section 3.10, proper names have senses that are too thin to determine reference, because the sense of a name '*N*' is simply an instance of (3.44):

(3.44)   the thing that is a bearer of '*N*'.

The indefinite article in (3.44) allows for the possibility of multiple bearers, and the definite article expresses the condition that the referent in literal uses of a name must be exactly one of its bearers. Thus, a proper name has no type-reference because the information necessary to satisfy this uniqueness condition is not available at the level of type-reference. At the level of token-reference, the uniqueness condition is typically satisfied on the basis of descriptions that speakers use to distinguish their intended bearer from among the other equally salient bearers of the name. In this respect, there is a close correspondence between the role of descriptions on this account and their role on Wittgenstein's conception of naming (1953: section 79). Warren Goldfarb writes:

> [Wittgenstein] wants to elicit the plain facts that seem to point in the direction of [strong descriptivist theories]. What I mean by "plain facts" are the practices we have regarding names and explanations, clarifications of names, and justifications of assertions containing names when challenges to those assertions arise. . . . An important plain fact is this: if I am called upon to explain the use of a name in a particular case, I shall usually supply a description. . . . When certain matters of fact are put into question, then [providing a strong description] is mandatory if I am to support my statement, indeed, if I am to be deemed as "knowing what I'm talking about." (1997: 84)

Thus, although on Frege's theory descriptions are supplied by the senses of names independent of pragmatic factors, on mine descriptions are supplied by the users of names in response to the exigencies of the context. As a consequence, on my theory, the descriptions that identify the bearers of tokens of a name '*N*' vary enormously from context to context. Since different descriptions will typically be used by different users of the same name or by the same user in different contexts, when we survey the bearers of a name '*N*' across all its applications, the descriptions under which they were referred to will reflect extensive heterogeneity among the referents. Coupling this with the fact that a name can have bearers belonging to many different categories—that is, for example, 'Mary Jane' can be the name of one's friend, pet, baseball bat, a candy bar, a rose, a boat, an airplane, and so on—my theory predicts exactly the facts about family resemblance that Wittgenstein observes.

Given that names have sense and that the sense of an expression is a necessary condition for its reference, there will be something common to all the things to which we apply the name 'N'; but that common feature is only a nominal essence, namely, the content of (3.44). Wittgenstein's criticism of theories of meaning (1953: sections 65 and 66) is about real essences, and, on our intensionalism, there may be none. Collectively, the descriptions that speakers use to identify the bearers of tokens of a name will reflect too much heterogeneity to pick out a common real essence.

Elsewhere, I argued that the new intensionalism is also compatible with the observed facts about family resemblance in the case of common nouns like Wittgenstein's own example 'game' (1990b: 111–115). The dictionary says that the English word 'game' has, among others, the senses (1) 'a contest conducted according to rules governing the play of its participant(s)', (2) 'an amusement', and (3) 'a scheme employed in the pursuit of some objective'. (1) is the sense of the first occurrence of 'game' in 'The game of chess is no game for some people' and (2) is the sense of the second. (2) is also the sense of 'game' in 'Spying was a game for Mata Hari but not for Sorge'. (1) and (2) are the senses of 'game' in 'The game is over, Big Louie. (Put down your cards.)' and (3) is the sense of 'game' in 'The game is up, Big Louie. (Throw down your gun.)'. Given that the English word 'game' is ambiguous in these ways, there will be no property common to all the activities to which 'game' literally applies. Even without considering figurative uses of language, these activities we call 'games' will exhibit precisely the family resemblance Wittgenstein describes (1953: section 66).

Wittgenstein's family resemblance argument does not work against all theories of meaning that construe senses as objects, but only against Fregean theories, which claim, as Wittgenstein put it (1953: sections 68 and 81), that the application of words is "everywhere circumscribed by rules." In Fregean semantics, an expression's having a sense is its being associated with a rule that demarcates its extension from its anti-extension, and hence circumscribes its application. In my semantics, an expression's having a sense is only its being associated with an object the structure of which relates the expression to the senses of other expressions in the language. This allows words to have a sense without bringing them under extensional constraints that restrict the diversity of the things to which they are applied. Hence, we can acknowledge the truth of what Wittgenstein says about the use of the term 'game' without this in any way counting against the view that senses are objects.

3.15. Vagueness

Vagueness is like family resemblance in some respects and unlike it in others. Both are features of the extensions of words that, contrary to Frege, show that their application is not "everywhere circumscribed by rules," but family resemblance is a matter of the diversity of the things to which one and the same word applies, while vagueness is an indeterminacy in the application of a word. Family resemblance highlights the absence of an attribute common to the collection of things to which a word applies, whereas vagueness highlights the absence of sharp boundaries for the collection. The concept of childhood, for example, has no sharp extensional boundaries because there is no definite answer to the question of when a child becomes an adolescent.

Vagueness poses a general problem, a problem for everyone. All of us have to have something to say about the sorites paradoxes arising from vagueness. None of us want to say, literally, that no one ever becomes an adult or that everyone is bald. But, like family resemblance, vagueness is also a special problem just for Fregeans because of their definition of sense. In the *Grundgesetze*, Frege writes:

> A definition of a concept (of a possible predicate) must be complete; it must unambiguously determine, as regards any object, whether or not it falls under the concept (whether or not the predicate is truly assertable of it). . . . We may express this metaphorically as follows: the concept must have a sharp boundary. . . . The law of excluded middle is really just another form of the requirement that the concept should have a sharp boundary. . . . Has the question 'Are we still Christians?' really got a sense, if it is indeterminate whom the predicate 'Christian' can truly be asserted of, and who must be refused it? (1952: 159)

On Fregean semantics, sense without reference is possible only if the concept is complete but it happens that nothing in the domain of the language falls under the sense, e.g., the expression 'the least convergent series'. But, in the case of a vague term like 'childhood' or 'Christian', it is not that the domain of the language lacks for appropriate objects. Nursery schools are full of clear cases of children and old age homes are full of clear cases of non-children. Since the concept of childhood is not complete, Frege's characterization of sense commits him to saying that the term 'childhood' has no sense. If the term had a sense, it would be a function from objects in the domain to a determinate extension, and, in this case, there would be no incompleteness.

Frege's position is incoherent. On the one hand, vague terms have no sense because they do not have a sharp boundary, but, on the other hand, they have to have a sense because they have a fuzzy boundary, that is, because there are some things that belong to their extension, some that are outside, and some that are borderline cases. Since things that belong to the extension of 'children' are not numbers and so on but children, and things that belong to its anti-extension are not children but numbers and so on, vague terms must have some sort of sense. Further, the existence of some sort of sense is presupposed by discussions of borderline cases: there is something that is insufficient to decide whether certain youngsters are children or adolescents.

Wittgenstein picked up on the wrongheadedness in Frege's denial that vague terms have a sense: "Frege compares a concept to an area and says that an area with vague boundaries cannot be called an area at all. . . . But is it senseless to say: 'Stand roughly there'?" (1953: section 71). From the perspective of my theory of sense, there are arguments showing that vague terms have a sense in the straightforward linguistic sense of the term. 'Child', 'Christian', 'tall', 'rich', 'bald', and so on are not nonsense words like Lewis Carroll's 'brillig' and 'tove'. Some have more than one sense, as with the ambiguous term 'bald', which can also mean 'undisguised', as in 'bald egotism' or 'bald truth'. We can, moreover, say what their sense is. The sense of 'childhood' is the same as the sense of 'period of life between birth and adolescence' and the sense of 'Christian' is the same as the sense of 'a theist who believes Christ is divine and the revealer of God's thought'. Further, the words 'childhood', 'adolescence', and 'adulthood' form an antonymous triple under the superordinate 'period of life'. Also, 'tall' is an antonym of 'short', 'rich' is an antonym of 'poor', and 'bald' is an antonym of 'hairy'. Since these vague terms, in contrast to a nonsense word like 'tove', have sense properties and relations, they must have senses.

The special problem that vagueness poses for Fregean semantics arises because the Fregean definition of sense makes having a sense depend on sharp extensional boundaries. Thus, vagueness does not pose a special problem for my semantics because (D) cuts the connection between sense and reference. Since from the standpoint of my autonomous theory of sense, senses are not required to provide referential determination, the general problem of not being able to say precisely which people fall under a term such as 'childhood' has no bearing on whether the term is meaningful in the language. From the standpoint of my theory of sense, there is no question of completeness, since a term's being meaningful is entailed by its having the sense properties and relations it has, independent of its referential situation. Separating sense structure from logical structure means that the law of excluded middle does not function as a requirement on sense.

Being saved from the special problem that vagueness raises for Fregean intensionalism, my intensionalism does not have to embrace behavioristic semantics in either the description of senses or the description of speakers' sense competence. On the basis of an argument that there is no consistent system of principles for applying vague expressions, Crispin Wright advocates conceiving of our semantic competence "on the model of a practical skill, comparable to the ability to hit a good crosscourt backhand or ride a bicycle" (1987: 238). No such broad metaphilosophical claim as Wright's conclusion that we should stop thinking of semantics theoretically and start thinking of semantic competence as a skill can be drawn.[17] Not even the general problem of vagueness arises on my autonomous theory of sense. Furthermore, if the problem does not arise for a theory of the sense structure of the language, it also does not arise for a theory of speakers' knowledge of the sense structure of the language. We can thus philosophize about both sense in natural language and its representation in the psychology of speakers without having to cast such philosophizing in behaviorist terms, something that, since Chomsky's criticism of behavioristic linguistics (1959), is to be welcomed enthusiastically.

The theory of type-reference for natural language sketched in the second part of this book is also safe from the special problem of vagueness. This is because the statements of referential correlates are simply associations of referential properties and relations with sense properties and relations. Thus, even though the general problem of vagueness would cause problems in model-theoretically interpreting languages in worlds like ours where periods of human development and multiplicities of hair grade off without a mark separating their stages and states, the general problem does not prevent the formulation of a theory of type-reference any more than it prevents the formulation of a theory of sense. I can pursue the development of those theories without a solution to the general problem of vagueness.

3.16. The dilemma about color incompatibility

Sentences like (3.47) raise a problem for a logic-based semantics. (See Katz 1998a for earlier discussion.)

(3.47)   The spot is red and blue.

Wittgenstein says: "It is clear that the logical product of two elementary proposi-tions can neither be a tautology nor a contradiction. The statement that a point in the visual field has two different colors at the same time is a contradiction" (1961: sec-tion 6.3751).

Wittgenstein's statements, plausible by themselves, together seem implausible in the extreme. (3.47) is "the logical product of two elementary propositions," and hence, according to the first statement, it cannot be a contradiction. But (3.47) asserts that "a point in the visual field has two different colors at the same time," and hence, according to the second, it is a contradiction. But both statements seem to have strong support. The first seems vouchsafed by our logic, the second by our linguistic intuition. Linguis-tic intuition tells us not only that (3.47) is a contradiction, but also that (3.48) and (3.52) are incompatible, that (3.48) entails (3.49) and (3.50), and that (3.51) is a necessary truth.

(3.48)   The spot is red.

(3.49)   The spot is not blue.

(3.50)   The spot has a color.

(3.51)   Red is a color.

(3.52)   The spot is green.

But logic appears to contradict intuition. Not only do the sentential components of (3.47) express elementary propositions, but (3.48), (3.50), (3.51) and (3.52) them-selves express elementary propositions, and (3.49) expresses the negation of an ele-mentary proposition. Since elementary propositions are logically independent of one another, logic tells us that sentences like (3.47)–(3.52) do not have the intended logical properties and relations. We seem, therefore, to face a dilemma that forces us to choose between our logical and linguistic intuitions.

Moreover, the dilemma is not restricted to color vocabulary. It involves the en-tire extralogical vocabulary and all the semantic properties and relations of the lan-guage, not just color words and the property of contradiction. It surfaces whenever we try to explain the semantic contribution that extralogical terms make to simple sentences on the basis of logical forms that represent the sentences as elementary propositions, and hence as lacking the logical structure necessary to account for logical properties and relations. But, even though the conflict between our intuitions about color words and the logic of sentences containing them is only a special case of the general problem, its historical importance and the special difficulties it poses make it a test case for the general problem.

In his post-*Tractatus* reflections on the color incompatibility problem, Wittgenstein came to the conclusion that sentences like (3.47)–(3.52) cannot be handled within a logic-based approach to semantics. Here, as elsewhere, Wittgenstein led the way in revealing deeply problematic aspects of a logic-based semantics for natural languages. But making the, at the time, natural assumption that formal semantics is either Russell-style extensionalism or Frege-style intensionalism, Wittgenstein rejected all formal approaches to the semantics of natural language. From my perspective, this went too far. Formal semantics is just semantics done formally—that is, on the basis of formal representations of semantic structure in natural language. Those representations do not have to be of logical forms, as Wittgenstein supposed. Logical semantics is one kind of formal semantics, but, as we have seen, not the only kind. Mereological semantics, as understood here, is another. Wittgenstein misses the possibility that the color incompatibility problem, though unsolvable within logical semantics, is solvable within mereological semantics.

My principal concern here is to show two things. First, the problem of color incompatibility is solvable within our autonomous theory of sense. Second, Frege's logicizing of semantics—his new characterizations of sense and analyticity—is responsible for making the problem seem to be unsolvable within formal semantics. If I am right that our delogicizing of semantics makes the problem solvable, then, *ceteris paribus*, philosophers do not have to sacrifice the benefits of a formal semantics or swallow the positivistic moral Wittgenstein tried to draw from his new approach to the semantics of natural language in the *Philosophical Investigations*.

It was the dilemma about color incompatibility, more than any other difficulty with Frege/Russell logic-based semantics, that caused Wittgenstein to replace logic-based semantics with the use-based approach he set out in the *Philosophical Investigations*. Wittgenstein's radically new way of thinking about meaning, language, and logic in his late philosophy was a direct consequence of his failure to handle sentences like (3.47) within the essentially Fregean system of the *Tractatus*. To my knowledge, E. B. Allaire (1959) was the first to recognize this. Nowadays, the central role of the color incompatibility problem in the development of Wittgenstein's late philosophy is widely recognized among Wittgenstein scholars. Referring to Wittgenstein's attempt in "Some Remarks on Logical Form" (1929: 168) to revise the truth-table notation to express "exclusion," Max Black says, "Here, it may be said, Wittgenstein's system begins to crack" (1964: 368). P. M. S. Hacker (1972: 84–94) and Anthony Kenny (1973: 103–119), two other well-known Wittgenstein scholars, take essentially the same view of the centrality of the problem in the transition from the early to the late philosophy.

Wittgenstein's opposition to synthetic *a priori* knowledge (1967: 68) led him to equate being synthetic with being contingent, and, as a consequence, put him under pressure to declare sentences like (3.47) meaningless. But, as he still held a calculus picture of language during this period, the option of representing sentences like (3.47) as meaningless, while at the same time representing their negations as meaningful truths, was not open to him. Since the only kind of sentential well-formedness in logical calculi is syntactic well-formedness, the meaningful/meaningless distinction coincides with the well-formed/ill-formed distinction. Hence, (3.47) and its negation are either both meaningful or both meaningless.

Allaire suggests that the need to separate meaningfulness from syntactic well-formedness led Wittgenstein to abandon the calculus picture of language and develop his new use-based conception of meaning:

> One possible way of making it palatable [that (3.47) but not its negation is meaningless] is to identify meaning with use. This, as we all know, is one of the key ideas of the final phase. If I am right, it follows that with respect to one very major issue, at least, the 1929 paper marks a transitional stage between the thought of the *Tractatus* and that of the final stage. (1959: 104)

Since, on the new conception, the meaningfulness of signs is an aspect of their use in our linguistic practices, it is possible to reject the identification of the meaningful with the syntactically well-formed. Hence, the negation of (3.47) can be treated as meaningful, in virtue of having the status of a "grammatical rule," while (3.47) itself is treated as meaningless, in virtue of being the denial of a grammatical rule.

At the outset of "the final stage," Wittgenstein diagnoses his earlier bewilderment as follows: "We make a picture like that of the two colors being in each other's way, . . . but on looking closer we find that we can't apply the picture we have made" (1958: 56). In the *Philosophical Investigations* (1953: sections 115–132), Wittgenstein uses the idea of "[a] picture [holding] us captive" as his diagnosis of our metaphysical condition.

The color incompatibility problem has played a pivotal role in the history of twentieth-century philosophy. Not only Wittgenstein's late philosophy, but also the other two philosophical positions within which most analytic philosophy in the twentieth century was done, Carnap's neo-Humean empiricism and Quine's neo-Millian empiricism, were, in very large measure, responses to the problem of how to preserve logic-based formal semantics in the face of elementary propositions that appear to have logical properties.

Carnap's response was to replace Frege's vague and confusing notion of definition with the apparatus of meaning postulates, so that we have a formal means of specifying logical relations among extralogical terms that make it possible to treat sentences like (3.47) as contradictions and their denials as analytic. Since meaning postulates are constraints on the assignment of extensions to sentences, Carnap can explicate analytic truth as truth in all possible worlds (1956: 7–13). This explication has an ontological and an epistemological payoff for him. Since analyticity is necessary truth, the explication delivers logicism effortlessly and without Frege's commitment to mathematical realism, and since necessary truths have no factual content, it delivers empiricism without a commitment to John Stuart Mill's inductivist view

of logical and mathematical knowledge. Reflecting on the significance of this explication, Carnap wrote:

> What [is] important . . . [is] . . . that it became possible for the first time to combine
> the basic tenets of empiricism with a satisfactory explanation of the nature of logic
> and mathematics. Previously, philosophers had only seen two alternative positions:
> either a non-empiricist conception, according to which knowledge in mathematics
> is based on pure intuition or pure reason, or the view held, e.g., by John Stuart Mill,
> that the theorems of logic and of mathematics are just as much of an empirical na-
> ture as knowledge about observed events, a view which, although it preserved
> empiricism, was certainly unsatisfactory. (1963: 47)

Quine's response to the troublesome sentences was clean and simple: extralogical
words have no logical powers; hence, there is nothing for Carnapian meaning postulates to explicate. Carnap's assumption, that extralogical words have logical powers, is, as Quine famously put it, "an unempirical dogma of empiricists" (1953: 37).
This response opened up the prospect of an empiricism in the Millian spirit. Quine
found Mill's own empiricism unsatisfactory (1966: 107–108), particularly its conception of the certainty of logic and mathematics, but he found the Millian view of
their empirical status congenial, and, accordingly, found Carnap's empiricism a compromise of the empiricist principle that all our knowledge rests on experience. Without an intensionalist basis for the *a priori* to worry about, Quine was able to reinstate
the empiricist principle in terms of his semantic holism.

My non-Fregean intensionalism opens up the possibility of a new response to
the problem. I can exhibit this new response by showing how my mereological semantics avoids the failure of Carnap's response.

Carnap's response rejects the notion that logical properties and relations of sentences like (3.47)–(3.52) arise from the internal structure of their extralogical vocabulary. Carnap's reasoning can be reconstructed as follows. Wittgenstein had
supposed that the source of the contradiction in a sentence like (3.47) lies in the nature of the color words themselves; but that supposition is not forced on us. The
contradiction does not have to arise from structure internal to the color words in order
for it to be shown in a symbolism. After all, the logical property of being a tautology
exhibited in instances of $P \vee -P$ is not shown in a representation of the internal structure of the logical words in those instances. Rather, the property is shown in a symbolism of logical postulates that represents the external structure of logical words.
So, if we take the contradiction in the case of (3.47)—and other semantic properties
in other cases—to be genuinely logical properties like being a tautology, then we
ought to treat so-called extralogical words in the same way we treat logical words.
To do this, we need to introduce "meaning postulates" to represent the external semantic structure of so-called extralogical vocabulary on the basis of the same referential apparatus used for logical postulates.

The attractive feature of Carnap's response is that it sacrifices neither our linguistic nor our logical intuitions concerning the sentences in question. Wittgenstein's
and Quine's ways of handling the sentences both sacrifice our linguistic intuitions.

Both deny that (3.47) is a necessary falsehood, that (3.51) is a necessary truth and that (3.48) and (3.52) are inconsistent, and both deny that these things are known *a priori* on the basis of intuition.

But, as Quine showed, this way out fails as an explanation because "We understand what expressions the rules attribute analyticity to, but we do not understand what the rules attribute to those expressions" (1953: 33).

From Quine's extensionalist perspective, the failure to provide such understanding is due to there being *au fond* no notion of analyticity for meaning postulates to explicate. From my intensionalist perspective, it is due rather to the fact that meaning postulates are by nature unsuited to explicating the concept that is there. Meaning postulates are simply a device for enumerating sentences under the rubric 'analytic'. Since the sentences are specified in the manner of theorems of logic, not as instances of the prespecified concept of analyticity, meaning postulates can serve as constraints on the assignment of extensions to sentences, but they cannot explain the property common to the sentences they enumerate. Like Socrates's interlocutors, meaning postulates offer examples of the concept instead of the concept itself.

The reason the meaning postulate approach cannot explain the property of analyticity common to analytic sentences is that it is based on the view that the external logical structure of extralogical words is the source of analyticity, contradiction, and analytic entailment in connection with sentences. But in the cases of sentences (3.47)–(3.52) external logical structure is not available. Meaning postulates represent no more than the external, i.e., logical, structure of the extralogical words, whereas the analytic structure of sentences like (3.51) requires access to the internal sense structure of such words.[18] Here, then, is where a mereological semantics overcomes the limitation of a logical semantics. My theory of sense provides a source for analyticity, contradiction, and analytic entailment in connection with those sentences in the internal sense structure of their extralogical words, that is, their decompositional structure. I have already argued that decompositional sense structure explains the semantic powers of some logically elementary sentences on the basis of non-logical, internal sense structure. In the first part of this book, I described how such an explanation goes in the case of the analyticity of sentences like 'Squares are rectangles' and 'Bachelors are unmarried' and the contradictoriness of sentences like 'Squares are circles' and 'Bachelors are spinsters'.

The sentences involved in the present dilemma are, to be sure, not transparent cases of containment like 'Squares are rectangles' and 'Bachelors are unmarried'. Far from it. A sentence like (3.53):

(3.53) Red is not blue.

seems rather to be a transparent case of non-containment. For (3.53) to be analytic, the sense of its subject 'red' must literally contain the sense of its predicate 'not blue', which is not easy to accept. Worse yet, the sentences in (3.54):

(3.54) Red is not green, Red is not yellow, Red is not brown, . . .

by the same token, must be represented as analytic, too, and this requires that the senses of 'not green', 'not yellow', 'not brown', and so on must likewise be packed into the sense of the subject 'red'. Hence, it appears, quite implausibly, that the sense of 'red', and by parity of reasoning, the sense of every basic color term, must contain the senses of all the other basic color terms.

Not surprisingly, this implausibility has spawned arguments that the sense of a basic color word cannot contain the sense of another basic color word. One such argument is C. L. Hardin's:

> There need be no occasion for a reflective green-seer to have had contact with red, . . . [hence] there is no reason to suppose that the concept of not being red is thereby part of her concept of being green; after all, not being a mastodon isn't part of the concept of being a lampshade, even though reflective people would be readily able to distinguish mastodons from lampshades. (1986: 122)

The special problem that color words pose for me is now clear. Since the existence of a way out of the dilemma based on literal containment provides the only alternative to Carnap's unacceptable way out, the preservation of our linguistic intuition depends on a way out based on literal containment. But literal containment presents a problem of its own: the implausibility of holding that the sense of a basic color term literally contains the senses of all the other basic color terms. This problem seems *prima facie* at least as bad as the counterintuitiveness of Wittgenstein's way out or Quine's.

But the problem can be solved by making use of the resources for representing decompositional structure in an autonomous theory of sense. To explain the solution, I must now depart from the informal mode of presentation adopted up to this point and introduce a formal symbolism for sense structure. The symbolism, which will be kept to a minimum, will also prove useful in discussing some of the philosophical issues to be raised in subsequent sections.

In earlier work (1972), I developed a formal symbolism for sense structure. The symbols representing sense structure, called "semantic markers," are tree structures,

(3.55)

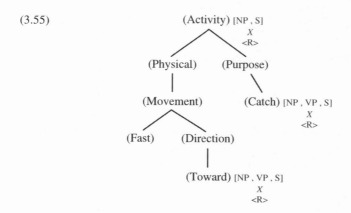

but, unlike the domination relations in the familiar tree notation for syntactic phrase markers, which represent constituent/sub-constituent relations in sentences, the domination relations in semantic markers represent sense/sub-sense relations in senses. The tree structures (3.55) and (3.56) are semantic markers that represent, respectively, the senses of the verbs 'chase' and 'follow'. In terms of such a symbolism, we can define one sense to be the superordinate of another, its subordinate, just in case the latter is a same-rooted subtree of the former. Since (3.56) is a same-rooted subtree of (3.55), the semantic markers (3.55) and (3.56) represent the sense of 'follow' as a superordinate of the sense of 'chase'.

In explaining the compositional meanings of sentences, the way semantic markers combine represents the way in which the senses of the parts of syntactically complex constituents combine. One mode of marker combination is attachment of a semantic marker representing the sense of a modifier as a branch under the semantic marker representing the sense of its head. The compositional meaning of the expression 'follow with the purpose of catching the followee' could be obtained in this way, starting with (3.56) as the representation of the head and attaching a representation of the modifier to form (3.55).

Another form of marker combination involves the aspect of semantic markers that represents the argument structure of predicates. In this form, semantic representations of compositional meanings are obtained from embedding one semantic marker within another. Argument places in a predicate are marked with occurrences of "categorized variables," $X, Y, Z, \ldots$, having syntactic information in brackets above the variable, such as in (3.55) and (3.56). Note that the same categorized variable can occur more than once in a semantic marker. In this way, we can represent, *inter alia*, the fact that the sense of 'chase' identifies the object of the chaser's purpose with what directs the course of the chaser's activity. The placedness of a relation is, accordingly, specified by the number of distinct categorized variables in its representation.

The syntactic information in the brackets specifies the semantic representations that can be values of the variable in terms of the syntactic constituents to which those

(3.56)

$$
\begin{array}{c}
\text{(Activity)} \ [\text{NP}, \text{S}] \\
X \\
<\text{R}> \\
| \\
\text{(Physical)} \\
| \\
\text{(Movement)} \\
\diagup \quad \diagdown \\
\text{(Fast)} \qquad \text{(Direction)} \\
\diagdown \\
\text{(Toward)} \ [\text{NP}, \text{VP}, \text{S}] \\
X \\
<\text{R}>
\end{array}
$$

representations are assigned. This ensures that the semantic representations of terms go in their proper argument places in a predicate (so that, e.g., 'John loves Mary' is not represented as synonymous with 'Mary loves John'). For convenience, such syntactic information may be represented in the form of Chomsky's (1965) grammatical functions. They pick out a constituent on the basis of its syntactic role in the sentence, e.g., the functions [NP, S] and [NP, VP, S] pick out, respectively, the subject of a sentence (the noun phrase that is a constituent of the whole sentence but of no other constituent in it) and the direct object of the sentence (the noun phrase that is a complement constituent of the verb phrase).

The angles under an occurrence of a variable state the condition under which an embedding can take place. These "selection restrictions" (<R>) ensure that the semantic representation resulting from a combination of semantic representations represents a *bona fide* sense. Requiring that the semantic representations have a particular content and structure to be the value of the variable, selection restrictions provide a formal means of blocking so-called 'category mistakes'. For example, the senses of the subject and direct object in (3.57) are of the appropriate category to combine with the sense of the verb 'chase'

(3.57)   The police chased the fugitive.

but, as the deviance of (3.58) shows

(3.58)   The police chased the number seventeen.

the senses of its subject and direct object are not. Thus, we want the selection restriction in (3.55) to require that the semantic marker '(Concrete)' appear as the label of the root in the representations for subjects and direct objects of 'chase'. Such a requirement blocks the semantic representations of the subject and direct object of (3.58) from being values of the variables in (3.55), and, consequently, (3.58) receives no semantic representation. In this way, selection restrictions enable us to mark the degree of ambiguity of expressions and sentences, that is, to assign n semantic representations to sentences with n senses.

A formal theory of decompositional and compositional sense structure consists of a dictionary in which each lexical item is associated with semantic markers representing its senses, a principle for assigning semantic markers from dictionary entries to occurrences of lexical items in sentences, and rules for compositional operations such as attachment and embedding. Assuming an appropriately formal dictionary, principle, and rules, the definitions of sense properties and relations can be stated formally, too, in terms of formal features of semantic markers. Hence, the informal generalization (A) can be restated as (A*):

(A*)   A semantic representation represents an analytic sense if it is of the form $P\{T_1, \ldots, T_n\}$, where $P\{x_1, \ldots, x_n\}$ is the predicate and $T_1, \ldots, T_n$ are the terms occupying its argument places, and one of those terms, T_i, is of the form $P'\{T'_1, \ldots, T'_n\}$, and $P\{x_1, \ldots, x_n\}$ is a same-rooted subtree of $P'\{x_1, \ldots, x_n\}$ and each term in $T_1, \ldots, T_{n-1}, T_{n+1}, \ldots, T_n$ is a same-rooted subtree of the corresponding term in $T'_1, \ldots, T'_n$.

Given (A*) and (3.55) and (3.56), we can say that sentences like 'The police follow those they chase' are analytic. A definition for analytic entailment parallel to (A*) would take the relation that the representation of the entailed sense must bear to the representation of the entailing sense to be, in effect, the containment relation that (A*) requires $P\{T_1, \ldots, T_n\}$ to bear to a term T_i (see Katz 1972: 171–197).

I am now in a position to take the first step toward representing the senses of basic color terms.[19] Since the sense *color* is the superordinate of *red*, as well as of the other basic color terms, we can represent the senses of 'red' and 'blue' with the semantic markers (3.59) and (3.60):

(3.59)   (Color)
                                      |
                                    (Red)

(3.60)   (Color)
                                      |
                                    (Blue)

These markers represent the senses of these words as primitive concepts, that is, as not definable in the system of senses. Nonetheless, (3.59) and (3.60) say that the senses of 'red' and 'blue' are complex concepts: the semantic markers representing primitive senses have domination relations representing superordinate/subordinate structure. Since the terminal components in (3.59) and (3.60) have no status in the symbolism independent of their status in (3.59) and (3.60), (3.59) and (3.60) represent the intrinsic connection that the senses *red* and *blue* have to their superordinate *color*.

With the semantic marker '(Color)' as the semantic representation of the sense of the word 'color', (3.59) and (3.60) enable us to mark (3.51) and similar sentences as analytic on the basis of (A*). The analytic entailment of (3.50) by (3.48) and similar analytic entailments can also be marked on the same basis. But (3.59) and (3.60) are not sufficient to enable us to mark the analyticity of sentences like (3.53). This can be seen when we note that the English words appearing in semantic markers serve a purely mnemonic function, and hence, that the semantic markers (3.59) and (3.60) are simply distinct symbols for distinct senses, and do not represent the antonymy of 'red' and 'blue', but only their nonsynonymy. (3.59) and (3.60) are thus incomplete representations of 'red' and 'blue'.

Thus, in order to represent (3.53) as analytic in the sense of (A*), another branch representing the antonymy of 'red' and 'blue' must be added to (3.59) and (3.60). Moreover, since (3.61) raises the same difficulty as (3.53)

(3.61)   Blue is not red.

the parts of the semantic markers for the senses of 'red' and 'blue' that represent their antonymy relations must be the same *modulo* the difference between (3.59) and

(3.60). Moreover, since there is a set of sentences for (3.61) corresponding to (3.54), i.e., 'Blue is not green', and so on, the semantic representation of a basic color term must show its incompatibility with all other basic color terms. Hence, the decompositional sense of a basic color term has somehow to embody the antonymy structure of the system of basic color terms.

Here we come to the key point. A basic color term must express its incompatibility with all the other basic color terms without the senses of the latter themselves occurring in the sense of the former. This is the element of truth in the claims of Hardin and other philosophers that one color concept is not part of another. But they go beyond this truth when they conclude that sentences like (3.53) are not analytic on the basis of containment. This truth has no such implication. What is overlooked is the possibility that the antonymy structure of color words is embodied in their senses in a sufficiently abstract form so that, on the one hand, a basic color term like 'red' can express its incompatibility with all other basic color terms without the senses of the latter themselves occurring in the sense of the former, and, on the other hand, a *sentence* like (3.53) can be analytic.

To represent the antonymy structure of color words as abstractly embodied in their senses, the semantic markers (3.59) and (3.60) have to contain a further branch, call it "*Br*," that expresses the antonymy of the color concept it represents with the other color concepts in the language without containing the semantic markers for those color concepts. Since *Br* is the same for the representation of every color word, we need only determine what *Br* is for (3.59). Our assumption that (3.53) is analytic in the sense of (A*) suggests a strategy for determining *Br*. Since, on this assumption, there must be a step in the derivation of the representation of (3.53) at which *Br* is transformed into a branch *Br** that represents the antonymy of the sense *red* with the sense *blue*, we need to look ahead to this step, see what the representation of *Br** is, and then work back from *Br** to *Br*. The strategy is to work out what *Br* has to be to have been the source of *Br**, on the basis of *Br** and the fact that the derivation of *Br** takes place within a formal theory of decompositional and compositional sense structure of the sort just sketched.

The first thing we note is that, since *Br* itself does not contain a representation of the sense *blue*, the semantic marker for the sense of 'blue' that enters *Br* at the step in question must be the value of a categorized variable in *Br*. Second, we note that the value of this variable must come from the representation of the sense of an occurrence of the word 'blue' elsewhere in (3.53). Third, we note that the only place from which the value can come is the verb phrase of the sentence. Since, as (3.54) shows, the verb phrase of such a sentence can contain any color term in the place where 'blue' occurs, the variable in *Br* must be categorized for the constituent of the verb phrase that contains the color term. This means that *Br* is a branch whose topmost marker '(Color)' dominates a variable the values of which are semantic representations of the constituent in a verb phrase containing the color term. To embody the antonymy structure of the system of basic color terms abstractly, this variable must be within the scope of an operator that specifies that the color that (3.59) supplemented with *Br* represents is different from the colors represented by the semantic markers belonging to the same antonymous *n*-tuple as (3.59) supplemented with *Br*. We have such an operator at hand.

In the first part of this book, I argued that internal negation is an operation on a sense that produces another sense belonging to the same antonymous n-tuple. All of the members of an antonymous n-tuple have a common superordinate, which distinguishes the antonymous n-tuple from other antonymous n-tuples, but each member stands in an exclusion relation to every other member. The sense of an internal negation is an operator, which we symbolize as 'A/ . . .', that, when applied to a sense, yields an exclusive disjunction of the other senses in its antonymous n-tuple, together with a term precluding any color at all.

Hence, Br is a branch the topmost marker of which, '(Color)', dominates a complex symbol consisting of an occurrence of 'A/ . . .' associated with a variable that is syntactically categorized for the constituent in a verb phrase containing the color term. Assume that the syntax of (3.53) is as depicted in (3.62). (The syntactic formalism in (3.62), though superseded, is preferable here to the formalisms of current versions of syntactic theory: there is a wide variety of the latter, they change often, philosophers are less familiar with them, and they are less transparent on first encounter.)

(3.62)

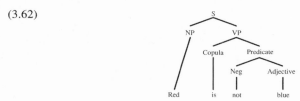

(3.63) replaces (3.59) as the semantic representation of the lexical item 'red'.

(3.63)

The syntactic information in [F] specifies the predicate adjective in the verb phrase and, together with the selection restriction, tells us that values of the variable in (3.63) are semantic representations of the predicate adjective just in case their superordinate marker is '(Color)'. Finally, parallel considerations dictate adding Br to (3.60) to provide (3.64) as the semantic representation of the color term 'blue'.

(3.64)

(Color)

(Blue)   [F]
      A/   X
      < (Color) >

Given (3.63) and (3.64), it can be shown that (3.53) is analytic in the sense of (A*). To show this, we have to exhibit a compositional derivation that begins with representations of the senses of the lexical items in (3.53), i.e., 'red', 'is', 'not', and 'blue', and ends with a representation of the sense of the sentence on which the sense of its subject 'red' contains the sense of its predicate 'not blue'. Further, the presentation of this derivation must be such as to indicate how, *mutatis mutandis*, similar derivations for the other color sentences in question can be given.

Since the derivation of a representation of (3.53) gives its compositional meaning, the representation is a function of the aforementioned representations of 'red', 'is', 'not', and 'blue' and their syntactic relations as depicted in (3.62). Since compositional principles work up from the most deeply embedded constituents of a sentence (its lexical items) to the least deeply embedded constituent (the entire sentence), the first step in the derivation assigns semantic markers from dictionary entries to terminal symbols of (3.62). Thus, (3.63) and (3.64) are assigned to the occurrences of 'red' and 'blue' in (3.62), 'A/ . . .' is assigned to the lexical item 'not' in (3.62), and (3.65) is assigned to the lexical item 'is'.

(3.65)

$$[\text{Predicate, S}]$$
$$X$$
$$<R> \qquad [\text{NP,S}]$$
$$X$$
$$<R>$$

(3.65) is modeled on the familiar notion of the application of the predicate concept in a subject-predicate sentence to the subject concept. The grammatical function [Predicate, S], which is read as "the constituent dominated by 'Predicate', dominated by 'S'," picks out the predicate 'not blue' in (3.23). The function [NP, S], as indicated earlier, picks out the subject of the sentence. (3.65) becomes the representation of (3.53) when the categorized variables in (3.65) are, respectively, replaced with the representations of the predicate and the subject of (3.53).

The second step combines the representation of 'not' with the representation of the adjective 'blue' to get (3.66):

(3.66)

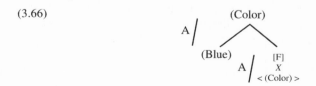

and assigns (3.66) as the representation of the Predicate 'not blue' in (3.62).

In the third step, the semantic marker (3.66), just assigned as the semantic representation of the Predicate, becomes the value of the variable categorized for representations of Predicates in the semantic marker (3.65). The result is (3.67):

(3.67)

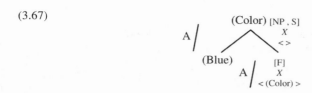

which is assigned as the semantic representation of the VP constituent in (3.62).

The fourth step provides a value for the categorized variable in the representation of the subject in (3.62). Since the semantic representation of the Predicate, (3.66), has the marker '(Color)' as its topmost marker, it satisfies the selection restriction of the variable in (3.63), and becomes its value. The result, (3.68), is assigned to the subject in (3.62).

(3.68)

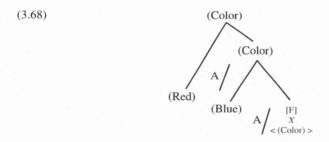

In the final step of the derivation, (3.68)—which was just assigned as the representation of the subject in (3.62)—is made the value of the variable categorized for the subject in (3.67), and the result, (3.69), is assigned to the sentence constituent in (3.62), and hence to (3.53).[20]

(3.69)

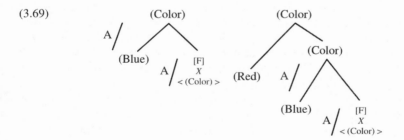

(3.69) is of the form $P\{T_1, \ldots, T_n\}$, $n = 1$. The semantic marker on the left of (3.69), which represents the predicate $P\{x_1, \ldots, x_n\}$, is a same-rooted subtree of the semantic marker on the right, which represents the term T_i, and, hence, (A*) marks the sense that (3.69) represents as analytic. Similarly, sentences like (3.47) and (3.70):

(3.70)   Red is not red.

can be marked as contradictory on the basis of representations like (3.63) and (3.64). On the definition of contradictoriness, (C), a sense of a sentence is contradictory if either there is an antonymy among its predicates or there is an antonymy between its predicates and its terms. (3.47) is an example of the former type of contradictoriness, and (3.70) is an example of the latter. In the case of (3.47), (3.63) and (3.64) are each values of the occurrence of the variable in the other. When these saturated semantic markers become the value of the variable categorized [Predicate, S] in the occurrence of (3.65) assigned to the copula of (3.47), the sentence will be represented as having an antonymy relation between its component predicates, and so be marked contradictory. In the case of (3.70), each occurrence of (3.63) will be the value of the variable in the other occurrence. When these saturated semantic markers replace the variables categorized [Predicate, S] and [NP, S] in the occurrence of (3.65) assigned to the copula of (3.70), the result is a semantic marker that represents (3.70) as having an antonymy between its predicate and term. Thus, (3.70) will be marked contradictory.

Since, in my view, analyticity and contradictoriness reflect structures internal to sentences of the language, not relations between language and the world, we have to go beyond the derivation to explain why and in what sense analytic sentences like (3.53) are necessary truths and contradictory sentences like (3.47) and (3.70) are necessary falsehoods. This is straightforward. Given the referential correlates for analytic sentences, (3.53) is a weakly necessary truth, as well as secured against falsehood, and, given the referential correlates for contradictory sentences, (3.47) and (3.70) are weakly necessary falsehoods, as well as secured against truth. Thus, evaluated at worlds where there is something for them to be true or false of, 'red' is necessarily exclusive of 'blue' and necessarily exclusive of 'not red'.[21]

I can now explain why it initially seemed impossible for the sense of 'red' in (3.53) to contain the sense of 'not blue'. It seemed impossible because no distinction was drawn between the meaning of a word *in isolation* and the meaning of a word *in a sentence*. To be sure, it is impossible for the sense of the lexical item 'red' to contain the sense *not blue*, but the case of a word in a sentence is different from the case of the word in isolation. It is different because the sense of a word in a sentence can have sense components that are not part of its sense as a lexical item, but come in from the senses of other constituents in the sentence. Compositionality makes the difference. Failing to take account of compositionality, philosophers assimilated the case of words in a sentence to the case of words in isolation, thereby taking a perfectly genuine impossibility intuition concerning words in isolation to apply to words in a sentence, where it does not apply at all.

Restricted to lexical concepts, Hardin's claim that "the concept of not being red is . . . [not] part of [the] concept of being green" expresses an uncontroversial truth. But such claims are intended to apply generally, and they must do so in order for them to support the view that Wittgenstein's problem has no solution. But if the claims do apply generally, they apply to senses of words in sentences, and then, as we have seen, they are false.[22]

Wittgenstein's problem was seen as posing a dilemma between intuition and logic because it was assumed that semantic structure is logical structure. On this assumption, we are restricted to one of two alternatives: we must either follow Wittgenstein and Quine and deny that extralogical words have semantic powers, or follow Carnap and try to explain their powers in logical terms. If we take the first alternative, we sacrifice our linguistic intuitions, and if we take the second alternative, we buy into an account of those intuitions that has been shown to be explanatorily empty. My way out drops the assumption, making it possible to go between the horns of the dilemma. Sentences like (3.47)–(3.52) have the semantic properties and relations that intuition tells us they have. Also, the components of (3.47) are logically elementary propositions, (3.48), (3.50), (3.51), and (3.52) are themselves logically elementary propositions, and (3.49) is the negation of a logically elementary proposition. Hence, it is true that those sentences cannot have their semantic properties and relations on the basis of their logical structure. But there is no conflict between intuition and logic and no need to resort to empty explanations, because the sense structure on the basis of which the sentences have those properties and relations is not logical structure. The alleged conflict between intuition and logic disappears once we cease thinking of sense structure in Fregean terms.

3.17. Analyticity, epistemology, and skepticism

It was a central thesis of logical positivism that sentences about color like (3.53) are merely analytic *a priori* truths. Such sentences provide no support for metaphysics because, as Moritz Schlick once put it, they "say nothing . . . about the nature of anything, but rather only exhibit the content of our concepts" (1949: 285). Now, my account of the analyticity of such sentences shows them to be analytic *a priori*, and hence it rules out precisely what logical positivists like Schlick wanted to rule out, namely, the metaphysical claim that our knowledge of those sentences is synthetic *a priori* knowledge. Hence, it looks *prima facie* as if we have vindicated the central thesis of logical positivism for one significant class of sentences.

This may be counted as something of a victory for logical positivism, but it is not one that logical positivists can take much comfort in. First, the semantics that delivers it is not theirs, and, second, from the standpoint of their central thesis itself, the victory is a Pyrrhic one. The logical positivists were right for the wrong reason. They were right in thinking that no special faculty of intuiting essences is required to explain what we know about the semantics of color sentences like (3.53), but wrong in thinking that this is because the semantic properties of such sentences can be explained on the basis of the Frege/Carnap logical notion of analyticity. As it turns out, it is the mereological notion of analyticity that explains the semantic properties of those sentences. From the larger standpoint of the controversy between empiricism and rationalism, this makes all the difference. For the failure of the Frege/Carnap notion of analyticity and the success of the mereological notion puts a thin analytic/synthetic distinction in place, which, although it counts one special class of truths as analytic *a priori*, counts many others with which the positivists were concerned, such as logical and mathematical truths, as synthetic *a priori*.

Unlike the Frege/Carnap notion, which expands the class of analytic truths to encompass the necessary truths, the mereological notion contracts the class of analytic truths so that virtually all logical and mathematical truths are synthetic. Thus, the success of the mereological notion of analyticity entails, for the empiricist, the undesirable consequence that the problem of synthetic *a priori* knowledge re-emerges for a wide range of sentences that the mereological notion marks as non-analytic. Hence, the arguments I have put forth for this notion in the course of this book, not the least of which is that it solves Wittgenstein's problem of color incompatibility, provide grounds for saying that the problem of synthetic *a priori* knowledge, particularly in logic and mathematics, is back to bedevil the empiricist thesis that all knowledge rests on experience.

In his narrow aim in "Two Dogmas of Empiricism" of establishing that the Frege/Carnap notion of analyticity cannot be used to show that some of our knowledge is *a priori*, Quine was entirely successful. However, in his broad aim of refuting the rationalist thesis that we have knowledge that is entirely independent of experience, he was not successful. This is because the mereological notion of analyticity provides an alternative to the Frege/Carnap notion of analyticity. As I argued earlier, the fact that Quine's assumption that Fregean intensionalism is all that intensionalists have available to them is false means that his criticisms of intensionalism fail, and hence so does his attempt to deny rationalism the conceptual tools it needs for its epistemology.

If this line of argument is right, then the various attempts we see made from time to time to save the *a priori* from Quinean criticisms are pointless. It does not need saving because Quine's criticisms are too narrowly focused on Frege/Carnap semantics to put it in danger. As Chalmers Clark (1998) reports, Quine himself seems to acknowledge that his criticisms do not apply to a theory of meaning such as ours.

Paul Boghossian's attempt to save the *a priori* (1996) is not only an attempt to defeat Quinean skepticism, but to defeat other forms of skepticism as well. Although this attempt, being general, is not pointless in the manner of attempts to save the *a priori* from Quine, it works only within the discredited framework of Frege/Carnap intensionalism. Indeed, it is just what one should say within that framework. But Boghossian's attempt does not work outside it because his argument, which is a purported linguistic justification for *a priori* knowledge, assumes that certain matters of theory, in particular, principles of logic, are part of the meaning of expressions in the language. This is the Frege/Carnap view of the language/theory distinction. Against it, I have argued that the principles of logic are extralinguistic matters of theory. If this is right, the assumption about meaning in natural language that drives Boghossian's argument is wrong.

Boghossian states that his aim is to show that ". . . in an important sense to be specified later on, our grasp of the meaning of logical claims can explain our a priori entitlement to holding them true. . . . [I]f someone knows the relevant facts about [the meaning of certain sentences], *then* that person will be in a position to form a justified true belief about their truth" (1996: 374, 386). He says that ". . . knowledge of the meaning of A . . . includes not merely knowledge of what A means, strictly so called, but also knowledge of how that meaning is fixed" and that "A logical constant C expresses that logical object, if any, that makes valid its meaning-constituting inferences or sentences" (1996: 386, 385). Given this, Boghossian argues against the skeptic that knowledge of the meaning of a constant C suffices for *a priori* knowledge of the validity of the arguments A expressing C's "meaning-constituting inferences." For "If C is to mean what it does, then A has to be valid, for C means whatever logical object in fact makes A valid. C means what it does. Therefore, A is valid."

Can we have *a priori* knowledge that C is meaningful? That it means what it does? Here Boghossian argues that we cannot coherently doubt that C is meaningful because such doubt is self-refuting. We are entitled to believe *a priori* that C is meaningful because we can see *a priori* that doubting it is self-refuting. An attempt to express meaning skepticism about logical negation, for example, would be something like (MS):

(MS)   If something is a token of the logical constant 'Not', then it is meaningless (does not have a meaning).

But either the negation in the consequent of (MS) has a meaning or it does not, so either (MS) is false or meaningless.

This argument supposes that the negation of the privative suffix '-less' in the consequent of (MS) is a token of the logical constant 'Not' of the antecedent. Given the language/theory distinction in the Frege/Carnap framework, all forms of negation are logical, and, hence, the supposition is true. In this case, meaning skeptics trip themselves up in the very attempt to express their position. But if, as I have argued, that distinction is untenable because logic is an extralinguistic theory—the theory of deduction—then the supposition that the negation of the privative suffix '-less' in the consequent of (MS) is a token of the logical constant 'Not' of the antecedent is false. In this case, (MS) can be meaningful and true, and skeptics can use it to express skepticism about logical negation.

What enables (MS) to be meaningful is the distinction, which goes along with the language/theory distinction as I have drawn it, between logical negation and sense negation. The 'Not' of the antecedent is logical negation, and its meaning consists in the principles for extensionally interpreting sentences in the scope of the operator. The privative suffix '-less' is sense negation, the meaning of which consists in the principles for intensionally transforming senses within its scope. As the point about sense negation was put earlier, it is a sense-to-sense toggle. Since skeptics can take the negation in the consequent of (MS) as sense negation, they can use (MS) to express the skeptical supposition that the set of coherent principles for extensionally interpreting tokens of the logical constant 'Not' is empty. Hence, Boghossian's attempt to refute semantic skepticism fails because it wrongly assumes a language/

theory distinction on which natural languages have principles of theories—in this case, logic—built into them.

From my perspective, Boghossian's criticism of the skeptic is similar to Quine's criticism of the anthropological posit of "prelogicality":

> . . . let us suppose that certain natives are said to accept as true certain sentences translatable in the form 'p and -p'. Now this claim is absurd under our semantic criteria. And, not to be dogmatic about them, what criteria might one prefer? Wanton translation can make natives sound as queer as one pleases. Better translation imposes our logic upon them, *and would beg the question of prelogicality if there were a question to beg.* (Quine 1960: 58 [italics mine])

Just as Quine sought to rule out prelogicality on semantic criteria that build principles of logic into language, so Boghossian sought to rule out skepticism with such criteria. On my view, it is contrary to their nature for natural languages to have a particular set of theoretical principles built into them: their nature is to be a means of expressing principles of all theories without favoritism. Even skepticism about logic gets a fair shake. My answer to Quine's question "[W]hat [other] criteria might one prefer?" is: semantic criteria on which there is no theory built into the language, and, hence, on which sense properties and relations are no more than mereological structures in the senses of sentences.

3.18. Existence

3.18.1. The Cogito dilemma

Descartes, to the best of my knowledge, was the first philosopher to have the idea that the cases I am categorizing as analyticities and analytic entailments are not matters of logic. He did not try to provide an account of analyticity and analytic entailment that would explain the difference between the two kinds of inference, but he went quite far toward expressing the difference in reflecting on particular cases, especially the Cogito. In such cases, the conclusion is not arrived at by deductive steps but by a single intuition. He says that one does ". . . not deduce existence from thought by syllogism, but by a simple act of mental vision, recognizes it as if it were a thing that is known *per se*" (1969: ii, 38) and that ". . . each individual can mentally have an intuition of the fact that he exists, and that he thinks; that the triangle is bounded by three lines only, the sphere by a single superficies, and so on. Facts of such a kind are far more numerous than many people think, disdaining as they do to direct their attention to simple matters" (1969: ii, 7).

A comparison with Frege is interesting. Descartes's distinction between simple matters and complex, logical matters—syllogistic matters, as he understood matters of logic—is, in effect, Frege's distinction between inference based on "beams in a house" containment and inference based on "plant in the seed" containment. Frege's metaphor for mereological facts is certainly more revealing than Descartes's, since the term 'simple' is only a negative characterization, telling us little about the nature of non-logical inferential structure. A further similarity is that Descartes and Frege both make the distinction in the service of an ambitious foundational project in philosophy. Each project depends on the special features of its own inference relation. Descartes's reconstruction of knowledge requires simplicity to provide a presuppositionless starting point for his foundational project. Frege's logicism requires complexity to provide a fruitful form of analyticity for his logicism.

Descartes's concern with his project allowed him to leave the concept of analytic entailment unexplained and address just the one special instance of the relation that would provide him his starting point. Due to Descartes's failure to explain analytic entailment, the enormous superiority of Frege's and Russell and Whitehead's logic over syllogistic logic, the importance of this work in subsequent philosophy, and the widespread acceptance of Frege's fruitfulness criticism, Descartes's distinction between inferences based on sense and inferences based on logic was not recognized for the radical insight it is. Instead, philosophers read Descartes's notion of syllogistic deduction quite narrowly as referring only to Aristotelian logic. Reading this notion as referring to a species of logical deduction, they read Descartes's distinction between simple and complex inferences as nothing more than the distinction between deduction in Aristotelian logic and the new predicate logic. As a consequence, Descartes's prime example of analytic entailment, the Cogito, had to be taken as either invalid, since, as presented, it has the form P [*'I think'*], *therefore*, Q [*'I exist'*], or as a complex inference within predicate logic.

Few philosophers (one example I will discuss in section 3.20 is Carnap) are prepared to say that the Cogito is invalid. Those who do not wish to take this implausible position have to treat it as enthymematic and reconstruct it as a valid logical inference with something like the general principle 'whatever thinks exists' as a suppressed premise. Arnauld, reflecting the then current notion, describes an enthymeme in the *Port-Royal Logic* as "a syllogism which though complete in the mind is incomplete in expression" (1964: 228). Hence, since the Cogito is not complete in expression, its validity must be established on the basis of a recasting of it with the premises 'I think' and 'Whatever thinks exists'. But the cost of this way of saving validity is high. It makes nonsense of what Descartes says about the inference in passages like the one quoted above, which explicitly says that 'I exist' is inferred from just the premise 'I think'. Furthermore, if we recast the Cogito as a logical inference with a suppressed premise, we also make nonsense of the use to which Descartes puts it as a grounding for his philosophy. Since its conclusion now rests on a general principle, as well as a law of logic, the argument is no longer the presuppositionless starting point that his reconstruction of knowledge requires.

Moreover, we do not really explain the validity of the Cogito, since we do not explain the truth of the allegedly suppressed premise, 'whatever thinks exists', which is, of course, the Cogito. Further, we distort Descartes's intention in saying that one does "not deduce existence from thought by syllogism, but by a simple act of mental vision." Further, Descartes took (3.71) and (3.72) to express necessarily false assertions

(3.71)   I am not thinking.

(3.72)   I do not exist.

but he did not take them to be logical contradictions.

Fregeanism thus presents us with yet another dilemma. If we treat the Cogito as the argument we actually find in Descartes's writings and do not recast it as a logical deduction, we have to say that it is invalid. What, then, do we say by way of explanation? That it is possible to think about existing but not exist while doing so? If we want to say the Cogito is valid, we have to treat it as an enthymeme and recast it as just the kind of deductive argument Descartes is at such pains to deny it is. Hence, we have to dismiss Descartes's plausible claim that its conclusion depends on a simple insight and deny that the starting point in his reconstruction of knowledge is the indubitable 'first principle' that he says it is.

The way out of such a dilemma is now familiar: we go between the horns. In the present case, we reject the Fregean assumption that all valid inference is logical deduction. My non-Fregean intensionalism opens up the possibility of explaining the validity of logically simple arguments like the Cogito without recasting them as logically complex, enthymematic, arguments. If, as I have argued elsewhere (1986b; 1990c) the Cogito can be understood as a case of analytic entailment, it is valid as it stands: there is no suppressed premise that requires deducing its conclusion by an application of logic. The inferential connection between its premise and conclusion can be, as Descartes put it, "a thing that is known *per se*."

Moreover, if the Cogito is taken as an analytic entailment, we can account for its indubitability. Descartes says that the inference is "so solid and secure that the most extravagant supposings of the skeptics could not overthrow it" (1969: iv). Since, for Descartes, such "extravagant supposings" include skepticism about the truth of our logical principles (1970: 150–151, 236–237), this solidity and security can only be explained if the Cogito is an analytic entailment—that is, if the conclusion 'I exist' cannot but be true when the premise 'I think' is true, because the sense of the former is contained in the sense of the latter in such a way that the truth of the premise is *ipso facto* the truth of the conclusion. Only in this case is the Cogito independent of the laws of logic, which, for Descartes, God has the power to change, and hence, only in this case is it secure from the skeptical claim that we can doubt laws of logic.

Things fall nicely into place *if* the Cogito is an analytic entailment. The problem is that *prima facie* it does not look like one. On the surface, it is not like the familiar examples of analytic entailment. The sense of 'I exist' is not contained in the sense of 'I think' in the predicate-to-predicate way that the sense of 'John is unmarried' is contained in the sense of 'John is a bachelor'. Even assuming that we can treat 'exists' as a predicate, its sense does not seem to be part of the sense of 'thinks' in the way that the sense of 'unmarried' is part of the sense of 'bachelor'.

But the fact that the sense of 'exists' is not part of the sense of 'thinks' *in the same way that* the sense of 'unmarried' is part of the sense of 'bachelor' does not imply that it is not part of it in another way. Hence, before we conclude that the benefits of construing the Cogito as an analytic entailment are unobtainable, we need to look again at sense structure to see in what other ways containment can occur. Such an examination will show that, although the kind of containment that we find in the Cogito does differ from the predicate-to-predicate containment in familiar cases of analytic entailment, there is a way in which the sense of 'I exist' is contained in the sense of 'I think'.

The definition (PP) of presupposition in section 3.8.3 specifies the presupposition of a sentence in terms of a prior division of argument places into referential and non-referential ones. The former are argument places the occupying terms of which contribute a clause to the presupposition of the sentence, and the latter are argument places the terms of which do not. For example, (3.73) presupposes the existence of police and a jewel thief,

(3.73)   The police chased the jewel thief.

(3.74) only presupposes the existence of a child,

(3.74)   The child imagined a candy mountain.

and (3.75) presupposes the existence of a Mary but not of her children.

(3.75)   If Mary has children, then Mary's children play the piano.

As written thus far, the semantic marker for 'chase', (3.55):

(3.55)

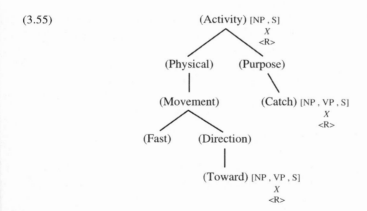

does not mark the argument places of the predicate as referential. As they stand, such semantic markers for activity verbs like 'chase' do not provide a formal specification of the presuppositions of sentences in which the verbs appear. To put the point in slightly different terms, we have not as yet provided the formal distinction necessary to represent the semantic difference in the recipient argument place in verbs like 'chase' and 'imagine'. In earlier work (1972: 167; 1979b), I suggested a formalism for distinguishing referential and non-referential argument places. The idea was to use "heavy parentheses," '**( )**', enclosing a categorized variable to represent a referential argument place and a categorized variable not enclosed by such parentheses to represent a non-referential argument place. With this formalism, the semantic marker (3.55) for 'chase' is rewritten as (3.76):

(3.76)

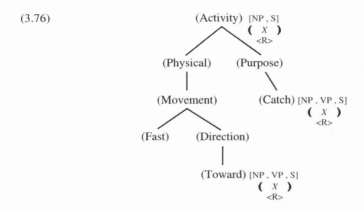

Heavy parentheses should be considered as much a part of the representation of a sense of a lexical item as whether a verb has one, two, or more argument places. That referentiality or non-referentiality of an argument place of a verb is a full-fledged feature of its sense is clear from the semantic difference between the recipient argument places in verbs like 'chase' and 'imagine'.

The referentiality of the agent and recipient argument places in the sense of 'chase' and the agent argument place in the sense of 'imagine' are inherent features of the senses of these verbs. Similarly, the non-referentiality of the recipient argument place of 'imagine' is an inherent feature of its sense. Thus, the appearance or non-appearance of heavy parentheses is part of the representation of the sense of a verb. As (3.75) and (3.77) show,

(3.77)   Mary's children play the piano.

some cases of non-referentiality are derived. (3.77) presupposes that Mary has children while (3.75) does not. The agent place of the sense of 'play' is inherently referential, but loses its referentiality in the scope of the hypotheticality that occurs in the antecedent. Hence, provision has to be made for changing the status of argument places from referential to non-referential in the compositional process. There are also changes from non-referentiality at the lexical level to referentiality higher up in the compositional process. In an earlier discussion of presupposition and compositionality (1979b), I described these changes in terms of rules that remove and install heavy parentheses in the derivation of the compositional meanings of sentences.

Given that the clauses of a presupposition make claims about existence, the terms occupying the referential argument places that contribute clauses to the presupposition have existential import. Hence, such terms ought to give rise to entailments of existence sentences—and they do, as can be seen from the fact that (3.73) entails (3.78) and (3.79):

(3.78)   Police exist.

(3.79)   A thief exists.

Correspondingly, the absence of existential import in the case of argument places like the recipient argument place in the sense of 'imagine' ought not to produce parallel entailments of existence sentences. That this is so can be seen from the fact that (3.74) does not analytically entail (3.80):

(3.80)   A candy mountain exists.

My task now is to show that these entailments and non-entailments can be explained in terms of analytic entailment. To do this, I have to show how the apparatus of heavy parentheses can be deployed to explain how a premise with a term occurring in a referential argument place can contain a conclusion asserting the existence of the referent of the term. Since containment is mereological inclusion, this requires me to represent the sense of 'exists' with the same formalism that I used to express the existential import of a term occupying a referential argument place. The formalism for the word 'exists' in sentences like (3.78)–(3.80) and the formalism for referential argument places must differ only in that the former does not represent the existential import of the term as a clause of a presupposition, but as an assertion. This difference is obtained if the sense of 'exists' in existence sentences is represented as the "empty" predicate (3.81):

(3.81)   ( ) [NP, S]
                                       X
                                      <R>

The fact that the heavy parentheses in (3.81) are empty—that they contain neither semantic markers nor a categorized variable—allows us to give 'exists' its grammatical due as a predicate. Note that 'exists' has perfectly good grammatical credentials for being a predicate. It has the syntactic form of an intransitive verb belonging to the class containing 'occurs', 'happens', and 'appears'. And, as I have observed elsewhere (1986b: 103), it behaves syntactically like such predicates. Further, the empty heavy parentheses in (3.81) allow us to accord 'exists' this status without running afoul of Kant's famous discussion. In fact, this formalism is a reasonable explication of Kant's claim that 'exists' is not a "real predicate." He never claimed that 'exists' is not a predicate at all, but only that it involves no content which, in application to a subject concept, "is added to the concept of the subject and enlarges it" (1929: 504).

At this point, all that is required to capture the analytic entailment of existence sentences is the addition of a clause to the definition of the same-rooted subtree relation that appears in (A*). The definition, as it stands, says that one semantic marker is a same-rooted subtree of another if they have a common root and the former is part of the latter. We supplement this definition with a further clause which says that ( ) (*M1*) is a same-rooted subtree of any semantic marker having a node with the label (*M2*) ((*M3*)) just in case (*M1*) is a same-rooted subtree of (*M3*) in the sense of its original clause. Given (3.81) as the representation of 'exists', (3.76) as the representation of 'chase', and this supplementation, we can mark (3.73) as analytically entailing (3.78) and (3.79).

The referentiality of the agent argument place is a feature of activity verbs generally. Thus, we should take 'think', 'doubt', and so on, which are mental activity verbs, to have a referential agent argument place in their senses like 'chase' and 'imagine'. This move will be opposed by philosophers such as G. E. M. Anscombe (1990: 135–153), who are influenced by Wittgenstein's Lichtenbergean view that the first-person pronoun does not make reference, but only functions like the expletive 'it' in 'It is raining'. I have argued that this view can be refuted on straight syntactic evidence (1990c: 175–177).

Given this formalism for the agent argument place in the premise of the Cogito, the sense of the first-person pronoun in 'I think' is represented as occurring in a referential argument place. Given (3.81) as the representation of 'exists' and the supplementation of the definition of same-rooted subtree, this formalism shows that 'I think' analytically entails 'I exist' on the basis of the same sense containment that is responsible for (3.73)'s analytically entailing (3.78) and (3.79). Of course, this containment is not the predicate-to-predicate containment on the basis of which 'John is a bachelor' analytically entails 'John is unmarried'; but, as I have now shown, that form of containment is not the only one to be found in sense structure.

This account of the Cogito does justice to Descartes's use of it and confirms what he says about it. If the Cogito is an analytic entailment, it is, as Descartes insisted, not a "syllogism"; that is, it is not derived on the basis of logical laws. Its conclusion is not a plant that grows logically from seeds, but a beam that is already part of a house. Since the Cogito is not enthymematic, Descartes faces no difficulty in the way he uses it in his reconstruction of knowledge. Moreover, the Cogito is valid (as it stands), and we can explain this as follows. The premise of the Cogito asserts that an activity of thinking is taking place at the speech point the agent of which is the speaker, and, hence, the premise presupposes the existence of this speaker. As a consequence, the conclusion of the Cogito, which asserts the existence of such a speaker, makes a redundant assertion. Hence, the conclusion makes a true statement whenever the premise does.

If this account of the Cogito is right, there is no Cogito dilemma. The difficulties philosophers have had in making sense of the Cogito are due to their having assumed that all valid inference is logical deduction. This created the dilemma. Taking the Cogito to be valid, so that its conclusion must be logically deduced from its premise, makes it enthymematic, which cannot be squared with either Descartes's characterization of it as lacking the complexity of logical inference or the role it is assigned in his epistemological project. Taking the Cogito to be invalid is simply turning a blind eye to virtually everyone's intuition that 'I exist' cannot be false whenever 'I think' is true. Abandoning the assumption and adopting the view that some inferences are non-logical, that is, simple matters, we can go between the horns. Given my account of the Cogito, its validity depends just on a containment relation, and, hence, can be grasped, as Descartes puts it, in "a simple act of mental vision."

3.18.2. Analytic existence sentences

Pelletier (1982: 322) makes the claim, attributing it to Leonard Linsky (1972: 473–482), that there is a difficulty with my account of analyticity because 'My father is not a queen', which is analytic, analytically entails 'Someone is not a queen' "which is not analytic."[23] The point could be made even more forcefully. It could be claimed that the fact that, on my account of analyticity, (3.82a) and (3.82b) are analytic and analytically entail (3.83):

(3.82a)   Some witches are female.

(3.82b)   Some witches are witches.

(3.83)   Witches exist.

shows that my account is incoherent. As the earlier discussion of (3.73)'s analytically entailing (3.78) and (3.79) shows, analytic entailments like that from (3.82a) to (3.83) and from (3.82b) to (3.83) are consequences of my theory. Since, further, (3.83) is false, it looks as if I am committed to saying that a true sentence entails a false one.

   In fact, there is no such difficulty. To be sure, that (3.82a) and (3.82b) each analytically entail (3.83) is a consequence of my theory, and, to be sure, (3.83) is false. But the falsehood of (3.83) does not deliver the *reductio* without the further assumption that (3.82a) and (3.82b) are true. On my presuppositionalist approach, however, the falsehood of (3.83) precludes the truth of (3.82). To put the matter from the standpoint of the formalization, the entailment runs off the heavy parentheses in the representation of the sense of the subject term in (3.82a) and (3.82b). Thus, the falsehood of (3.83) means that the presupposition of (3.82a) and (3.82b), that there are witches, is not satisfied. In this case, (3.82a) and (3.82b) have no truth value. The idea that inferences like that from (3.82a) or (3.82b) to (3.83) pose a difficulty for my account arises because inference is seen through the lens of Fregean semantics, according to which the referential interpretation of analyticity is necessary truth.

   There is no problem with analytic sentences' analytically entailing non-analytic sentences so long as the former are not true under circumstances where the latter are false. Thus, there is no problem about the fact that the analytic sentence 'My father is not a queen' analytically entails the non-analytic 'Someone is not a queen', since the latter cannot be false if the former is true.

3.18.3. Frege's fruitfulness criticism again

Frege denied that "[Kant] can speak of a subject concept and ask—as his definition requires—whether the predicate concept is contained in it or not. But how can we do this, if the subject is an individual object? Or if the judgment is an existential one? In these cases there can simply be no question of a subject concept in Kant's sense" (1953: 99–100). Frege was right to claim that Kant's "division of judgments into analytic and synthetic is not exhaustive" (1953: 100), but wrong to take this limitation to show that his own account of analyticity with its more fruitful notion of containment is mandatory. As with the objection that Kant's notion of analyticity does not apply to relational sentences, the two objections Frege makes in the above quotation do not raise problems intrinsic to the mereological notion of analyticity.

Assuming what Frege has in mind in talking about "an individual object" are cases of subjects that are proper names, my account of their senses shows that we *can* ask "whether the predicate concept is contained in" a proper name. On (3.44), the predicate *is a bearer of 'Socrates'* is (mereologically) contained in the sense of the subject of 'Socrates is a bearer of Socrates'. Further, as is evident, my explication of the Cogito and my discussion of analytic existence sentences answers the last of Frege's specific objections to a "beams in the house" notion of containment. Hence, the problems Frege raises for Kant's way of explicating analyticity, especially, as Frege points out, for taking analytic judgments to be exclusively "universal affirmative judgments," are not problems for other ways of explicating it. What is called for to remove them is, therefore, not, as Frege insists, a "more fruitful" explicandum for analyticity, but a better explicans for mereological analyticity.

3.19. The paradox of non-being

Roderick Chisholm quotes Meinong as saying: "Those who like paradoxical modes of expression could very well say: There are objects of which it is true to say that there are no such objects" (1960: 8). More fully, the paradox may be posed as follows. (3.84a) and (3.84b) are truths.

(3.84a)   Golden mountains do not exist.

(3.84b)   Santa Claus does not exist.

Hence, they are about something. If so, the something that they are about must exist, but, of course, if it exists, the sentences in question must be false. Therefore, on pain of acknowledging true sentences that are false, we have to concede that we are unable to express facts about non-existence.

Like most philosophers, I agree with Russell's judgment that Meinong's solution represents "a failure of that feeling for reality which ought to be preserved even in the most abstract studies" (1919: 169). On the other hand, as indicated in the earlier discussion of Russell's theory of descriptions, I do not find his solution to the paradox of non-being attractive. My new intensionalism provides an alternative to Russell's alternative to Meinong.

My account of the predicate 'exists' in the treatment of Descartes' Cogito coupled with the notion of aboutness in (ABT) enables us to block the argument to the paradox of non-being by rejecting the premise that if a sentence is true, it is about something. (ABT) says that negative existentials like (3.84a) and (3.84b) and positive existentials like (3.84c) and (3.84d) are not about anything.

(3.84c)   Golden mountains exist.

(3.84d)   Santa Claus exists.

This makes good intuitive sense, since, after all, there is nothing out there in the world for them to be about. As Gilbert Ryle puts it:

> Suppose I assert of (apparently) the general subject 'carnivorous cows' that they 'do not exist', and my assertion is true, I cannot really be talking about carnivorous cows, for there are none. So it follows that the expression 'carnivorous cows' is not really being used, though the grammatical appearances are to the contrary, to denote the thing or things of which the predicate is being asserted. (1952: 15–16)

This leaves the question: if sentences like (3.84a) and (3.84b) are not about anything, how can they say what is the case about how things are? My account of the predicate 'exists' explains how they can. On my account, 'exists' is the language's device for just this purpose. As I have argued, the predicate expresses the same existence condition as a referential argument place. In the case of a referential argument place with a term occupying it, the condition is a clause of the presupposition saying that the term must refer to something in the domain of the language for the sentence to have a truth value. In the case of the predicate 'exists' associated with a term, the condition is a truth condition of the sentence rather than a clause of the presupposition, since, as I argued earlier, existence sentences have no presupposition. Hence, a positive existential sentence is true in case the term with which its predicate is associated refers to something in the domain of the language and false in case the term refers to nothing. A negative existential sentence is true in case the term with which its predicate is associated refers to nothing in the domain of the language and false in case the term refers to something. Accordingly, (3.84a) and (3.84b) are true and (3.84c) and (3.84d) are false *tout court*.

Since my account of existence sentences says they are not about anything in the world, there is no need to posit so-called negative events and negative facts to explain how sentences like (3.84a) and (3.84b) are true. As Richard Gale put it, the principal line of argument for positing them is that "[t]he correspondence theory of truth seems to require the postulation of something in the world to serve as the correspondent of a true proposition about the world. Since there are true negative propositions *about absences, lacks, and privations in the world*, there must be such negative events or states to serve as their correspondents" (1976: 1 [italics mine]). On my view, this argument is unsound. True negative existence sentences are not about anything, so we do not have to say that there are absences, lacks, or privations that they are about. The correspondence theory of truth requires us to say that the truth of a proposition asserting that an object has or does not have a property is a matter of its having or not having the property; but the theory does not require us to say that existence sentences express propositions asserting that an object has or does not have a property. They express propositions asserting that a term has or does not have reference.[24]

It might be said that sentences like (3.84a)–(3.84d) are about something because they make an assertion about the world. There is some plausibility in this, and it is consistent with (ABT)'s thesis that true negative existence sentences are not about anything in the world, such as absences, lacks, or privations. Moreover, (ABT) could, of course, be written to reflect this way of speaking. But (ABT) was written as it was because this way of speaking is not entirely acceptable. If a sentence like (3.84c) expresses a statement about the world, the statement must be (3.85):

(3.85)   The world contains golden mountains.

but then the former sentence ought to be synonymous with the latter. But it is not. If there had been nothing rather than something—a possibility that all reflective cosmogonists recognize—then (3.84a) would be true, while (3.86):

(3.86)   The world does not contain golden mountains.

would not be true (because if there were nothing, there would be no world).

Finally, there is a further issue that is sometimes run together with the analysis of existence sentences. Richard Cartwright says that we feel "linguistic outrage . . . at being told that [(3.87)] is not about dragons" (1987b: 27).

(3.87)   Dragons do not exist.

The "outrage" stems from the fact that, on his view, (3.87) and (3.88) are both true.

(3.88)   Dragons do not have fur.

Cartwright says: ". . . to deny [(3.88)] is to exhibit an ignorance of mythology as pathetic as the ignorance of natural history displayed by denying [(3.87)]" (1987b: 27–28). But it is hard to see why what is true in myth should be a basis for saying anything about the truth value of (3.88), construed as a non-generic statement about the world. (If we construe sentences like (3.88) as generic sentences about a kind, and if, as I have argued [1979b: 113–119], generic sentences are presuppositionless, there is a basis for counting sentences like (3.88) as true in the actual world.) The mythological and the real are different domains in which to evaluate the sentences of a language. If we take (3.88) to be a statement about the actual world, then it comes out as not having a truth value, but if we take it to be a statement about mythology, then our analysis of existence sentences delivers Cartwright's conclusion that (3.88) is true.

It *would* be outrageous to take a use of (3.88) to be truth-valueless in the context of informing a small child about Puff the Magic Dragon; but this is, as it were, a pragmatic outrage. The assertion is made subject to the pretense about dragons in mythology and in children's stories. I thus agree with Cartwright's truism that "un-reality . . . is not another reality" (1987b: 30): an assertion about something that we entertain under a pretense is an act that is part of reality.

3.20. Regimentation revisited

One important strand in my argument for an autonomous theory of sense and a non-Fregean intensionalism has been the completion of the objection some philosophers and linguists have made to the practice of regimenting simple sentences. As I have noted, their objection left defenders of the practice with a forceful response. The defenders can concede that representing simple sentences as compound sentences misrepresents their grammatical structure, but justify it by saying that the increase in the explanatory scope of their semantics compensates for this element of grammatical counterintuitiveness. Without such recasting, the defenders of regimentation can say, there is no way to account for the semantic properties of simple sentences inside a logic-based semantics. This is not a response that the philosophers and linguists in question are in much of a position to counter, sharing, as they do, the defenders' commitment to a logic-based semantics.

I have argued that the response can be rebutted because there is a way of accounting for the semantic properties of simple sentences outside a logic-based semantics. I have argued that my autonomous theory of sense and my new intensionalism—in particular, the mereological treatment of analyticity—accounts for such properties without distorting the grammatical structure of simple sentences. This being so, the rationale for tolerating grammatical counterintuitiveness disappears. So what if there is no way to account for the semantic properties of simple sentences *inside* a logic-based semantics? Once this rationale goes, the distortions of grammatical structure become a powerful argument against the general claim that the standard practice of regimentation is adequate for sentences of natural language, or can be made so without fundamental change.

In this section, I present some additions to this argument against regimentation. One is that the standard practice of regimentation fails to account for the analyticity of sentences like (3.82a) and (3.82b):

(3.82a)   Some witches are female.

(3.82b)   Some witches are witches.

Such sentences make redundant predications, but cannot be marked as analytic on the standard regimentations '$(\exists x)(\text{Witch } x \ \& \ \text{Female } x)$' and '$(\exists x)(\text{Witch } x \ \& \ \text{Witch}$

x)', where they come out as implying the synthetic claim that there is at least one witch. Note, furthermore, that restricted quantifier notation, in and of itself, does not capture their analyticity either. Using this notation for (3.82a), '[some x: Witch x] (Female x)', avoids distorting the grammar of this simple sentence and provides the truth condition that the intersection of the extensions of the two predicates is not empty, but it does not tell us whether the sentence is analytic. Hence, markerese representations of the senses of the expressions in (3.82a) and the definition (A*) are necessary to block the regimentation-defenders' explanatory-scope response.

Once such representations and this definition are in place, there is nothing left for the regimentation-defenders to do but deny that we have the intuitions that (3.82a) and (3.82b) are analytic. This is, however, a lame rejoinder. There are various sure signs that we do indeed have such intuitions. For example, the "So, what else is new?" reaction is just as appropriate to someone who says (3.82a) or (3.82b) as it is to someone who says "Witches are female" or "Witches are witches." Also, the noun phrase 'some female witches' is clearly redundant, which could not be the case unless the corresponding sentence (3.82a) were analytic. Further, since it will be conceded that the unquantified sentences that are part of (3.82a) and (3.82b), that is, 'Witches are female' and 'Witches are witches', are analytic, it is hard to see how we lose analyticity when the scope of reference is narrowed from all witches to some witches. Finally, are we to say that the negations of (3.82a) and (3.82b) are synthetic claims that there is not even one witch?

Quine writes: ". . . existential quantification . . . is a logically regimented rendering of the 'there is' idiom. The bound variable 'x' ranges over the universe, and the existential quantification says that at least one of the objects in the universe satisfies the appended condition—in this case the condition of being the object a [in '$(\exists x)(x = a)$'] (1969: 94). Quine offers a reason for regimentation in terms of existential quantification. He appeals to a suggestion of John Bacon's: "just as 'a eats' is short for 'a eats something', so 'a is' is short for 'a is something'." This parallel actually works against the Quinean regimentation. 'A eats' means *a eats something*, but 'a cries (dies, barks)' does not mean *a cries (dies, barks) something*. This is because the intransitive verbs in the former cases but not the latter have a decompositional meaning containing a component expressing the concept of the recipient of the action. That this is the case is shown by the fact that the component expressing the concept of the recipient of the action can even be more specific than *something*, as, for example, in the case of 'a drinks', where the component is *a liquid*. But the 'is' in 'a is something' is not a verb at all; it is the copula. Unlike verbs, the copula expresses bare predication (as I describe in (3.65)). Unlike transitive and intransitive verbs, the copula does not have a sense containing a concept for an action or a concept for the recipient of an action.

There also seems to be a confusion between the 'is' of identity required in the regimentation and the 'is' of predication presupposed in Bacon's analogy. (The 'is' of identity presupposed in logical recastings identifies the referents of the terms flanking the sign.) These considerations suggest that it is better to say that sentences like 'a is'—if indeed strings like 'A thief is' (rather than 'There is a thief') are really sentences—are not "short" for 'a is something'. Extensionalists such as Quine need have no qualms about taking the standard regimentation line on existence sentences, since they require no more for regimentation than preservation of truth value. Intensionalists ought to have the higher standards, ones requiring the preservation of sense. But, as virtually all of them are Fregeans, they automatically recast existence sentences in terms of existential quantification, in spite of the fact that such recasting does not preserve sense. For example, the sense of (3.79) is not that the universe contains something identical to a thief, but simply that there is a thief—on a par with the way that 'There is something' says that there is something.

Taking the logical recasting of existence sentences as an unquestioned truth of philosophical analysis, Carnap accuses Descartes of two errors. Carnap elaborates the first as follows:

> Descartes' "I am" has always been interpreted in this sense [of existence]. But in that case this sentence violates the . . . logical rule that existence can be predicated only in conjunction with a predicate, not in conjunction with a name (subject, proper name). An existential statement does not have the form "*a* exists" (as in "I am", i.e. "I exist"), but "there exists something of such and such a kind." (1959: 74)

To be sure, Descartes's 'I am' does not conform to this "logical rule": but it is only Fregean dogma that requires conformity. Failing to take account of Descartes's explicit warning to philosophers against "disdaining . . . to direct their attention to simple matters" and his clear statement that simple matters are not subject to logical treatment, Carnap begs the question. In fleshing out Descartes's notion of simple matters as mereological structure, I have explained why simplicity is not subject to logical treatment.

Carnap elaborates Descartes's second error as follows:

> The second error lies in the transition from "I think" to "I exist". If from the statement "P(a)" ("a has the property P") an existential statement is to be deduced, then the latter can assert existence only with respect to the predicate P, not with respect to the subject *a* of the premise. What follows from "I am a European" is not "I exist", but "a European exists". What follows from "I think" is not "I am" but "there exists something that thinks." (1959:74)

Again, Carnap is arguing from his own theory, and hence, again, he begs the question against Descartes. Furthermore, the consequence of Carnap's position that only statements like "A European exists" follow from statements like "I am a European" is a *reductio* of that position. Assuming coreference, the further inference from the statement "I, Rudolf Carnap, am a European" to "I, Rudolf Carnap, exist" is valid. 'I, Rudolf Carnap, think' could not be true while 'I, Rudolf Carnap, exist' is false. If Carnap's intensionalism prevents us from capturing such inferences, then it is in error.

These considerations show that, in the case of existence sentences, too, grammatical considerations argue against recasting in logical terms. Thus, with (3.81) and the other semantic apparatus for capturing the analyticities and analytic entailments of existence sentences, we can add existence sentences to the list of simple sentences with inferential structure that can be captured without distorting their grammatical structure by recasting them in logical terms.

Finally, let us consider another highly influential example of regimentation, Donald Davidson's regimentation of action sentences (1967b), and explain why it goes the way of the other examples we have considered. Davidson claims that action verbs in simple sentences have an event argument place over and above their agent and recipient argument places. For example, the verb 'butters' in (3.89) is supposed to have an argument place for the event of Jones's buttering the toast

(3.89)   Jones buttered the toast.

and (3.90) an argument place for the event of Jones's killing his boss.

(3.90)   Jones killed his boss.

Davidson introduces this novel argument place into the logical form of action verbs in order to enable us to derive certain obvious entailments of action sentences. Thus, regimenting (3.91) as (3.92):

(3.91)   Jones buttered the toast in the bathroom with a knife at midnight.

(3.92) $(\exists x)[(\text{Buttering (Jones, Toast, } x)) \ \& \ (\text{In (Bathroom, } x)) \ \& \ (\text{With (knife, } x)) \ \& \ (\text{At (Midnight, } x))]$

enables us to derive sentences that say (1) that the event in question took place in the bathroom, (2) that it was accomplished with a knife, and (3) that it occurred at midnight.

Recalling the earlier discussion of regimentation, we can identify two problems with Davidson's approach to action sentences. First, sentences like (3.89) are simple sentences, not compound sentences like (3.93):

(3.93)   There exists something such that it is the event of Jones's buttering toast.

Of course, the response to this will be to concede the divergence from English grammar—Davidson himself describes the event place as one "that [action verbs] do not appear to [contain]" (1967b: 92)—but to argue that introducing this argument place into the semantics of 'butter' is necessary to account for the entailments (1)–(3). It was Davidson's insight to see that a logic-based semantics can explain these and similar entailments on the basis of such an argument place and that such a semantics is otherwise at a loss to explain the entailments.

Second, although this response is a strong one within a logic-based semantics, Davidson cannot assume that the only semantics in which we might explain such entailments is a logic-based semantics. A mereological semantics can explain them as analytic entailments. (See Katz 1987: 214–226.) More than this, however, it can explain entailments that Davidson's logic-based semantics with its novel logical forms cannot explain. For example, the sentence (3.94) entails the sentences (3.95)–(3.97):

(3.94)   Jones sipped the cider.

(3.95)   Jones drank.

(3.96)   Jones drank cider (a liquid, and so on).

(3.97)   Jones did not gulp down the cider.

Since my mereological semantics is decompositional, I can represent the sense of 'sip' as something like *drink in small amounts*, and, hence, explain these entailments as analytic with no extension of the grammatically apparent argument structure of the verb 'sip'. Hence, if the criterion of whether sentences like (3.89), (3.90) and (3.94) are to be regimented as compound sentences, in the manner of (3.92), is how adequately the regimentation enables us to capture their entailments, then Davidson's semantics is inadequate by his own criterion.

To reinforce this point, I shall illustrate how a decompositional semantics captures the facts that (3.98) entails (3.99) and (3.100):

(3.98)   Jones killed his boss with a knife.

(3.99)   Jones used a knife (to kill his boss).

(3.100)   Jones's boss is dead.

Let the semantic marker (3.101) represent the sense of 'kill',

(3.101)

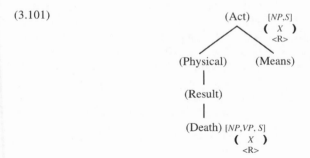

(3.102) the sense of the preposition 'with',

(3.102)   (Means) [NP, PP, VP, S]

                                      (X   )

                                        <R>

and (3.103) the sense of 'knife'.

(3.103)

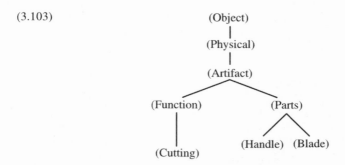

Finally, let (3.104) represent the syntax of (3.98).

(3.104)

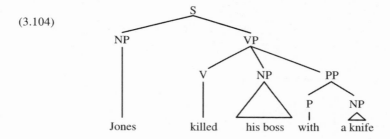

We can now form a representation of the compositional meaning of (3.98). First, the semantic representations of the lexical items in (3.98) are assigned to the occurrences of those items in (3.104). Next, with the compositional principle for argument places stated above, namely, replace an occurrence of a categorized variable with the semantic marker that satisfies both its syntactic condition and selection restriction, (3.103) becomes the value of the variable in (3.102), the semantic representation for 'Jones', say, '(Jones)', becomes the value of the variable categorized for subjects, and the semantic representation for 'his boss', say, '(Boss)', becomes the value of the variable categorized for direct objects.

In an earlier publication (1987: 217), I stated two compositional principles for cases of modification. One of them is (3.105):

(3.105)   If the semantic marker (M_h), which is the representation of H, contains a branch terminating in the semantic marker (M_i) and if the topmost marker in the semantic marker (M_m), which is the semantic representation of M, is (M_i), then attach (M_m) to (M_h) at this common point (M_i), merging redundant markers.

where H is a head and M its modifier. Applying (3.105), we get (3.106):

(3.106)

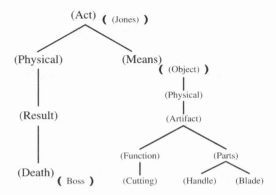

Given (3.106) and assuming that (3.99) has the right-hand branch of (3.106) as its semantic representation, we can explain the fact that (3.98) entails (3.99), which Davidson explains on the basis of simplification, as analytic entailment. Assuming that (3.100) has the semantic representation '(Death) (Boss)', we can explain the fact that (3.98) entails (3.100), which Davidson cannot explain, as another analytic entailment, since the semantic representation of (3.100) is a same-rooted subtree of (3.106).

Like other analytic philosophers influenced by the linguistic turn, Davidson tried to obtain substantive metaphysical conclusions from language. To be sure, he was more cautious than many in this regard, distinguishing between a linguistic theory and a metaphysical theory: "On the score of ontology, too, the study of logical form can carry us only a certain distance. . . . Given this much, a study of event sentences will show a great deal about what we assume to be true concerning events. But deep metaphysical problems will remain . . ." (1970: 146–147). Nonetheless, Davidson claims that his study of the logical form of action sentences has been carried far enough to show that events are values of bound variables, and must, for familiar Quinean reasons, be admitted into our ontology as particulars to which we can refer by various descriptions. Given my criticism of Davidson's regimentation of action sentences, this piece of metaphysical theorizing does not get off the ground.[25]

3.21. The dilemma of the logical and the extralogical

Tarski posed the challenge of distinguishing between logical and extralogical terms:

> [The division of terms into logical and extralogical] is certainly not arbitrary . . . . If, for example, we were to include among the extra-logical signs the implication sign, or the universal quantifier, then our definition of logical consequence would lead to results which obviously contradict ordinary usage. On the other hand, no objective grounds are known to me which permit us to draw a sharp boundary between the two groups of terms. It seems to be possible to include among logical terms some which are usually regarded by logicians as extra-logical without running into consequences which stand in sharp contrast to ordinary usage. In the extreme case we could regard all terms of the language as logical. (1956b: 418–419)

Broadly speaking, there are two current solutions to this problem. There is Frege and Carnap's solution, which maintains that there is no logical/extralogical distinction. This solution is Tarski's "extreme case" in which all meaningful items in the vocabulary of the language are taken as having logical powers. The logical powers of ordinary nouns, verbs, and so on are formally represented in terms of Carnapian meaning postulates. Then there is Quine's solution, which maintains the standard distinction between logical and extralogical vocabulary. The former is the only true *logical* vocabulary; the latter is *non*-logical. For Quine, the idea that extralogical vocabulary has logical powers is a dogma of empiricism.

In the case of the choice between these solutions, as with the other dilemmas, we are required to choose between two views, neither of which is satisfactory. Quine pointed out that, without an explanation of analyticity, the inclusion of a statement as a meaning postulate is arbitrary: "Obviously any number of classes K, M, N, etc. of statements of L_0 can be specified for various purposes or for no purpose; what does it mean to say that K, as against M, N, etc., is the class of the 'analytic' statements of L_0?" (1953: 33). Ironically, Quine's account of the logical vocabulary is subject to essentially the same criticism he makes of Carnap's account of analytic truth. Quine's account is similarly given on the basis of a list with no principle expressing a membership condition. As Quine says in comparing his conception of the scope of logic with Strawson's: "Logical vocabulary is specified only, I suppose, by enumeration. If this element of apparent arbitrariness is a shortcoming, it is a shortcoming also in Mr. Strawson's characterization . . ." (1966: 141). Given the venerable precept that two wrongs do not make a right, we can ask what it means to say that K, as against M, N, and so on, is the "logical vocabulary" for the language L_0. In what seems to be an attempt to put a brave face on things, Quine says:

> . . . the position [of enumerating the logical vocabulary] is not intolerable. We well know from modern logic how to devise *a* technical notation which is admirably suited to the business of 'or', 'not', 'and', 'all', 'only', and such other particles as we would care to count as logical. . . . [If all science is] fitted within that stereotyped logical framework—and there is no hardship in so doing—our notion of logical vocabulary is precise. (1966: 128)

Carnap's enumeration of meaning postulates is precise, too. Nevertheless, precision does not absolve Carnap's enumeration from the sin of arbitrariness; and it does not absolve Quine's enumeration of logical vocabulary from it, either. Hence, we are faced with another dilemma, this time one in which we have to choose between two unsatisfactory views of the logical vocabulary.

As in the case of the other dilemmas, dropping the equation of intensionalism with Fregean intensionalism broadens our range of choices, freeing us from a choice between alternatives neither of which provides for a principled logical/extralogical distinction. A non-Fregean intensionalism provides a principled way of drawing the distinction: it is drawn on the basis of the difference between logical and mereological structure. The inferential powers of items in the logical vocabulary derive from "plant in the seed" containment, whereas the inferential powers of items in the extralogical vocabulary derive from "beams in the house" containment. Thus, instead of an enu-meration of items, there is a distinction based on the difference between deduction and mereology. Deduction is a dynamic process involving operations that comprise the steps in, as it were, the growth of a conclusion from premises, while mereological structure is static, involving part-whole relations among senses of expressions.

On this view, Carnap was wrong to claim that there is no distinction between logical and extralogical vocabulary, and Tarski and Quine were right to say that there is. Tarski was right to believe that the distinction is not an arbitrary one. Quine was right to say that the logical particles, or something close enough to them, are the only properly *logical* vocabulary. But Quine was wrong to say that, because the extralogical vocabulary is non-logical, its members have no genuine inferential powers.

Curiously, Carnap and Quine were wrong for the same reason. Thinking that extralogical words have inferential powers, Carnap automatically took them as hav-ing logical powers. Thinking that extralogical words have no logical powers, Quine automatically took the view that those words have no inferential powers. Carnap and Quine thus took the views they took because each assumed that intensionalism is Fregean intensionalism, and hence was left with no way of understanding the source of inferential powers other than as deriving from logical structure. On my non-Fregean intensionalism, however, the source of the inferential powers of extralogical words is the mereological structure of their senses.

Note two things. First, I leave open the question of what the scope of logic is. I have established the lower limit, but not even addressed the vexed question of the upper limit. Second, my proposal offers no criterion for sorting the words of a lan-guage into logical and extralogical vocabulary. It is only an attempt to say what the basic difference between the two vocabularies is. Sorting the vocabulary of a lan-guage into logical and extralogical words is to be worked out in the course of devel-oping the theories of sense and reference. An example of this sorting is the distinction drawn earlier between external, logical negation and internal, sense negation.

3.22. What was the problem with linguistic philosophy?

The difficulties with a large number of linguistic answers to philosophical questions stem from a common problem with linguistic philosophy and the forms of analytic philosophy based on Frege, Russell, the early work of Wittgenstein, and subsequently Carnap and Quine ("L/AP," as I shall refer to them). The problem is of more than historical interest, since at present the closest thing the English-speaking world has to a broadly accepted view of the nature of philosophy is L/AP.[26]

The basic problem is L/AP's effacement of the language/theory distinction. As argued in this book, the effacement began with Frege's replacement of the traditional "beams in the house" notion of analyticity with his "plant in the seed" notion. He thereby redrew the boundaries of language to allow the principles studied in logic, the theory of deduction, to fall within them. Intensionalists such as Carnap adopted Frege's notion of analyticity with only a few minor revisions. Extensionalists such as Quine adopted it, too, but with a major revision—the omission of definitions and the restriction of analyticity to provability from laws of logic. Thus, Quine says, ". . . the major difficulty lies not in the first class of analytic statements, the logical truths, but rather in the second class, which depends on the notion of synonymy" (1953: 24). In the present connection, the hotly contested issue between intensionalists and extensionalists—namely, whether there are senses—is something of a red herring. Both sides adopt the core of Frege's logical notion of analyticity.

Frege's descendants further inflated the conception of language in the interests of one or another philosophical agenda. Carnap, for example, took the next step by capitalizing on the development of modal logic, which took place after Frege's time, to extend the boundaries of language even further. Wittgenstein in his later work and Quine carried the process about as far as it can go. Wittgenstein's comparison (1953: section 18) of a language to a city with unchecked urban sprawl provides an apt metaphor for his view that virtually nothing can be excluded from language. Quine strikes a similar note: ". . . we learn logic in learning language. But this circumstance does not distinguish logic from vast tracts of common-sense knowledge that would generally be called empirical" (1970: 100–101).

L/AP involves a collection of inflated conceptions of language on which principles of various substantive domains of knowledge count as linguistic. Frege put his inflated conception of language to use in his logicist program, Carnap put his to use in trying to fashion an empiricism that avoids the implausibility of Millian empiricism, Wittgenstein put his to use in devising a new concept of meaning for his late critique of metaphysics, and, finally, Quine put his to use in creating a novel and more plausible form of Mill's uncompromising empiricism. The rationale in each case is that the conception of language provides answers to philosophical questions with *linguistic* credentials, and the importance of this is that such answers are not supposed to be irredeemably controversial in the manner of philosophical answers. Herein lies the source of the difficulties with a large number of L/AP's linguistic answers to philosophical questions. Resting as they do on principles that are taken to be linguistic but that in fact are not, these answers to philosophical questions in actuality have no genuine linguistic credentials. Language does not provide grounds for the principles that linguistic answers assume, and, as we shall see, in certain cases, it undermines such answers.

Wittgenstein in his early work and the logical positivists failed to draw a linguistic distinction between metaphysical sentences and the sentences of natural science because, contrary to their claims, very few of the former are linguistic nonsense. Perhaps only Carnap's much overworked example 'The nothing nothings' might rightly be said to transcend the limits of language. But, for other metaphysical sentences such as those that express skepticism about induction or the external world, those that assert the existence of abstract objects, and so on, there is nothing in natural language to appeal to in order to support the claim that they are nonsense. In natural language, nothing more is required for a sentence to be meaningful than that it have a sense that is a compositional function of the senses of its constituents. Hence, answers to philosophical questions about skepticism and the like require more in the way of warrant than natural languages, properly understood, can provide. Natural languages do not contain principles of substantive domains of knowledge.

As I have argued, there is a reason that natural language cannot sanction such principles: they are maximally effable. As a universal means of expression, natural languages equally, and without bias, can express every theory we can construct about the phenomena in a domain of knowledge. Unlike theories that, for explanatory purposes, favor one set of principles about the domain over others, natural languages express all principles—even, as I shall explain shortly, without a bias against inconsistent principles. Natural languages are theory-neutral systems that enable us to formulate all competing theories about the phenomena in a domain.

I have explored the conflict between my conception of language and Quine's indeterminacy thesis; but I have said nothing yet about the related incommensurability thesis and the view based upon it that the tradition that emerges from a scientific revolution cannot be said to refute the old tradition, but only to replace it. As Thomas Kuhn puts it: ". . . the normal-scientific tradition that emerges from a scientific revolution is not only incompatible but often actually incommensurable with that which has gone before" (1962: 103). Incommensurability obtains when the semantic resources of old and new scientific traditions do not suffice to translate certain central theoretical terms.

This untranslatability is held to result from the fact that the semantic resources of a theory come from its principles. Paul Feyerabend makes this crystal clear: ". . . the meaning of every term we use depends upon the theoretical context in which it occurs. Words do not 'mean' something in isolation; they obtain their meaning by being part of a theoretical system" (1965: 180). It is thus easy to see why radical differences between competing theories produce incommensurability: theoretical terms obtain their meaning from their place in the principles of a theory, and, as a consequence, if two theories are different enough, the nexus of principles in each confers quite different meanings on what orthographically might seem the same term.

I have argued against the Kuhn-Feyerabend incommensurability thesis elsewhere (1979a), and there is no need to repeat the full argument here. However, I should point out that the thesis rests on just the language/theory conflation that I have been criticizing. Kuhn and Feyerabend understand natural languages as, to a large extent, dependent on theories for the semantic resources necessary to construct meanings for theoretical terms. This understanding contrasts with the understanding we have if we maintain the distinction between language and theory. Maintaining that distinction, we can understand natural languages as independent linguistic systems with their own intrinsic sense structure that allows the (compositional) construction of meanings for theoretical terms independently of how radically the theories which use those terms differ as scientific explanations.

The Kuhn-Feyerabend view, on which language relies on the principles of a theory to provide meanings for theoretical terms, comes, I submit, from seeing natural languages through the lens of artificial languages developed in logic. Rather than being seen as grammatical systems in which syntactic rules generate a class of sentences and semantic rules assign each member a set of senses, languages are seen as logistic systems with formation rules, transformational rules, and postulates. The transformational rules and the postulates come, respectively, from theories in the formal and natural sciences.

This perspective on natural language is, of course, one that we associate with Carnap. He uses it *inter alia* to try to show the meaninglessness of "external questions." Hence, this positivistic thesis rests on the same language/theory confusion as the Kuhn-Feyerabend incommensurability thesis. Carnap writes:

> If someone wishes to speak in his language about a new kind of entities, he has to introduce a system of new ways of speaking, subject to new rules; we shall call this procedure the construction of a linguistic *framework* for the new entities in question. And now we must distinguish two kinds of questions . . . questions of the existence of certain entities of the new kind *within the framework*; we call them *internal questions* . . . [and] questions concerning the existence or reality *of the system of entities as a whole*, called *external questions*. (1956: 206)

Carnap denies that external questions, such as those about the existence of abstract objects like properties, classes, numbers, and propositions, have a sense. His reason is that they do not construe such entities as "element[s] of the system; hence this concept cannot be meaningfully applied to the system itself" (1956: 207).

This reason is based on the same conflation of language and theory as the Kuhn-Feyerabend incommensurability thesis. Given that there is no overarching, theory-neutral linguistic framework within which an external question can receive a meaning, particular systems must provide meanings for terms like 'property', 'class', and so on in terms of their role in the principles of the system, and, hence, relative to the system. So, in the absence of a common, theory-neutral framework, there are no common principles to provide an absolute meaning for such terms in each system.

Given that natural languages have a compositional sense structure that allows theory-independent construction of meanings, someone who wishes to speak in his or her language, say English, about a new kind of entity—a property, class, number, or proposition—does not have "to introduce a system of new ways of speaking, subject to new rules." English is all they need. This ought to be obvious, since philosophers of various persuasions have had no trouble constructing absolute meanings for terms referring to properties, classes, numbers, or propositions in their language. Russell did not have "to introduce a system of new ways of speaking, subject to new rules" when he wanted to speak about new entities such as self-membered classes and non-self-membered classes. The term 'class' itself has a common meaning for realists, nominalists, and conceptualists. What varies from one philosophy of mathematics to another is a philosophical theory about the ontological status of the entities picked out by the common linguistic meaning of the term.

I am not denying that we can make an internal/external distinction in connection with sentences of a natural language; but if we do, questions about the language system itself are not meaningless. If they were meaningless, there would be no science of linguistics as we know it.

In his late period, Wittgenstein, like Carnap, continued to pursue his former positivist aim of showing that metaphysical sentences are nonsense. Wittgenstein was like Karl Marx. He made the most penetrating criticisms of the system he opposed, but advocated an alternative as bad or worse. Basing his notion of meaning on use produced an extreme inflation of language. Of their nature, accounts of meaning based on use produce extreme inflations of language. This is because a wide range of factors play a role in determining the use of an expression, e.g., connotative properties of words, syntactic properties of sentences, psychological properties of speakers, cultural properties of the community, and social properties of the context. Use accounts of meaning *ipso facto* make these factors part of meaning. Hence, meaning includes any such factor on which a speaker's application of language depends. This bloating of meaning runs roughshod over intuitions about sense properties and relations such as meaningfulness and meaninglessness, sameness and difference of meaning, and so on.

Let me briefly review some of the considerations showing that a use-based notion of meaning does not square with our intuitions about sense properties and relations of expressions in natural language. Many words have a connotation that suggests their appropriateness for conversation with children: for example, 'bunny', 'doggie', 'wee-wee', 'doo-doo', and 'toesies'. Such connotations of words constrain their use. For example, no urologist would inform an adult patient of the results of his or her urine test by saying, "The results of your wee-wee test were normal." But each such word has a synonym which lacks its connotation: 'rabbit', 'dog', 'urine', 'feces', and 'toes'. As a consequence, we get the counterintuitive result that the words in the former set are not synonymous with their synonyms in the latter. No wonder *Webster's New International Dictionary* explains connotation as "the suggestive significance of a word apart from its explicit and recognized meaning." Proponents of use-based accounts of meaning owe us a non-question-begging statement of what the difference *in meaning* between pairs like 'wee-wee' and 'urine' is supposed to be.

Consider the case of syntactic properties, in particular, arrangement, length, and complexity. The arrangement of words in sentences governs aspects of their use. Hence, (3.107) cannot, but (3.108) can, be used in a poetic context to provide a rhyme with 'slumber'

(3.107)   Mary looked the number up.

(3.108)   Mary looked up the number.

and (3.108) cannot but (3.109) can be used as an illustration of the phenomenon of apparent particle movement.

(3.109)   Someone gave many a buck to Jane.

(3.110)   Someone gave Jane many a buck.

Further, (3.109) cannot, but (3.110) can, be used to rhyme with the subsequent line "Jane has all the luck," and (3.110) cannot, but (3.109) can, be used as an illustration of a sentence with a prepositional phrase. But, despite these and other differences in use, (3.107) and (3.108) are synonymous, as are (3.109) and (3.110). Here, too, proponents of use-based accounts of meaning owe us a statement of the *meaning* difference between the members of these two pairs of sentences.

It has long been recognized that there is no upper limit on sentence length in natural language. The recursive mechanisms of sentence formation in natural language generate longer and longer sentences without bound. English thus contains sentences with more words than there are seconds in all our lifetimes put together. Proponents of use-based accounts of meaning must count such megasentences—and, of course, many shorter and longer ones—as meaningless because they are too long to have a use; but nonetheless many of these sentences will be perfectly meaningful, having meanings formed from the meanings of their lexical items on the basis of compositional operations that preserve meaningfulness (e.g., conjunction).

George Miller points out (1962) that the form of syntactic complexity known as center-embedding produces meaningful sentences that are extremely difficult to understand and, with enough center-embedding, fully incomprehensible. (3.111) is an example of center-embedding.

(3.111)   The rat the cat the dog the cow with the crumpled horn tossed worried killed ate the malt that lay in the house that Jack built.

If (3.111) is not incomprehensible, it is certainly very difficult to understand, and adding further center-embeddings would make it absolutely incomprehensible. Nonetheless, many such complex sentences are perfectly meaningful, as can be shown from the fact that they are synonymous with their easily understood meaningful right-branching counterparts, for example (3.112):

(3.112)   The cow with the crumpled horn tossed the dog that worried the cat that killed the rat that ate the malt that lay in the house that Jack built.

One problem for accounts of meaning based on use is that megasentences and center-embedded sentences having no use must be counted as having no meaning. Another problem is that multiply center-embedded sentences and their right-branching counterparts, which clearly have different uses, are synonymous.

The philosophers who follow Wittgenstein in understanding meaning in terms of use include most ordinary language philosophers of the mid-twentieth century as well as more recent philosophers such as G. E. M. Anscombe, Norman Malcolm, Rogers Albritton, Peter Winch, H. P. Grice, P. F. Strawson, John Canfield, Warren Goldfarb, Burton Dreben, Cora Diamond, Robert Brandom, and Paul Horwich. To be sure, not all of these philosophers follow Wittgenstein in all aspects of his later thinking. Some, for example, Grice (1989) and Horwich (1998), abandon Wittgenstein's view about the nature of philosophical problems (1953: section 109) and try to provide a use-based *theory* of meaning.

Such an approach holds out the hope that such a theory will provide a response to the counterexamples. Grice says nothing about how a theory of the meaning of sentences might handle their sense properties and relations. This, I believe, is very likely not a matter of oversight on his part, but rather a consequence of his failure to find a way to explain the notion of the meaning of an expression-type in terms of his basic notion of a speaker's (nonnaturally) meaning something by an utterance—the familiar Gricean notion of speakers intending to produce an effect by means of their audience recognizing the intention. Grice himself concedes (1989: 127–128) the inadequacy of the reductive definitions he has come up with (one of which assigns the meaning M to a sentence-type s on the condition that people usually use s to mean M, and another of which is a variant of this with 'conventionally' in place of 'usually'). Grice counts this inadequacy as one of the two significant problems with his program (1989: 298–299).

Given this concession, the question arises, "Why stick to the program? Why continue to insist on a reductive analysis of the concept of meaning, when the status of the notion of a speaker's (nonnaturally) meaning something by an utterance does not depend on a successful reduction?" Grice does, at one point, consider an alternative program:

> The only alternative which I can think of would be that of treating "meaning" as a theoretical concept which, together perhaps with other theoretical concepts, would provide for the primitive predicates involved in a semantic system, an array whose job it would be to provide the laws and hypotheses in terms of which the phenomena of meaning are to be explained. (1989: 358)

An interesting alternative indeed, which, as Grice surely knew, had been advocated by certain MIT linguists and philosophers since the early '60s. Without the slightest discussion of their proposals for such a treatment of the concept of meaning, Grice rejects the alternative simply on the grounds that "[i]f this direction is taken, the meaning of particular expressions will be a matter of hypothesis and conjecture rather than of intuition, since the application of theoretical concepts is not generally thought of as reachable by intuition or observation" (1989: 358–359). For Grice to reject the proposal on these grounds is quite remarkable in light of the fact that he also surely knew of the theory of generative grammar developed by Chomsky (1965) and of the theory of the semantic component of such grammars developed by me (1964; 1965; 1972) and my MIT colleagues. This theory took grammars and their semantic components to be *both* hypothetico-deductive *and* responsible to speakers' intuitions about the phonological, syntactic, and semantic structure of sentences.

To be sure, such grammars are not "reachable by intuition" if this is taken to mean being directly derivable from the intuitively given facts. But they are "reachable by intuition" if this is taken to have the more straightforward meaning of being determinable from such facts together with the usual principles of scientific theory construction and methodology. Since *Syntactic Structures* (1957), Chomsky took great pains to stress that such determinability was one of the features of his new theory that distinguished it from the theory of taxonomic grammar of the earlier American structuralist linguistics.

Horwich presents a reply (1998: 78–79) to one of the syntactic objections to use-based accounts of meaning, the one based on meaningful sentences that are too long to have a use. The reply fails, but even if it were to succeed, use-based accounts of meaning would not get off the hook. This is because the more telling of my objections, the one based on the synonymy of multiply center-embedded sentences and their right-branching counterparts, is entirely ignored. Without a response to this objection, the game is up.

In the case of meaningful megasentences, Horwich argues that although they may be meaningless to speakers, they are meaningful in the language, and that his theory can account for this. He says:

> . . . it must be conceded that the meaning of a complex expression in a speaker's language is *not* necessarily manifested in his use of it. However, a use-theoretic property is none the less associated with it: namely, that it is constructed in a certain way from words with certain uses. And this, we can suppose, is the property in which its meaning in the language consists. (1998: 79)

True enough, we can say that a megasentence has the property, call it *P*, of being constructed in a certain way from words with certain uses; but Horwich says nothing in this context to legitimate taking *P* to be "the property in which its meaning in the language consists." There is, moreover, a very good reason for not doing so, namely, that taking *P* to be a property of the kind that can serve as the meaning of a sentence has the consequence that straight-out meaningless sentences would count as meaningful. For example, Chomsky's famous case (3.113) is meaningful.

(3.113)   Colorless green ideas sleep furiously.

The core sentence 'Ideas sleep' is "constructed in a certain way from words with certain uses," and, hence, on Horwich's assumptions, it is (falsely) ascribed a "meaning in the language." But to take such sentences to be meaningful in virtue of having the "use-theoretic property" *P* associated with them makes every sentence in the language meaningful, and the distinction between meaningful and meaningless sentences goes out the window.

Moreover, a property of a sentence that involves the use regularities associated with its lexical items is not *ipso facto* a property that expresses a possible use. To be sure, the use features of the lexical items can confer something that we might refer to as a use property of the sentence, but it is not a property that guarantees a possible use for a megasentence, thereby conferring a meaning upon it. Such sentences, having no possible use, have no meaning in the sense that is required for explaining meaning in terms of use.

I have taken Horwich's formulation "constructed in a certain way from words with certain uses" to mean *constructed in a syntactically acceptable way*; but, of course, it might be taken to mean *constructed in a semantically compositional way*. Horwich (in conversation) suggests this interpretation: instead of *P*, the property in which the meaning of a megasentence *s* in the language consists is the compositional meaning *M* of *s* based on the uses of its lexical items and the way the sentence is constructed from them. It is hard to evaluate this suggestion, because Horwich (1998) provides no explanation of compositionality based on lexical meanings taking the form of use regularities, and it is not obvious that there is such a thing. No matter. If there were a compositional meaning for a megasentence, it would predict that the sentence is meaningful, and, hence, a use theory of meaning would falsely predict that it has a use. Furthermore, since a multiply center-embedded sentence *s* and its right-branching version *s'* are synonymous, they have the same compositional meaning. In this case, a use theory of meaning predicts that they have the same use. But they do not: *s'* has a use, but *s* has none.

Let me mention two further examples of how an inflated conception of language leads to mistaken philosophical analysis, each from a major figure in the analytic tradition. The first example is Ryle's (1937/1938) famous discussion of categories. He claims to provide a criterion that tells us when two expressions belong to different categories. Ryle's criterion is a substitution test that counts two expressions as belonging to different categories when one but not the other can fill the unfilled portion of a chosen sentential schema without "absurdity." On this criterion 'Socrates' and 'Saturday' belong to different categories since only the former term can fill '. . . is in bed' without absurdity. Ryle's criterion also counts 'he' and 'the writer of this book' as belonging to different categories because the former but not the latter can without absurdity fill the unfilled portion of the schema '. . . has never written a book'.

Ryle offers no criterion for when two expressions belong to the same category. Indeed, there is none for him to offer, since, on his criterion, no two expressions can belong to the same category (a point first noted by J. J. C. Smart [1953]). It is easy to see that this is so. For any two non-synonymous expressions, we can construct a schema in which the insertion of one but not the other produces absurdity (in Ryle's loose sense of that term). We simply locate a concept *C* in the sense of one with respect to which they differ in meaning and frame a schema in which the predicate is a concept incompatible with *C*. For example, with the pronouns 'he' and 'she', we locate the concept *female* and frame the schema '. . . is female', which then shows that 'he' and 'she' belong to different categories. Ryle's criterion makes a mockery of the notion of a category.

What has gone wrong is that the property to be preserved in Ryle's substitution test, absurdity, covers both cases of conceptual conflict that result in meaninglessness and cases of conceptual conflict that result in contradiction. This equivocation runs meaningful sentences, contradictions like (3.114) and (3.115):

(3.114)   Sam drew a round square.

(3.115)   The square Sam drew is round.

together with meaningless sentences like (3.113). But contradictions are not meaningless. Sentences expressing a contradiction are linguistically no more problematic than others. To be sure, they cannot be true; but, as this is for extralinguistic reasons, it does not make them linguistically deviant. Indeed, they could not be false if they had no meaning.

Let us restrict ourselves to contradictions arising from internal negation, since external or logical negation presents no issue here. On the logical semantics of the Frege/Russell tradition, contradictions like (3.114) and (3.115) fall together with meaningless sentences like (3.116) and (3.117):

(3.116)   Sam drank a prime number.

(3.117)   Sam killed his boss with a prime number.

There is no way to separate the two cases of conceptual conflict. On my mereological semantics, however, the separation is automatic. In the case of internal contradiction, the conflict is between members of the same antonymous n-tuple. Such conflicts are "horizontal" in that they occur at the same level, namely, between co-subordinates under the same superordinate. In the case of meaninglessness, the conflicts are "vertical" in that they occur at different levels, namely, between the level of subordinate and superordinate.

To understand this difference, think of the compositional process whereby senses of complex syntactic constituents are formed from the senses of their subconstituents. In the case of the contradiction (3.114), the sense of the modifier 'round' combines with the sense of the head 'square' because, as indicated in (3.105), the sense of 'round' is a subordinate of the same superordinate as the sense of 'square', namely, *figure*. Similarly in the case of the contradiction (3.115). Hence, both sentences have a sense. But in the case of (3.116) and (3.117), the sense of 'prime number' is not a subordinate of the concept governing its combination with the sense of the verb. Both the verbs 'drink' and 'kill' have a selection restriction that requires the senses of their direct objects to be subordinates of the superordinate *concrete object*. Since this restriction is not met in the case of (3.116) and (3.117), there is no compositional sense for the verb phrases of the sentences, and, hence, the sentences themselves do not have a sense.[27]

The second example is Strawson's linguistic solution to the problem of induction. According to Strawson (1952), our practice of making predictions about the future on the basis of what has been predicted successfully in the past is justified because we know the practice is reasonable and we know this purely *linguistically*, because being reasonable in this case just means *acting on a degree of belief in a statement that is proportional to the strength of the evidence in its favor*. The claim that the reasonable predictive practice is inductive, being analytic, can no more receive a substantive justification than can the claim that bachelors are unmarried.

An alternative view is that 'reasonable' just means *in accord with reason* or *in accord with the standards that govern reasoning*. The fact that the standards vary with the nature of the subject prevents any particular standards from being part of the sense of 'reasonable'. Thus, the inductive standard cannot, contrary to Strawson, be part of the meaning of 'reasonable', since the standard of reasonableness in logic or mathematics, where there is proof but not evidential support, is different.

Looked at for what it is—a claim about the sense of the word 'reasonable'— Strawson's claim is that in application to non-demonstrative inference it is synonymous with 'having a degree of belief in a statement that is proportional to the strength of the evidence in its favor'. But the sentences (3.118) and (3.119) are not synonymous, as they would have to be for Strawson to be right.

(3.118)   Sam doubts that Mary's inductive predictions are reasonable.

(3.119)   Sam doubts that Mary has a degree of belief in her inductive predictions that is proportional to the strength of the evidence.

(3.118) might be false, while (3.119) is true. If Sam is a skeptic about induction, or suffers from the delusion that only Nostradamus can predict the future, he might very well have no doubts about the complement of (3.119) but have serious doubts about the complement of (3.118).

Against the argument that there might be other methods of predicting the future the success of which makes it rational to prefer them to induction, Strawson makes the—from his position, obligatory—rejoinder that there could not be such methods because the description 'successful method of finding things out that has no inductive support' is the denial of an analytic proposition, and hence a contradiction. But, clearly, there is nothing contradictory about this description. This is what skeptics about induction claim on behalf of certain counterinductive rules. Skepticism cannot be refuted on the grounds that the skeptic has made a contradictory claim. Is it not logically possible that soliciting a prediction from a particular swami, one who has never been asked about the future, is a successful method of prediction?

3.23. A balance sheet

In this final section, I want to indicate the net philosophical worth of non-Fregean intensionalism. To this end, I will first consider the possible liabilities of replacing Fregean intensionalism with non-Fregean intensionalism, and then the possible assets.

3.23.1. The debit side of the ledger

I will argue that the debit side of the ledger is blank. But before making this argument, it is necessary to look at why intensionalists have been so sure for so long that sense and analyticity *must* be Fregean sense and analyticity. The appeal of Fregean intensionalism will indicate what intensionalists fear we stand to lose if the Fregean notions of sense and analyticity are abandoned.

The appeal of Fregean intensionalism is based on the supposition that these notions possess a unique constellation of virtues. First, the Fregean definition of sense explains the function of senses. They are there to fix reference. Second, senses solve the Fregean puzzles about identity and opacity, and solving them provides the rationale required for positing the existence of senses as entities over and above the expressions of a language and their extensions. Third, the Fregean definition of sense assigns the task of explaining sense to the theory of reference. Taking the task out of the hands of traditional theories of meaning, which were widely thought to be rather nebulous, and handing it over to the new theory of predicate logic seemed at last to meet the modern standards of philosophical rigor. Fourth, the Fregean definition of sense provides the simplest and most direct account of the relation between sense and reference. Fifth, Frege's definition of analyticity overcomes undeniable difficulties with traditional definitions, such as the apparent psychologism of Kant's definition of analyticity and the quite real failures of Locke's and Kant's definitions to account for the analyticity of analytic relational and existence sentences. Finally, Frege's fruitful notion of analyticity promises philosophical applications that unfruitful notions like Locke's and Kant's could by no stretch of the imagination provide.

Given this constellation of virtues, it looks as if philosophy stands to lose something of irreplaceable value in relinquishing Fregean sense and analyticity. But, in fact, nothing valuable is lost. The "virtues" that do go when Fregean intensionalism is replaced with the new intensionalism were never genuine virtues in the first place, and the genuine virtues do not go. They are preserved in the new intensionalism, and, in fact, some are even improved upon.

It would certainly count as a debit if abandoning the Fregean idea that the function of sense is to determine reference left us with no account of the function of sense. But it does not. (D) provides us with an account of the function of sense, only a different one. The function of sense is not to determine referential properties and relations; it is to determine sense properties and relations. This account of the function of sense provides a better parallel to the function of the other aspects of grammatical structure: the function of phonology is to determine phonological properties and relations (rhyme, alliteration, and so on), and the function of syntax is to determine syntactic properties and relations (well-formedness, agreement, sentence-type, and so on).

The new intensionalism does not sacrifice solutions to the Fregean puzzles about sense, since, as I have argued, it is not *Fregean* senses that are necessary for solving those puzzles, but only senses. Frege's puzzle about sentences like 'Hesperus is Hesperus' and 'Hesperus is Phosphorus' (1952: 56–57) was that neither the referential nor the orthographic differences between the names provide semantic values fine-grained enough to account for the fact that sentences like the former "[hold] *a priori* and, according to Kant, [are] analytic," whereas true sentences like the latter "contain very valuable extension[s] of our knowledge." If there are senses for names, even such thin ones as the metalinguistic senses that I identified, then there are semantic values that are fine-grained enough to account for this fact.

Frege's puzzle about the meaningfulness of vacuous expressions (1952: 58) is a problem for extensionalism generally and for the Millian account of names in particular. Since a name like 'Santa Claus' has no referent, a true, hence meaningful, sentence like (3.42) ('Santa Claus does not exist') is a counterexample to Millianism. For, if, as Millians say, all names are senseless, bearerless names have nothing to contribute to the compositional meaning of sentences, and, hence, Millians must deny that sentences like 'Santa Claus does not exist' are meaningful, or else say that their subjects refer to a fictional object and that they are false. On my theory of sense, bearerless names like 'Santa Claus' are not senseless, and, hence, such sentences have a compositional meaning.

Frege's puzzle about substitution of coreferential names in opaque contexts (1952: 64–67) is standardly lumped together with his puzzles about identity statements with names and the meaningfulness of bearerless names. This is a mistake—one that is made, I suspect, because Frege himself treated the puzzle about substitution as a problem that is solvable with the notion of sense. Of course, on Frege's notion of sense, the puzzle about substitution of coreferential names in opaque contexts does belong with the others. But once the widespread assumption that senses are reference-determiners is abandoned, it does not. Once (D) is assumed, the puzzle must be recognized as being of a different kind from the puzzles about identity statements with names and the meaningfulness of bearerless names. The latter two puzzles are about *sense* properties—analyticity in the one case and meaningfulness in the other—whereas the former problem, being about the conditions for valid substitutional inference, is not. Since that problem is about the property of truth, it falls within the theory of reference. Hence, a theory of sense based on (D) is under no obligation to solve it.

Moreover, in certain cases, the solutions involving non-Fregean senses improve upon Frege's solutions. First, taking 'Hesperus' and 'Phosphorus' to have senses that are instances of *the thing that is a bearer of 'N'* explains why the one sentence has a repetitive sense and the other does not. Further, not only are Fregean senses not required to solve the Fregean puzzle about names, but also they do not provide satisfactory solutions for it, as Mill's and Kripke's counterfactual counterexamples show. As I argued above, the thin senses of names succeed where Frege's thick senses fail.

Given these considerations, it is clear not only that the new intensionalism provides essentially the same kind of rationale for positing the existence of senses as Frege, namely, solutions to the Fregean puzzles about sense, but that the particular rationale it provides in the case of each of these puzzles is a more philosophically satisfactory one than Frege provides.

To be sure, Locke's theory of ideas, Kant's theory of concepts and judgments, and Moore's account of analysis fall short of what modern standards of rigor demand in the way of philosophical clarity and precision. It is true, but not exculpatory, that the focus of philosophers such as Locke, Kant, and Moore was not primarily semantic and that they wrote at a time when the standards of clarity and precision in such matters were less demanding than they are now. But even if we hold these philosophers fully responsible, it does not follow that to bring intensionalist semantics up to modern standards of clarity and precision it is necessary to explain sense in the theory of reference. Measuring up to modern standards of clarity and precision in semantics is a matter of articulation and formalization of theory, and a mereological theory of sense such as the one developed here can, as I have shown, be formulated with as much clarity and precision as the logical theories of sense in the Fregean tradition, including those of contemporary neo-Fregeans.

No doubt, some of Frege's criticisms reveal genuine flaws in the Lockean and Kantian notion of analyticity. That notion does not cover relational or existence sentences. But, as I argued earlier, those flaws are not ones that call for extirpation of the notion, only explication of it. Generalizing containment from a condition applying exclusively to subject terms to a condition applying to any term enables us to capture analytic relational sentences. And the formal apparatus that explains the Cogito as an analytic entailment enables us to capture analytic entailments with existence sentences as conclusions. Therefore, my explications of analyticity and analytic entailment enable the new intensionalism to meet Frege's criticism about the scope of Lockean and Kantian analyticity without taking his step of replacing the mereological notions of analyticity and analytic entailment with logical notions.

Though it is perhaps obvious, it should be noted that a mereological notion of analyticity provides the same protection against psychologism as Frege's logical notion. Both can be understood as representing an objective, mind-independent structure—just as both can also be understood as representing a subjective, mind-dependent structure. It is not the nature of the formal relations taken to be constitutive of analyticity that makes the difference between psychologism and realism, but the ontological interpretation that is put on those relations, whether, that is, we interpret the theory of the semantic objects that exhibit those relations as a theory of abstract objects or as a theory of mental objects.[28]

It looks as if Frege's thesis that sense determines reference is simpler than my mediation thesis, because, in expressing the relation between sense and reference in the definition of sense, the former kills two birds with one stone. Thus, since my mediation thesis requires an independent statement in the theory of reference relating sense and reference, replacing the Fregean definition of sense with (D) seems to entrain a loss in simplicity.

However, on closer examination, this is not so. Simplicity decides between competing claims only when all other things are equal, when the claims are equivalent in other relevant respects. If the more complex claim is better in other relevant respects— if, for example, the additional complexity buys less conceptual trouble or more explanation—the simpler claim is too simple. Hence, if, as argued in this book, my account of the relation between sense and reference is better than Frege's in dealing with linguistic and philosophical problems—for example, the three problems addressed in the first part of the book or the various problems addressed in the third part—then the appeal to simplicity is spurious. There is no simplicity to be lost in replacing his determination thesis with my mediation thesis.

Finally, it is worth saying explicitly that rejection of the Frege/Carnap view of analyticity does not entail rejection of logical truth. Quine rejected that view of analyticity, but certainly did not thereby reject logical truth. On my view, rejecting the Frege/Carnap view of analyticity sharply separates the theory of sense from the theory of reference, but both remain as independent theories. The position I arrive at is Quine's position minus his skepticism about the theory of meaning. Thus, Quine was right to insist that the semantic structure of the extralogical vocabulary is not logical structure, but wrong to insist also that there are no meanings and no analytic/synthetic distinction in the traditional sense. His argument—recall his metaphor of "a closed curve in space"—rests on assuming that intensionalism is Fregean intensionalism, and hence assuming that the theory of sense must be reduced to the theory of reference. Without this assumption, Quine's argument depends upon a misguided reductionism that arbitrarily treats a theory of sense differently from other formal theories.

In section 3.21, I argued that the new intensionalism provides a principled way of drawing the distinction between the logical and the extralogical. Further, I argued that the study of an independent, linguistic domain of sense structure makes a contribution to understanding the nature of logic. It also makes a contribution to the topics of implication and necessary truth. The obvious point is that the new intensionalism enables us to recognize these topics as general topics, rather than as branches of logic *per se*. Less obviously, the new intensionalism enables us to account for the fact that sentences like (3.120)–(3.122) are necessary truths.

(3.120)   If John is a bachelor, then John is an unmarried man.

(3.121)   If pigs fly, bachelors are unmarried.

(3.122)   If bachelors are married, pigs fly.

We can formulate a cross-theory concept of propositions that explains their modal status on the basis of both logical and mereological laws. Such a cross-theory concept is not, à la Frege, a replacement for the traditional concept of analyticity. We can take the cross-theory concept to have the same hybrid status as the corresponding cross-theory concept of propositions that explains the necessity of truths involving both logic and mathematics. Hence, what Frege accomplishes by conflating the theories of sense and reference can also be accomplished by the two theories as independent theories. Thus, we do not lose the ability to handle standard examples of implication and necessary truth.

The hopes that philosophers had that Frege's notion of analyticity would provide a "fruitful" conceptual tool in philosophical programs like Frege's logicism and the Vienna Circle's positivism turned out to be illusory. The demise of these philosophical programs turned out to be no loss to philosophy. Further, Frege's fruitfulness criticism of mereological semantics, as we have seen, was a *petitio principii* when used against Kant's mereological notion of analyticity, and it is not any less fallacious when modern-day philosophers use it against recent explications of Kant's mereological notion of analyticity.

3.23.2. The credit side of the ledger

The credit side of the ledger is by no means blank. Entries on this side can be grouped in these areas: sense, reference, and philosophy. In the first, there are three principal items: avoidance of the problem of too strong a constraint, avoidance of the problem of too weak a constraint, and avoidance of the problem of the wrong constraint. Together these three problems comprise the main case against intensionalism in twentieth-century philosophy. I have shown that all of them result from adopting

Frege's characterizations of sense and analyticity, and that once there are non-Fregean definitions to replace them, there is no longer a case against intensionalism.

The autonomous theory of sense that develops from those non-Fregean definitions counts in and of itself as an entry on the credit side of the ledger. Such a theory provides explanations of the sense properties and relations of expressions and sentences like meaningfulness, ambiguity, synonymy, antonymy, redundancy, and so on, without which a theory of natural language can hardly be complete. Given my arguments against extensionalism and Fregean intensionalism, an autonomous theory of sense is the only way to gain an understanding of such linguistic phenomena.

Further, the new intensionalism avoids the distortion of the grammar of simple sentences that results from their regimentation as compound sentences. As I have argued, Frege was forced to introduce such regimentation in order to bring analytic simple sentences under his logical definition, since, having eliminated the Kantian account of analyticity, he otherwise would have had no account of them at all. Once the mereological account of analyticity is reintroduced, no recasting of simple sentences as compound sentences is necessary to account for analyticity and other semantic properties and relations. Hence, no distortion of their grammatical structure has to be swallowed for the sake of having an account of these properties and relations.

Moreover, restricting regimentation to cases where it does not distort grammatical structure involves no cost to logic. Logic remains as it has always been, a *theory* of deduction. Given the language/theory distinction, what changes is the view we have of logic's application to natural languages. In the Frege/Russell tradition, particularly as developed by Quine, regimentation serves the aims of an exclusively referential conception of the semantics of natural language. When we note, as I have done in discussing Quine on regimentation, that departures from natural language are justified in terms of those aims, it seems fair to say that Frege's concept of a logically perfect language has survived in contemporary analytic philosophy in the form of regimentation. Thus, my restriction of regimentation to compound sentences accords well with the shift that has taken place in philosophy from the earlier form of thinking on which ordinary language needs to be "sublimed"—logically reconstructed—by philosophers to the current form on which it is to be scientifically understood by linguists.

In the area of reference, the gain is also considerable. Given an autonomous theory of sense together with referential correlates for each of the sense properties and relations, a model-theoretic semantics of natural languages acquires a significant range of new constraints on assignment of extensional structure to expressions and sentences. These constraints, which I have called to as "referential correlates," explain the contribution of the sense structure of a natural language to its referential structure. Without those correlates, the constraints on the model-theoretic interpretation of the language are considerably weaker than they could be. Finally, I should mention the suggestion that a system of referential correlates introduces a significant simplification of the compositional apparatus of the theory of reference, perhaps even its entire elimination.

In the third area, philosophy, the items on the credit side are the results of the re-examinations of the twenty or so philosophical questions taken up in the third part of the book. This reexamination shows that a non-Fregean intensionalism based on an autonomous theory of sense leads to significant progress on, for example, the dilemmas concerning confirmation and aboutness, the consistency and completeness of natural languages, proper names, the Cogito, the semantics of natural kind terms, the logical/extralogical distinction, and others. These dilemmas were shown to arise from the restriction of alternatives that comes from the equation of intensionalism with Fregean intensionalism. In each case, philosophers, intensionalists and extensionalists alike, are forced to choose between alternatives each of which forces them to sacrifice robust intuitions. In each case, my non-Fregean intensionalism introduces a way of going between the horns that sacrifices none of those intuitions.

Progress on these dilemmas and on a wide range of other philosophical issues shows that many of the issues in twentieth-century philosophy were decided without adequate consideration of the alternatives to the positions that were taken on them. At the very least, the present reexamination ought to prompt philosophers to reassess their decisions on the philosophical questions that have been considered. Beyond this, the progress here achieved on those questions by taking new positions into consideration provides philosophers with reason to expect similar progress on other philosophical questions where the equation of intensionalism with Fregean intensionalism has restricted consideration of alternative positions.

NOTES

1. Sense

1. I have focused here on Frege's claim that sense determines reference because of its importance for contemporary criticisms of intensionalism. Frege was not completely clear in his treatment of sense and its relation to reference. In particular, it is not clear whether he intended his characterization of sense as determiner of reference as a *definition* of sense. I will thus refer to this claim as the *Fregean* (rather than *Frege's*) definition of sense.

2. Other philosophers have criticized an autonomous theory of sense along lines similar to Dummett's, for example, David Lewis (1972), John Searle (1974), and Gareth Evans and John McDowell (1976). Lewis's agenda is a theory of possible worlds semantics in the Carnapian tradition; Searle's is a speech act theory of meaning in the Austinian tradition; and Evans and McDowell's is a truth-conditional theory of meaning in the Davidsonian tradition. I have responded to their criticisms elsewhere (1990b: 210–215).

3. I first proposed (D) to provide a semantics (1972) for Chomsky's (1957) early theory of generative grammar. Although Chomsky's theory told us next to nothing about the intuitive notion of sense, and in fact had no place for semantic structure, it provided examples of how to explicate grammatical notions that could serve as models for the explication of sense structure. On Chomsky's theory, the notions of syntactic structure and phonological structure are explicated in terms of the aspects of the grammatical structure of sentences that are responsible, respectively, for the syntactic and phonological properties and relations of sentences. (D) is the result of modeling the explication of sense structure on the explications of syntactic and phonological structure.

2. Reference

1. Neither (A) nor (A') is intended as more than a first approximation.

2. As C. S. Peirce drew the distinction between types and tokens, the former are unique (there is but one word 'word' in English), they cannot occur in time, they cannot appear on a

surface, they cannot have acoustic features, they cannot have causal properties, and so on, and the latter can be multiple (there are many utterances or inscriptions of the English word 'word'), they occur at fixed times and places, they can have acoustic features, they can have causal properties, and so on. Types are abstract objects; tokens are concrete objects. When we say that the English proper name 'London' has many bearers or that the English common noun 'unicorn' has no referent, we are talking about the word-type. When, on the other hand, we say that John's utterance of 'London is in Ontario, Canada' is false while Mary's is true, we are talking about linguistic tokens. Speakers stand in a special relation of possession to the tokens they produce, but not to sentence-types of the language.

3. It is not clear what Frege's view of the senses of indexicals and their relations to utterance contexts was.

4. I should note in this connection that my concept of meaning differs significantly from David Kaplan's. For Kaplan (1979; 1989), the meaning of an expression-token is divided into two components, one of which he calls "character" and the other of which "content." The latter is what is said in producing the token in the context, and the former is a rule—part of the linguistic competence of speakers—that determines the content of the token in context. Character is a function from context to content. (M1) and (M2) should make it clear that, on my view, if speakers have knowledge of functions from context to content, such knowledge is something more than knowledge of meaning, which lacks the information to determine what is said. On my view, speakers who know what 'the man drinking a martini' means do not *ipso facto* have knowledge of a function from contexts to what is said in them in uses of its tokens. From my perspective, such functions (as a component of meaning) are just more Fregeanism.

5. (SW) is a change from my earlier definition of a satisfier world (Katz 1997:24), which speaks only of terms. If the occurrence of 'Santa Claus' is actually a term in 'Some children believe that Santa Claus brings Christmas presents', then the unfortunate consequence follows that this world is not a satisfier world for this sentence even though it is true in this world. To allow such occurrences to be terms, I now state the definition of a satisfier world as in (SW). This has the following implication: on the earlier definition, sentences like 'Gorillas exist', 'Golden mountains exist', and so on express weakly necessary truths, since they have to be true in all their satisfier worlds insofar as the truth of a sentence of the form *a exists* in a world *w* requires only that *w* contain an *a*. Similarly, the negations of such sentences are weakly necessary falsehoods. This now changes because of (SW) and, as I explain in section 3.16, the subject term of such existence sentences does not occur in a referential position. (SW) does not imply that those sentences express weakly necessary truths nor that their negations express weakly necessary falsehoods.

3. Philosophy

1. Given the interdefinability of the notions of truth and reference in Tarskian semantics, deflationism based on the disquotational schema for the truth predicate must also be based on a corresponding disquotational schema for the reference relation, roughly, '"*w*" refers to *w*'. The problem with this schema is that there is no way to make it work in the simple form that deflationism requires. The variable *w* ranges over expressions of natural languages. Indefinitely many of them are ambiguous and indefinitely many others are non-ambiguous but have multiple reference. In the first case, we will have instances of the schema like '"The uncle of John and Mary" refers to the uncle of John and Mary'. We can see what has gone wrong when we ask how many uncles are in the extension of the expression. In the second case, we will have instances like '"John Smith" refers to John Smith', which pose the same

problem: is the name 'John Smith' coreferential with the expression 'all the people with the name "John Smith"'? In neither case can the expression be split into two or three or more expressions with unique reference. Neither of these cases is one of homonymy—that is, different words with the same pronunciation (like 'bare' and 'bear').

2. The point can be underscored by expanding the phrase in some such way as 'Of Mikhail Gorbachev, the former president of the Soviet Union who is sitting right there in front of you'. Note also that the counterexample does not depend upon the presence of the pronoun 'he', since everything remains the same when the pronoun is replaced with the proper name 'Mikhail Gorbachev' or an expression like 'the most important Russian since Stalin'.

Note further that the problem cannot be gotten around by denying that the reference of the proper name 'Mikhail Gorbachev' in the *de re* 'of' phrase is its customary referent, that is, by denying that its referent is the man Gorbachev himself. As (3.5) or (3.6) shows, that occurrence of 'Mikhail Gorbachev' is not in an oblique context, and, moreover, such a denial would leave us without a conception of the grammatical conditions for customary reference.

3. On the new intensionalism, the source of the validity of such inferences is sense structure, pure and simple. In contrast, the source of the validity of logical inferences that depend on substitution of a coreferential expression for an expression in extensional contexts is referential structure. From my perspective, extensionalists like Quine are quite correct to deny the existence of logical inferences in cases of substitution into oblique contexts, and thus to restrict the scope of the logical substitution principle. Their mistake was to go further and deny the existence of senses and the validity of inferences based on them.

4. No one I know of with a proper understanding of compositionality rejects it. Schiffer (1987), as I read him, does not reject the principle itself but rather certain arguments that have been given for it, in particular, arguments from linguistic creativity (the fact that speakers can in principle understand indefinitely many novel sentences). I share his view that these are bad arguments for compositionality.

5. In line with the sharp distinction here between the theory of sense and the theory of reference, I once distinguished between the effability thesis and the statability thesis (1972: 23, n. 6). The latter says that, if some condition obtains in the world, we can state a true sentence asserting that it does, and if some condition does not obtain in the world, we can state a true sentence asserting that it does not. I am advocating a treatment that denies statability. Of course, no incompleteness is something we are going to be happy about, but, from one perspective, the failure of referential completeness ought to strike us as the lesser of the evils. The intuition we have about the expressive completeness of the language does not carry over to a theory like the theory of reference, and there is no independent intuition of completeness in the case of theories.

Thus, once the language/theory distinction is drawn as it is drawn in the new intensionalism, we ought to be reconciled to incompleteness in the theory of reference. Hence, the sharp separation between sense and reference that results from my thin notion of sense enables us to avoid arguments that natural languages are ineffable, that noncontradiction has to be given up, and that natural languages are inconsistent.

6. In my *Semantic Theory* (1972: 127–150), I argued that Epimenidean sentences in natural language provide an argument for presupposition. (See also Katz 1979b.)

7. This is a new argument for presupposition based on an old example (see Katz 1972: 140, n. 7). Presupposition, as I understand the notion, is a grammatically determined condition satisfaction of which is necessary and sufficient for a sentence, depending on the kind of sentence, to make a statement, to ask a question, to issue a request, and so on (see Katz 1980: 88–117). Here, however, I restrict the treatment to assertive sentences, taking their presupposition to be a condition whose satisfaction is necessary and sufficient for them to make a true or a false statement.

8. It is not necessary to adopt an ontological dualism on which intensional and extensional propositions are two different kinds of entity, since nothing has been said to rule out the possibility that each extensional proposition is an intensional proposition. As I have suggested elsewhere (1972: 127–150; 1980: chapter 1), we might construe extensional propositions ontologically as intensional propositions (or sets of them). The suggestion might be implemented by saying, roughly speaking, that an extensional proposition E in the context C is the intensional proposition P such that the speaker communicates P in C and the presupposition of P, if there is one, is satisfied in C. (Often the sense P is not the sense of the sentence that communicates P in C, but, as I have argued, the sense of a sentence no more determines the sense of its tokens than it does their reference.)

I am not offering this suggestion as more than an indication of how the possibility in question might be fleshed out. My point here is not that this is the way to go, but only that propositional dualism is not a necessary consequence of the situation I have reached. If my suggestion is wrong, then there is an ontological issue between propositional dualism and propositional monism, and we have to take the less parsimonious side. But the difference in economy does not decide the issue, since dualism can be worth its price because of the philosophical work a thin notion of meaning does and because of the problems thick notions of meaning involve us in.

9. We can accommodate the intuition that (i) is a weakly necessary truth

(i)   All ravens are black if and only if all non-black things are non-ravens.

on the basis of a referential correlate for the negative prefix that says that the extension of 'non-T' is the complement of the extension of T. Given this correlate, a Venn diagram interpretation will show that (i) is weakly necessary.

10. Thus, a sentence with a presupposition is not about anything unless all of the clauses of its presuppositions are satisfied. It seems plausible to say that sentences like 'The tooth fairy left a quarter under Mary's pillow' and 'Mary found a quarter the tooth fairy left under her pillow' are not about anything. There is, of course, the alternative of taking them to be about Mary and her pillow but not about anything else. The definition of aboutness is easily modified to express such an alternative.

The provision for presuppositionless sentences is included to cover existential sentences like 'Snow-covered mountains exist' and 'Golden mountains exist'. See section 3.16.

11. In addition to the threat to philosophies generally of failing to do justice to one or the other of two strong sets of intuitions, there is also the threat to intensionalists of having to restrict their position to common nouns—and if Kripke and Putnam are right about the relation between natural kind terms and proper names, to non-natural kind common nouns as well. My thin notion of sense removes this threat to intensionalism.

I have doubts about the claim that natural kind terms are rigid designators like names. On my account, their differences allow us to say that natural kind terms do not designate rigidly. Natural kind terms, unlike names, have type-reference, and names, unlike natural kind terms, acquire their rigidity as a matter of stipulation in the use of language. Thus, on my account, a natural kind term like 'jade' could refer to the mineral jadeite and the mineral nephrite in the actual world, to jadeite in some possible worlds, and to nephrite in others. I need only allow that natural kind characterizations can determine more than one kind. Thus, instead of a real definition for 'jade', there would be a natural kind characterization that picks out the mineral jadeite or nephrite. Moreover, this seems to accord better with the way speakers use the term 'jade'.

12. There is of course ample controversy over whether or not Putnam's and Kripke's arguments do support this conclusion. (The literature is very large. Important contributions

to the debate may be found in Ludlow and Martin 1998, Wright, Smith, and Macdonald 1998, and Boghossian and Peacocke 2000.) The point that needs to be stressed here is that if Fregean intensionalism is abandoned, Putnam's and Kripke's arguments do not even raise the issue.

13. Again, there is considerable controversy and a large literature. (See the collections cited in the previous note for some of the important essays.)

14. This is also a problem with an enormous literature. Needless to say, no resolution of the controversies in this literature is possible here. The important point is that these controversies are finessed by the approach taken in the text.

15. Knowledge of the types of sense properties and relations in natural language has to be *a priori*, too. Such knowledge can be obtained independently of experience on the basis of intuitions about the meaning of metalinguistic terms in natural languages. There is a wide range of clear cases in which we can tell, intuitively, whether or not the meaning of such a term involves the notion of sense. We can see *a priori* that the predicate 'is nonsense' means *does not have a sense*, that the predicate 'is ambiguous' means *has two or more senses*, and that the predicate 'is synonymous with' means *has the same sense as*. The approach is to construct a theory on the basis of the clear cases of sense properties and relations and use it to settle the status of unclear cases.

16. This is because, for any deviant interpretation, there are non-structural properties available for distinguishing the numbers from the objects in the deviant interpretation. We are assured of having the properties we need for any particular case of deviant interpretation because they are required to distinguish the deviant interpretation from the intended one. A skeptical claim that the numbers cannot be distinguished from a particular deviant interpretation D must include considerations that show that the deviant interpretation in question is not merely the intended model under a deviant description. Hence, the skeptic has to provide grounds for distinguishing the object assigned to the number term 'N' on the deviant interpretation from the number N. Thus, the skeptic has to exhibit a property that one but not the other of them has. If the skeptic cannot exhibit such a property, we have no reason to think that the object assigned to 'N' is not just N itself; if the skeptic can provide such a property, we are handed a distinction between the intended and deviant interpretations on a silver platter.

Dethroning Fregean semantics does not, of course, prevent mathematical structuralists from trying to come up with another argument for restricting the properties that might be used to individuate numbers to structural properties. This, as I understand him, is what Benacerraf (1983) tries to do when he argues that the use of non-structural properties to individuate numbers is illegitimate because it "misses the point of what arithmetic, at least, is all about." In response to this argument, I argued (1998b: 85–116) that what arithmetic is all about can be understood in two ways: from the perspective of mathematics and from the perspective of philosophy. Benacerraf's claim that the philosopher is "mistaken" to seek answers to questions about the ontology of mathematics makes sense only if the philosopher's quest is judged from the mathematical perspective. But why shouldn't it be judged from the philosophical perspective—that is, from the perspective of the traditional metaphysician's concern with the nature of reality? Benacerraf's answer, I believe, is that this perspective is excluded on the basis of the naturalist metaphilosophy—widely held at the time he wrote "What Numbers Could Not Be"—that there are no questions about the nature of reality for philosophy to address. This is because there are no questions about reality that go beyond the scope of science. Philosophy on this metaphilosophy is a second-order discipline that does not provide knowledge of the world but only analyzes the linguistic/conceptual structure of the first-order disciplines that do. But this answer only raises the further question of why we should accept this naturalist metaphilosophy rather than the traditional metaphysical metaphilosophy.

Although dethroning Fregean semantics does not preclude other lines of argument against realism, it brings their metaphilosophical and metaphysical assumptions out into the open. We no longer see those lines of argument as resting on application of technical results about the model-theoretic interpretation of formal mathematical systems, but rather as resting on the metaphysical and metaphilosophical assumptions. Hence, they appear far less convincing than when seen simply as applications of technical results in logic. (See Katz 2002.)

17. The conclusion is essentially the same as the one that Wittgenstein (1953: sections 71 and following [particularly section 75]) drew from his criticism of Frege's demand for exact concepts. (See Katz 1990b: 21–134.)

18. Carnap's notion of intensional isomorphism (1956: 56–64) and its progeny do not overcome the difficulty because they assume an isomorphism between sense structure and syntactic structure. I have discussed this assumption earlier, but see also Katz 1996 (612–613) on the notion of intensional isomorphism.

19. I characterize basic color terms as those with decompositional sense structure that involves nothing more than the determinable 'color' with a single hue designation as its determinate. If the determinate is qualified in terms of degree of saturation or brilliance, or if more than one hue determinate occurs, the term is not a basic color term. Thus, the lexical items 'red' and 'blue' (as represented in (3.63) and (3.64)) are basic color terms, but 'mauve', being the term for a color of a bluish blue-red of high saturation and of medium to low brilliance, is not a basic color term.

20. When there is no semantic representation to provide the value of a variable, its value is the semantic marker in its own selection restriction. This principle is independently required to handle analytic entailments such as that from 'The dog drank' to 'The dog drank a liquid'. See Katz 1972 (107).

21. Weakly necessary truth is not only the referential correlate for these analytic sentences; it is also the correlate for the denials of the corresponding contradictory sentences. Hence, the sentences 'The spot is not red and blue' and 'It is not the case that the spot is red and blue' are both weakly necessary truths. Correspondingly, weakly necessary falsehood is not only the referential correlate of such contradictory sentences; it is also the referential correlate for sentences that are the denials of the corresponding analytic sentences. Hence, the sentence 'It is not the case that red is not blue' is a weakly necessary falsehood.

22. Hardin is correct to claim that "not being a mastodon is not part of the concept of being a lampshade." But his example 'A lampshade is not a mastodon' is hardly a parallel case to (3.53). Hardin's example is not analytic, whereas, as we have seen, (3.53) is. The difference lies in the fact that the sense of 'red' and the sense of 'blue' are members of the same antonymous n-tuple, whereas the sense of 'lampshade' and the sense of 'mastodon' are not members of the same antonymous n-tuple, but only contain senses (i.e., the senses *artifactual* and *natural*) that are. This difference allows the sense of 'mastodon', the predicate in Hardin's example, to contain senses that do not appear in the sense of 'lampshade', the subject in that example. Thus, Hardin's example is not analytic. But, although it is not analytic, it is a weakly necessary truth because it is the denial of the contradictory sentence 'A lampshade is a mastodon', and being a weakly necessary truth is also the referential correlate of being the denial of a contradictory sentence.

23. It is worth taking a moment to look at some of Pelletier's other criticisms. He criticizes my account of anomaly as follows:

> . . . both the subject and the object of *chased* must be marked as "inherently spatiotemporal particulars" . . . yet . . . "The thought of bed chased all concern with linguistic theory from my mind" is clearly grammatical [sic]. There seems to be no

way of changing the selection restriction without also letting in Katz's anomalous "Truth chased falsehood". So we must posit another sense of *chase* . . . [and] ST has no theoretical mechanism to prevent an endless proliferation of readings and markers. . . . (1982:321)

On the one hand, it makes good linguistic sense to posit another sense of 'chase' in connection, for example, with sentences like Pelletier's 'The thought of bed chased all concern with linguistic theory from my mind'. (Compare Rylean cases of oddity, like 'They chased the thought from my mind and the customers from my store'.) On the other hand, Pelletier is simply mistaken when he says that "ST has no theoretical mechanism to prevent an endless proliferation of readings and markers." He ignores the theoretical mechanism that is in place. The principle is: "Posit as many senses for a word as is necessary to account for the sense properties and relations of the sentences in which it occurs in the simplest and most revealing fashion."

Pelletier is right to say that my theory of sense ". . . makes use of some syntactic theory in order to state the selection restrictions and co-occurrence relations," but this is not the full story concerning the role of syntactic information. Since my theory involves compositionality in the standard sense (it says that, in general, the sense of a sentence is a function of the senses of its constituents and their syntactic relations), it presupposes a syntactic theory that provides an account of syntactic relations in sentences. This is something that, I would presume, any adequate syntactic theory must do. My theory of sense has never assumed any particular syntactic theory. I have only assumed that there is some syntactic theory that is adequate.

Contrary to this, Pelletier says: "[Katz's theory] is strictly tied to a syntactic parsing which will yield the sort of semantic trees he has presented us with. One wonders what level of syntactic description [Katz's theory] operates on" (1982:321). These statements make Pelletier's confusion evident. He mistakenly thinks that my semantic trees are stages of *syntactic* derivations in generative grammars—as if my theory of sense were one or another system of the sort called "Generative Semantics" back in the late '60s and early '70s. Quite the contrary. I then defended and continue to defend the opposite view—"Interpretive Semantics"—on which semantic derivations are independent of syntactic derivations and constitute an interpretation of syntactic derivations parallel to their phonological interpretation. Hence, my theory is not "strictly tied" to any particular class of syntactic theories. Chomsky's (1965) theory has always been used just as an illustration. Any syntactic theory that provides the relevant information about the grammatical relations required for the conditions expressed in the brackets over categorized variables will do.

The last of Pelletier's criticisms that I will consider is his version of the fruitfulness criticism. It begins with a mischaracterization that needs to be corrected. Pelletier says, *without citing a source*, that "[on Katz's theory] analyticity is defined in terms of 'the representation of the predicate being included in the representation of the subject'." Since Katz 1972—that is, ten years prior to the publication date of Pelletier's essay—I have taken pains to make it clear that I reject this Kantian definition of analyticity in favor of one like (A), according to which the containing term may be any term in the sense of the sentence.

Be that as it may, Pelletier, after observing against Thomason that "the semantic relations Katz wishes to capture are not those of predicate logic," states that my "[semantic] relations [do not] perform any useful service in understanding the semantics of natural language" (1982: 321–322). Pelletier states this without presenting anything to back it up. He thus overlooks Katz and Postal 1964 and Katz 1972; 1978; 1979b; 1980; 1981—to mention some of the work published prior to his 1982 article—in which reasons are provided for thinking that my theory does help us to understand the semantics of natural language.

24. Note that another of Gale's reasons for positing negative facts is undercut by our discussion of the semantics of color terms. His reason is that "a thing cannot have a positive property without lacking certain other properties," as, for example, with the sentence 'If a thing is red, then it is not blue'. But, I have argued, the term 'not blue' does not have to be understood as expressing a lack, but as expressing the notion of the subject's being some color other than blue.

25. Before we leave the topic of regimentation, I want to remind the reader of Arnold Koslow's comment, based on Koslow 1992, that "[t]he resources of an abstract concept of implication are incredibly rich. . . . Results that were once closely linked to languages that assumed some syntactic or semantic regimentation are now available without those constraints" (1999: 152). Note that my analyticity and analytic entailment are implication relations in Koslow's sense. In fact, Koslow cites mereological implication—though not my notion of analyticity or analytic entailment in particular—as an example of an implication relation in his abstract sense (1999: 118). Note also that the broad notion of logic that Koslow uses in connection with his "abstract theory of implication" is—to indulge in a bit of British under-statement—quite a bit broader than the notion of logic in the Frege-Russell tradition, which has been my focus here. The latter is a special case of the former. Koslow's notion of impli-cation is closer to my notion of inference.

26. The term 'analytic philosophy' is sometimes also taken to apply to philosophizing that puts a high premium on clarity and rigor. This is the contrastive sense in which Anglo-American philosophers frequently distinguish themselves from Continental philosophers. But there is no logical connection between the two senses of the term. Some of the great figures in the history of philosophy were analytic philosophers in the latter sense but not the former and some of the lesser figures in contemporary philosophy are analytic philosophers in the former sense but not the latter. Everyone endorses analytic philosophy in the latter sense. Who is for obscurity and sloppiness?

27. A mereological semantics also provides an account of the categories of a language. In the tradition of Aristotle and Kant, categories are understood as the most general concepts in a conceptual system. Since the superordinate/subordinate relations represented in the domi-nation structure of semantic markers provide the notion of one sense's being more general than another, we can say that the semantic categories of a language are those senses that are superordinates of some senses but subordinates of none. Katz (1987: 194–197) suggests a formalization for this notion of category.

28. My ontological view differs from Frege's in taking natural languages as well as senses to be abstract objects. The construal of sentences as abstract objects, which I have defended elsewhere (1981; 1998b), requires little more than that sentences be types and that their senses be part of their grammatical structure.

BIBLIOGRAPHY

Allaire, Edwin B. 1966. *Tractatus* 6.3751. In *Essays on Wittgenstein's* Tractatus, edited by Irving M. Copi and Robert W. Beard, 189–94. New York: Macmillan.

Anscombe, G. E. M. 1990. The first person. In *Demonstratives*, edited by Palle Yourgrau, 135–53. Oxford: Oxford University Press.

Armour-Garb, Brad, and J. J. Katz. 1998. What's in a name. Typescript.

Arnauld, Antoine. 1964. *The art of thinking*. Indianapolis: Bobbs-Merrill.

Austin, J. L. 1961. Other minds. In *Philosophical papers*, 44–84. Oxford: Oxford University Press.

Bell, David. 1990. *Husserl*. London: Routledge.

Benacerraf, Paul. 1981. Frege: The last logicist. *Midwest Studies in Philosophy* 6:17–35.

———. 1983. What numbers could not be. In *The philosophy of mathematics: selected essays*, second edition, edited by Paul Benacerraf and Hilary Putnam, 272–94. Cambridge: Cambridge University Press.

Black, Max. 1964. *A companion to Wittgenstein's* Tractatus. Ithaca: Cornell University Press.

Block, Ned. 1986. Advertisement for a semantics for psychology. *Midwest Studies in Philosophy* 10:615–78.

Boghossian, Paul. 1994. Sense, reference, and rule following. *Philosophy and Phenomenological Research* 54:139–44.

———. 1996. Analyticity reconsidered. *Noûs* 30:360–91.

Boghossian, Paul, and Christopher Peacocke, editors. 2000. *New essays on the a priori*. Oxford: Oxford University Press.

Boolos, George. 1998. *Logic, logic, and logic*. Cambridge: Harvard University Press.

Brandom, Robert. 1994. *Making it explicit*. Cambridge: Harvard University Press.

Burge, Tyler. 1979a. Frege and the hierarchy. *Synthese* 40:265–81.

———. 1979b. Individualism and the mental. *Midwest Studies in Philosophy* 4:73–121.

Carnap, Rudolf. 1956. *Meaning and necessity*, second edition. Chicago: University of Chicago Press.

———. 1959. The elimination of metaphysics through the logical analysis of language. In *Logical positivism*, edited by A. J. Ayer, 60–81. Glencoe, Ill.: The Free Press.

———. 1963. Intellectual autobiography. In *The philosophy of Rudolf Carnap*, edited by P. A. Schilpp, 3–84. La Salle, Ill.: Open Court.

Cartwright, Richard. 1987a. On the origins of Russell's theory of descriptions. In *Philosophical essays*, 95–133. Cambridge: MIT Press.

———. 1987b. Negative existentials. In *Philosophical essays*, 21–31. Cambridge: MIT Press.

Chisholm, Roderick M. 1960. Editor's introduction. In *Realism and the background of phenomenology*, 3–36. Glencoe, Ill.: The Free Press.

Chomsky, Noam. 1957. *Syntactic structures*. The Hague: Mouton and Co.

———. 1959. Review of *Verbal behavior*. *Language* 35:26–58.

———. 1965. *Aspects of the theory of syntax*. Cambridge: MIT Press.

Church, Alonzo. 1954. Intensional isomorphism and the identity of belief. *Philosophical Studies* 5:65–73.

———. 1956. *Introduction to mathematical logic*. Volume 1. Princeton: Princeton University Press.

Clark, Chalmers. 1998. Quine and the speculative reach of philosophy in natural science. *Dialectica* 52:275–90.

Davidson, Donald. 1967a. Truth and meaning. *Synthese* 17:304–23.

———. 1967b. The logical form of action sentences. In *The logic of decision and action*, edited by Nicholas Rescher, 81–95. Pittsburgh: University of Pittsburgh Press.

———. 1970. Action and reaction. *Inquiry* 13:140–8.

Descartes, René. 1969. *The philosophical works of Descartes*. Translated and edited by Elizabeth Haldane and G. R. T. Ross. Cambridge: Cambridge University Press.

———. 1970. *Descartes: Philosophical letters*. Translated and edited by Anthony Kenny. Oxford: Clarendon Press.

Donnellan, Keith. 1962. Necessity and criteria. *The Journal of Philosophy* 59:647–58.

———. 1966. Reference and definite descriptions. *The Philosophical Review* 75:281–304.

Dummett, Michael. 1973. *Frege: philosophy of language*. London: Duckworth.

———. 1975. What is a theory of meaning? In *Mind and language*, edited by Samuel Guttenplan, 97–138. Oxford: Clarendon Press.

———. 1981. *The interpretation of Frege's philosophy*. Cambridge: Harvard University Press.

———. 1991. *Frege: philosophy of mathematics*. Cambridge: Harvard University Press.

Evans, Gareth, and John McDowell. 1976. Introduction. In *Truth and meaning*, vii–xxiii. Oxford: Clarendon Press.

Feyerabend, Paul. 1965. Problems of empiricism. In *Beyond the edge of certainty*, edited by Robert G. Colodny, 145–260. Englewood Cliffs, N.J.: Prentice Hall.

Field, Hartry. 1977. Logic, meaning, and conceptual role. *The Journal of Philosophy* 74: 379–409.

———. 1994. Deflationist views of meaning and content. *Mind* 103:249–85.

Fodor, Jerry A. 1980. Fixation of belief and concept acquisition. In *Language and learning: The debate between Jean Piaget and Noam Chomsky*, edited by Massimo Piattelli-Palmarini, 143–9. Cambridge: Harvard University Press.

———. 1982. Cognitive science and the twin-earth problem. *Notre Dame Journal of Formal Logic* 23:98–118.

———. 1994. Concepts: A potboiler. *Cognition* 50:95–113.

Fodor, Jerry A., Merill F. Garrett, Edward C. T. Walker, and Cornelia H. Parkes. 1980. Against definitions. *Cognition* 8:263–367.

Fogelin, Robert J. 1976. *Wittgenstein*. London: Routledge and Kegan Paul.

Frege, Gottlob. 1952. *Translations from the philosophical writings of Gottlob Frege*. Edited by Peter Geach and Max Black. Oxford: Basil Blackwell.

———. 1953. *The foundations of arithmetic*. Translated by J. L. Austin. Oxford: Basil Blackwell.

———. 1968. The thought: A logical enquiry. In *Essays on Frege*, edited by E. D. Klemke, 507–35. Urbana: University of Illinois Press.

———. 1972. *Conceptual notation and related articles*, translated and edited by Terrell Ward Bynum. Oxford: Clarendon Press.

———. 1979. *Posthumous writings*, edited by Hans Hermes, Friedrich Kambartel, and Friedrich Kaulbach. Oxford: Basil Blackwell.

———. 1984. *Collected papers on mathematics, logic, and philosophy*, edited by Brian McGuinness. Oxford: Basil Blackwell.

Gale, Richard. 1976. *Negation and non-being*. Oxford: Basil Blackwell.

Gardam, Jane. 1971. *A long way from Verona*. London: Little, Brown.

Gemes, Ken. 1994. A new theory of content I: Basic content. *Journal of Philosophical Logic* 23:595–620.

Goldfarb, Warren. 1997. Wittgenstein on fixity of meaning. In *Early analytic philosophy: Frege, Russell, Wittgenstein*, edited by W. W. Tait, 75–89. Chicago: Open Court.

Goodman, Nelson. 1972. *Problems and projects*. Indianapolis: Bobbs-Merrill.

Grice, H. P. 1989. *Studies in the way of words*. Cambridge: Harvard University Press.

Hacker, P. M. S. 1972. *Insight and illusion*. Oxford: Oxford University Press.

Hardin, C. L. 1986. *Color for philosophers: Unweaving the rainbow*. Indianapolis: Hackett.

Harman, Gilbert. 1967. Quine on meaning and existence I. *The Review of Metaphysics* 21: 124–51.

———. 1987. (Nonsolipsistic) conceptual role semantics. In *New directions in semantics*, edited by Ernest LePore, 55–81. London: Academic Press.

Hempel, Carl G. 1965. *Aspects of scientific explanation and other essays in the philosophy of science*. New York: The Free Press.

Herzberger, Hans. 1965. The logical consistency of language. *Harvard Educational Review* 35:469–80.

———. 1970. Paradoxes of grounding in semantics. *The Journal of Philosophy* 67:145–67.

Herzberger, Hans, and J. J. Katz. 1967. *The concept of truth in natural language*. Typescript.

Horwich, Paul. 1998. *Meaning*. Oxford: Clarendon Press.

Hume, David. 1978. *A treatise of human nature*, second edition, edited by L. A. Selby-Bigge. Oxford: Oxford University Press.

Isaacson, Daniel. 1994. Mathematical intuition and objectivity. In *Mathematics and mind*, edited by Alexander George, 118–40. New York: Oxford University Press.

Kant, Immanuel. 1929. *Critique of pure reason*. Translated by Norman Kemp Smith. New York: St. Martin's Press.

———. 1951. *Prolegomena to any future metaphysics*. Edited by Lewis White Beck. New York: The Liberal Arts Press.

Kaplan, David. 1979. On the logic of demonstratives. *Journal of Philosophical Logic* 8:81–98.

———. 1989. Demonstratives. In *Themes from Kaplan*, edited by Joseph Almog, John Perry, and Howard Wettstein. Oxford: Oxford University Press.

Katz, J. J. 1964. *An integrated theory of linguistic descriptions.* Cambridge: MIT Press.
————. 1965. *Philosophy of language.* New York: Harper and Row.
————. 1972. *Semantic theory.* New York: Harper and Row.
————. 1978. Effability and translation. In *Meaning and translation,* edited by F. Guenthner and M. Guenthner-Reutter, 191–234. New York: New York University Press.
————. 1979a. Semantics and conceptual change. *The Philosophical Review* 88:327–65.
————. 1979b. A solution to the projection problem for presupposition. In *Syntax and semantics: Presupposition,* edited by Choon-Kyu Oh and D. A. Dinneen, 91–126. New York: Academic Press.
————. 1980. *Propositional structure and illocutionary force.* Cambridge: Harvard University Press.
————. 1981. *Language and other abstract objects.* Totowa, N. J.: Rowman and Littlefield.
————. 1986a. Why intensionalists ought not be Fregeans. In *Truth and interpretation,* edited by Ernest LePore, 59–91. Oxford: Basil Blackwell.
————. 1986b. *Cogitations.* New York: Oxford University Press.
————. 1987. Common sense in semantics. In *New directions in semantics,* edited by Ernest LePore, 157–233. London: Academic Press.
————. 1988. The refutation of indeterminacy. *The Journal of Philosophy* 85:227–52.
————. 1990a. Has the description theory of names been refuted? In *Meaning and method: Essays in honor of Hilary Putnam,* edited by George Boolos, 31–61. Cambridge: Cambridge University Press.
————. 1990b. *The metaphysics of meaning.* Cambridge: MIT Press.
————. 1990c. Descartes's *Cogito.* In *Demonstratives,* edited by Palle Yourgrau, 154–81. Oxford: Oxford University Press.
————. 1992. The new intensionalism. *Mind* 101:689–720.
————. 1994. Names without bearers. *The Philosophical Review* 103:1–39.
————. 1996. Semantics in linguistics and philosophy: An intensionalist perspective. In *Handbook of contemporary semantic theory,* edited by Shalom Lappin. Oxford: Basil Blackwell.
————. 1997. Analyticity, necessity, and the epistemology of semantics. *Philosophy and Phenomenological Research* 57:1–28.
————. 1998a. The problem in twentieth-century philosophy. *The Journal of Philosophy* 95: 547–75.
————. 1998b. *Realistic rationalism.* Cambridge: MIT Press.
————. 2001. The end of Millianism: Multiple bearers, improper names, and compositional meaning. *The Journal of Philosophy* 98:137–66.
————. 2002. Mathematics and metaphilosophy. *The Journal of Philosophy* 99:362–90.
Katz, J. J., and Jerry A. Fodor. 1963. The structure of a semantic theory. *Language* 39:170–210.
Katz, J. J., and Paul Postal. 1964. *An integrated theory of linguistic descriptions.* Cambridge: MIT Press.
Kenny, Anthony. 1973. *Wittgenstein.* Cambridge: Harvard University Press.
————. 1995. *Frege.* London: Penguin.
Kneale, William. 1962. Modality de dicto and de re. In *Methodology and the philosophy of science,* edited by Ernest Nagel, Patrick Suppes, and Alfred Tarski, 622–33. Stanford: Stanford University Press.
Koslow, Arnold. 1992. *A structuralist theory of logic.* Cambridge: Cambridge University Press.
————. 1999. The implicational nature of logic: A structuralist account. *European Review of Philosophy* 4:111–55.

Kripke, Saul. 1971. Identity and necessity. In *Identity and individuation*, edited by Milton Munitz, 135–64. New York: New York University Press.

———. 1975. Outline of a theory of truth. *The Journal of Philosophy* 72:690–716.

———. 1980. *Naming and necessity*. Cambridge: Harvard University Press.

———. 1982. *Wittgenstein on rules and private language*. Cambridge: Harvard University Press.

———. 1988. A puzzle about belief. In *Propositions and attitudes*, edited by Nathan Salmon and Scott Soames, 102–48. Oxford: Oxford University Press.

Kuhn, Thomas S. 1962. *The structure of scientific revolutions*. Chicago: University of Chicago Press.

Langford, C. H. 1942. The notion of analysis in Moore's philosophy. In *The philosophy of G. E. Moore*, edited by P. A. Schilpp, 321–42. La Salle: Open Court.

Leeds, Stephen. 1973. How to think about reference. *The Journal of Philosophy* 70:485–503.

———. 1978. Theories of reference and truth. *Erkenntnis* 13:11–129.

Lewis, David. 1969. *Convention*. Cambridge: Harvard University Press.

———. 1972. General semantics. In *Semantics of natural language*, edited by Donald Davidson and Gilbert Harman, 169–218. Dordrecht: D. Reidel.

Linsky, Leonard. 1972. Analytic/synthetic and semantic theory. In *Semantics of natural language*, edited by Donald Davidson and Gilbert Harman, 473–482. Dordrecht: D. Reidel.

Locke, John. 1924. *An essay concerning human understanding*. Edited and abridged by A. S. Pringle-Pattison. Oxford: Clarendon Press.

Ludlow, Peter, and Norah Martin, editors. 1998. *Externalism and self-knowledge*. Stanford: CSLI Publications.

Mendelsohn, Richard. 1996. Frege's treatment of indirect reference. In *Frege: Importance and legacy*, edited by Matthias Schirn, 410–37. Berlin: Walter de Gruyter.

Mill, John Stuart. 1862. *A system of logic*. London: Parker, Son, and Born.

Miller, George A. 1962. Some psychological studies of grammar. *American Psychologist* 17:748–62.

Moore, G. E. 1942. A reply to my critics. In *The Philosophy of G. E. Moore*, edited by P. A. Schilpp, 535–677. LaSalle: Open Court.

———. 1944. Russell's "theory of descriptions." In *The Philosophy of Bertrand Russell*, edited by P. A. Schilpp, 177–225. New York: Harper and Row.

———. 1953. *Some main problems of philosophy*. London: George Allen and Unwin.

Neale, Stephen. 1990. *Descriptions*. Cambridge: MIT Press.

Parsons, Terence. 1981. Frege's hierarchies of indirect discourse and the paradox of analysis. *Midwest Studies in Philosophy* 6:37–57.

Passmore, John. 1957. *A hundred years of philosophy*. London: Gerald Duckworth.

Peacocke, Christopher. 1992. *A study of concepts*. Cambridge: MIT Press.

Pelletier, Francis Jeffrey. 1982. (X). *Notre Dame Journal of Formal Logic* 23:316–26.

Pitt, David. In defense of definitions. *Philosophical Psychology* 12:139–56.

———. In preparation. The Burgean intuitions.

Pitt, David, and J. J. Katz. 2000. Compositional idioms. *Language* 76:409–32.

Plato. 1935. *The sophist*. In *Plato's theory of knowledge*, edited by F. M. Cornford. London: Routledge and Kegan Paul.

Prior, Arthur N. 1967. Negation. In *The encyclopedia of philosophy*, edited by Paul Edwards, volume 5, 458–63. New York: Macmillan.

Priest, Graham. 1987. *In contradiction*. Dordrecht: Nijhoff.

————. 1993. Can contradictions be true?—II. *Proceedings of the Aristotelian Society Supplementary Volume* 67:35–54.

Putnam, Hilary. 1973a. Meaning and reference. *The Journal of Philosophy* 70:699–711.

————. 1973b. Explanation and reference. In *Conceptual Change*, edited by Glenn Pearce and Patrick Maynard, 199–221. Dordrecht: D. Reidel.

————. 1975a. The meaning of "meaning." *Minnesota Studies in the Philosophy of Science* 7:131–93.

————. 1975b. It ain't necessarily so. In *Mathematics, Matter, and Method*, 237–49. Cambridge: Cambridge University Press.

————. 1975c. Is semantics possible? In *Mathematics, Matter, and Method*, 139–52. Cambridge: Cambridge University Press.

Quine, W. V. 1953. *From a logical point of view*. Cambridge: Harvard University Press.

————. 1960. *Word and object*. Cambridge: MIT Press.

————. 1966. *The ways of paradox and other essays*. New York: Random House.

————. 1969. *Ontological relativity and other essays*. New York: Columbia University Press.

————. 1970. *Philosophy of logic*. Englewood Cliffs, N.J.: Prentice-Hall.

Routley, Richard, and Robert K. Meyer. 1976. Dialectical logic, classical logic, and the consistency of the world. *Studies in Soviet Thought* 16:1–25.

Russell, Bertrand. 1905. On denoting. *Mind* 14:479–93.

————. 1919. *Introduction to mathematical philosophy*. London: George Allen and Unwin.

Ryle, Gilbert. 1937–1938. Categories. *Proceedings of the Aristotelian Society* 38:189–206.

————. 1952. Systematically misleading expressions. In *Logic and language: First series*, edited by Antony Flew, 11–36. Oxford: Basil Blackwell.

Salmon, Nathan. 1998. Nonexistence. *Noûs* 32:277–319.

Schiffer, Stephen. 1987. *Remnants of meaning*. Cambridge: MIT Press.

————. 2000a. Meanings. Lecture presented at the CUNY Graduate School colloquium series in September 2000.

————. 2000b. Pleonastic Fregeanism. In *Proceedings of the Twentieth World Congress of Philosophy*. Vol. 6, *Analytic philosophy and logic*, edited by Akihori Kanamori, 1–15. Bowling Green, Ohio: Philosophy Documentation Center.

Schlick, Moritz. 1949. Is there a factual a priori? In *Readings in philosophical analysis*, edited by Herbert Feigl and Wilfred Sellars, 277–85. New York: Appleton-Century-Crofts.

Searle, John. 1958. Proper names. *Mind* 67:166–73.

————. 1968. Russell's objections to Frege's distinction between sense and reference. In *Essays on Frege*, edited by E. D. Klemke, 337–45. Urbana: University of Illinois Press.

————. 1974. Chomsky's revolution in linguistics. In *On Noam Chomsky*, edited by Gilbert Harman, 2–33. New York: Anchor.

Smart, J. J. C. 1953. A note on categories. *British Journal for the Philosophy of Science* 4:227–8.

Smiley, Timothy. 1993. Can contradictions be true?—I. *Proceedings of the Aristotelian Society Supplementary Volume* 67:17–33.

Strawson, P. F. 1950. On referring. *Mind* 69:320–44.

————. 1952. *Introduction to logical theory*. New York: John Wiley and Sons.

Tarski, Alfred. 1952. The semantical conception of truth. In *Semantics and the philosophy of language*, edited by Leonard Linsky, 13–47. Urbana: University of Illinois Press.

————. 1956a. The concept of truth in formalized languages. In *Logic, semantics, metamathematics*, 152–278. Oxford: Clarendon Press.

———. 1956b. On the concept of logical consequence. In *Logic, semantics, metamathematics*, 409–20. Oxford: Clarendon Press.

Wiggins, David. 1980. "Most" and "all": Some comments on a familiar programme, and on the logical form of quantified sentences. In *Reference, truth, and reality*, edited by Mark Platts, 318–46. London: Routledge and Kegan Paul.

Wittgenstein, Ludwig. 1929. Some remarks on logical form. *Proceedings of the Aristotelian Society Supplementary Volume* 9:162–71.

———. 1953. *Philosophical investigations*. Translated by G. E. M. Anscombe. Oxford: Basil Blackwell.

———. 1958. *The blue and brown books*. Oxford: Basil Blackwell.

———. 1961. *Tractatus logico-philosophicus*. Translated by David Pears and Brian McGuinness. London: Routledge and Kegan Paul.

———. 1967. *Ludwig Wittgenstein und der Wiener Kreis*. Edited by Brian F. McGuinness. Oxford: Basil Blackwell.

———. 1974. *Philosophical grammar*. Berkeley: University of California Press.

Wright, Crispin. 1987. Further reflections on the sorites paradox. *Philosophical Topics* 15:227–90.

Wright, Crispin, Barry C. Smith, and Cynthia Macdonald, editors. 1998. *Knowing our own minds*. Oxford: Clarendon Press.

Yourgrau, Palle. 1986–1987. The path back to Frege. *Proceedings of the Aristotelian Society* 87:169–210.

INDEX OF NAMES

INDEX OF SUBJECTS